PROFITING FROM WEEKLY OPTIONS

PROFITING FROM WEEKLY OPTIONS

How to Earn Consistent Income Trading
Weekly Option Serials

Robert J. Seifert

WILEY

Cover image: © iStock.com/adam smigielski
Cover design: Wiley

Published by John Wiley & Sons, Inc., Hoboken, New Jersey.
Published simultaneously in Canada.

Limit of Liability/Disclaimer of Warranty: While the publisher and author have used their best efforts in preparing this book, they make no representations or warranties with respect to the accuracy or completeness of the contents of this book and specifically disclaim any implied warranties of merchantability or fitness for a particular purpose. No warranty may be created or extended by sales representatives or written sales materials. The advice and strategies contained herein may not be suitable for your situation. You should consult with a professional where appropriate. Neither the publisher nor author shall be liable for any loss of profit or any other commercial damages, including but not limited to special, incidental, consequential, or other damages.

For general information on our other products and services or for technical support, please contact our Customer Care Department within the United States at (800) 762-2974, outside the United States at (317) 572-3993 or fax (317) 572-4002.

Wiley publishes in a variety of print and electronic formats and by print-on-demand. Some material included with standard print versions of this book may not be included in e-books or in print-on-demand. If this book refers to media such as a CD or DVD that is not included in the version you purchased, you may download this material at http://booksupport.wiley.com. For more information about Wiley products, visit www.wiley.com.

Library of Congress Cataloging-in-Publication Data:
Seifert, Robert J.
  Profiting from weekly options : how to earn consistent income trading weekly option serials / Robert J. Seifert.
     pages cm. – (Wiley trading series)
  Includes index.
  ISBN 978-1-118-98058-3 (Hardcover) – ISBN 978-1-118-98095-8 (ePDF) – ISBN 978-1-118-98094-1 (ePub) 1. Options (Finance) I. Title.
  HG6024.A3S437 2015
  332.64′53–dc23

                                                                                    2014037475

Printed in the United States of America

10 9 8 7 6 5 4 3 2 1

To Ryan, Aly, and Steph, how could I be so lucky?

CONTENTS

Todd "Bubba" Horwitz

I first walked onto a trading floor at the CBOE in September of 1982. I was 24 years old and I knew that I wanted to be involved in the option market. I was one of the original market makers in the SPX, and it was quite a thrill. When you trade for a living, every day is a new adventure; you never know what is going to happen next but you know that it will be interesting. Over 30 years later, I still can't wait for the opening bell!

So much has changed since I started to trade that it isn't the same business anymore. Now there is really no open outcry, the markets have shifted upstairs to the electronic platforms, and the trading pits are almost empty. When I started to trade, the option markets only had four expirations per year. Gradually, the powers that be figured out that if you had an expiration each month, that would bring more customers into the markets and provide greater liquidity. Another major policy change was to narrow the bid–offer spreads to $1, and that brought even more business into the market. All of the changes made it better for the retail customer.

In 2010, the SEC decided that it would allow customers to trade options on a weekly basis, bringing the expiration total to 52 times a year. Finally, three years ago, the exchanges were approved to list weekly options that would fill out the rest of the month so that they could be used for calendar spreading and rolling positions back one week instead of one month. The weekly option market has grown so much in the last year or so, it is now liquid enough to allow the retail trader to compete with the giants of Wall Street.

I am very pleased to have helped to educate scores of students on how to successfully integrate weekly options into their arsenal of trading tools, and I am very happy to be a part of this book. I have known Bob Seifert for more than 25 years, and we have collaborated on a great number of projects. I personally think that weekly options are the best investment tool that I have seen in that time. They are so versatile it is hard to believe that it took so long to bring them to the marketplace. If you have a stock position in place, the weekly options can be used to hedge your risk. If you have cash that is on the sidelines and you want to enhance your yield, weekly options offer you that opportunity, and if you want to speculate, the weekly options offer you the best possible opportunity.

When you read this book, you will probably need to study the material several times to take full advantage of the concepts presented. Anything that is worthwhile takes effort, and learning to trade weekly options is no different. Although the trades are very basic, they will offer you the chance to make money in any market condition.

I wish you good luck in your trading, and I can assure you that if you have the patience to learn the principles presented in this book, you will make your own luck!

For many years, it was difficult for individual option traders to compete with the banks and professional market makers in the derivative market. The bid–offer spreads were too big, the premium levels were so high that a retail trader could not afford to be involved, and finally, if their trade of choice was spreading, they had to wait months for the trade to mature.

Four years ago, weekly options didn't exist, and now they represent more than 30 percent of all options traded. There must be a reason for the phenomenal growth in such a short period of time. There is a reason, and it is very simple: Weekly options offer the best opportunity for any retail trader to get involved in the derivative market. This book is designed to reach any level of option trader, from the novice to successful traders that have yet to learn the power of weekly options.

The book is organized into sections, and after each part there is a quiz that reviews the key points that are emphasized in the chapter. The first section deals with market psychology and is designed to help you learn "the other side of the trade." If you think you can just pick up a book and magically defeat your opponent without understanding the psychology of the market, then you must also believe that if you can hit a golf ball you could beat Tiger Woods. In both cases, you are only fooling yourself.

The second section teaches you that underlying asset groups have different characteristics, and it is important to learn how each type of asset can be traded. It will show you that some markets are ideal for trading and other markets are simply impossible to beat. Once you learn what markets can be played, you need to see how they look when you study them, the patterns that constantly repeat, and how to spot those patterns. In addition, you must be able to communicate to the broker or to your software execution platform the trades that you want to make. Options have a distinct vocabulary and you must learn certain terms in order to participate in the market.

The third section is devoted to the option model, how it is unique in the world of finance, and why you must familiarize yourself with how it is priced in order to succeed. Simple mathematical examples are given to help you adjust your vision of markets to the viewpoint of an option trader. The option chain is introduced and how comprehension of this vehicle will be all-important to your trading success.

The second-to-last section deals with four simple trades that you can continuously make. It explains when and how the trades should be initiated, what market conditions give you the best chance for the individual trade to succeed, and how to manage the trade once it is in place.

The final section demonstrates how to manage your greatest asset—cash. It clarifies how to utilize your capital in a manner that will ensure that you don't run the risk of ruin when the inevitable capital drawdown occurs, and it identifies which trades can be employed using your available capital levels.

After the final chapter, there is a final exam made up primarily of questions that you have been asked before. If you can score 90 percent or better, you should be ready to tackle the big players in the option market!

ACKNOWLEDGMENTS

I would be remiss if I didn't start this section with mentioning the influence of my parents on my life and trading career. My father, "Lefty," and mother, Rita, introduced me to the wonderful world of numbers when I was a small child. My parents would best be described as "characters," immense personalities with a positive view on living that enhanced my life and all those who were fortunate enough to meet them.

Cards were the pastime in our house, and it was my father who introduced me to probabilities and odds. At the time I didn't know what they were, but Lefty taught me that if you held a pair of aces, you were a big favorite going into the draw. That simple explanation helped me to understand how to make certain decisions based on probability. I had a magical childhood, great parents, and have had good luck throughout my life.

I want to thank **Ablesys Corporation**, Dr. John Wang, Grace Wang, and Jesse Wang for their help in getting this book to be printed and for their permission to use the charts and graphs from the **AbleTrend** and **Abledelta** platforms as illustrations.

I want to thank Todd "Bubba" Horwitz for his Foreword section and for all of our years together working with students on how to trade, as well as for his input into many of my trading models.

I want to thank Ryan Seifert for his contribution and the time that he spent editing the manuscript. And finally, Bonnie Pittenger, without whose support this project would never have been completed. Not only did she help me with the text of the book, but her positive attitude toward life and her ability to overcome adversity continue to inspire me and all who know her.

Market Psychology: The Mind-Set of a Trader

"90 percent of the game is 5 inches wide, the length of the space between your ears."

—Bobby Jones, Golfer 1932

"Anyone who has never made a mistake has never tried anything new."

—Albert Einstein, Scientist 1937

"You can observe a lot by just watching."

—Yogi Berra, baseball player, New York Yankees 1956

"Greed is good."

—Gordon Gekko, *Wall Street* 1987

"Bulls and bears make money; pigs get slaughtered."

—Anonymous

"Coulda, woulda, shoulda."

—Every Investor 5000 BC to Present

The Herd Mentality: Bubbles

History is our great teacher. As Yogi Berra, the Yankees great, once said, "You can observe a lot just by watching." The past is the key to the present; if we do not learn from observing past events, we are doomed to repeat them.

In the spring of 2014, we still have a vivid memory of the financial meltdown in the summer and fall six years ago. TV commentators pleaded with investors to "get in there and sell, Wilson sell." Irate investors looked to hang their broker. Pictures of hysterical homeowners seeing years of hard work going out the window in a matter of months were gut-wrenching. Fingers pointed and tongues wagged. Crooked politicians, dishonest mortgage brokers, greedy Wall Street traders, shady rating agencies—there was enough blame to spread around.

Who could have possibly seen this one coming?

Comedians had a field day. Internet cartoons of stick figures explained to other stick figures where their money went. Hitler learning that his generals had tied up all of his cash in AIG and Lehman Brothers stock. Surely, this was the first time such a financial disaster had affected so many so quickly.

Or was it?

Because of its impact, it is crucial to recognize that the Great Recession was not an isolated incident. The market psychology that triggered this disaster goes back at least as long as history has been recorded. The panics will come in all forms and will start with many different patterns. Usually, the common thread is that some commodity or new technical revolution has no upper end. Demand for the product will be so great that it can only get bigger. There will be no upper limit to price, and any naysayers will regret their doubt. The thought process is:

"This time will be different."

Let's review a few of these "bubbles" that have occurred in the past 300 years and see what they have in common.

The South Sea Bubble 1711–1721: Trade, War, and Government Collusion

The South Sea Company was established in 1711 as a partnership between the British Treasury and the merchant class. England had been in a battle with Spain since the early 1700s in what is referred to as the "War of Spanish Succession." The war had been very costly; the Crown need to finance its debt, and the Lord Treasurer Robert Harley came up with a good idea: **Sell a franchise!**

He granted exclusive trading rights to a group of merchants in the "South Seas." It is a common misconception that the "South Seas" were in the Pacific, but in eighteenth-century Europe, the term referred to South America and the Caribbean Sea, not the Pacific.

The first round of financing granted the company "exclusive" trading rights for the sum of £10 million (approximately £500,000 million in 2014 £). In effect, the merchants convinced investors to take stock in the company and replace the bonds issued by the English Treasury. In exchange, the government granted the company a permanent annuity paying a little more than 5 percent. The merchants quickly resold the notes and guaranteed a profit to investors from the Treasury "in perpetuity." Today, we would call this *arbitrage,* and it is the way many investment banks generate billions in profit: Buy debt for one price, sell it for a discounted amount to investors, and take the difference and put it in their pocket.

The British government viewed the transaction as a layup. It would charge tariffs on trade from the "South Seas" to fund the interest and pocket the difference.

When the war with Spain was finally settled in 1713 by the treaty of Utrecht, the terms were not as favorable as the Crown or the merchants had hoped. Although there is no evidence the company had ever made dollar one, the Treasury was able to float another round of financing in 1717 for £2 million. The original notes were converted to the new debt and the government continued to pay the interest. Nowadays, financiers call this type of sovereign debt replacement *Brady bonds* in honor of the US Secretary of the Treasury whose ingenuity bailed out US banks and Latin America in the 1990s.

The new debt funded the original loans from 1711. Nevertheless, as time passed and the company still did not flourish, the Crown needed to raise more capital. In 1719, the company conceived of a new idea.

Exchange the existing debt for equity in the Crown!

The company proposed to buy the majority of the Treasuries debt for £30 million. In exchange, the government guaranteed to pay interest on the shares at a preferred rate of 5 percent for a period of eight years, and then 4 percent "in perpetuity." To sweeten the deal, the shares were allowed to be traded, and any "appreciation" could be used to buy more shares.

Needless to say, this arrangement benefited the company and the Crown. Rumors circulated that the trading rights granted the South Sea Company in the "New World" were far in excess of what was being revealed (can you say "new economy stocks"?), which caused frenzied speculation. Trading in the winter and spring of 1720 drove the price of the stock up almost 400 percent. Greed pulled in even more investors anxious to be in on the big payoff. Insiders and the Crown were rumored to have made a killing.

In June 1720, after scores of joint-stock companies joined in the feast, Parliament—fearing a revolt by the general population—passed the "Bubble Act," which forbad joint-stock companies from participating in unregistered issuance of stock. Unfortunately, this did not curb the bubble, but triggered even more aggressive buying of the South Sea Company stock. In a perverted way, the South Sea Company was viewed as a flight to quality!

Shares prices exploded, peaking at 1,000 percent of their issuance price from the final conversion of debt to stock in 1719. Finally, in August 1720, "No greater fool could be found," and the prices started to tumble. In six weeks, it was all over. The price was back to £150.

What became of the South Sea Company?

It continued to exist until 1763, when it was disbanded. In between wars, it continued to serve as a front for the Crown's debt. In times of war, it virtually disappeared.

The hangover lasted for decades. Scores of ordinary citizens were broken. Bitterness was unbridled and knew no class. One of the biggest losers in the scam was Sir Isaac Newton, one of the most brilliant minds of all time. He never recovered financially and died in virtual poverty March 31, 1727, in an apartment with his niece and her husband.

■ The Cotton Panic of 1837: Land, Commodities, and Government

The first bubble addressed took place in Europe. Let's turn our attention to the original panic in the United States. This bubble is not nearly as celebrated as its European counterpart, but it was equally as deadly. It occurred during the presidency of Andrew Jackson, 1829–1837. When the bubble burst on May 10, 1837, Martin Van Buren was the president, but make no mistake—the stage was set in the prior 10 years.

The war of 1812 was really America's second Revolutionary War. The British invasion was almost successful, and the United States came very close to being "the colonies" again. As with most wars, there is a positive effect on the economy, as manufacturing and commerce in general have a tendency to grow. Capital goods must be replaced at a far greater rate than during times of peace. Usually, the prosperity lasts a few years; however, once the "war effect" ends, a general slowdown is almost sure to occur. In the United States, it manifested itself with the downturn of 1819–1821.

By the middle of 1821, the country was on its way to a recovery. The United States was expanding it western borders; new agriculture opportunities and trade brought in an era of exceptional wealth. The population went up by almost 60 percent, primarily shifting to the West, where commerce flourished North and South along the Mississippi River valley.

When the Jacksonian Era began in 1829, the United States had expanded its borders, and had also built an infrastructure of roads and canals that allowed for a flow of goods not only North and South on the Mississippi but also from the East Coast ports to the western colonies as far as Ohio.

Jackson was a very tough and vengeful man. He had been a war hero, a US senator, a landowner—and his nickname "Old Hickory" said it all. It was the merciless streak that helped to set the wheels in motion for the disaster that was to follow.

As with any time of prosperity, the demand for commodities and the land to produce them continued to increase. By law, public land in the West and Mississippi Valley could be purchased for $1.25 per acre. Sales of land increased steadily in the 1830s, and landowners started to feel the first *wealth effect*. Land in some prime growing areas of the Mississippi more than quadrupled in value in five years (Iowa farmland in 2014?).

In government, a nasty personal feud between President Jackson and Nicholas Biddle, the owner of the Second Bank of the United States, resulted in the revocation of its charter. Jackson replaced the Second Bank of the United States (lender of last resort) with "Specie Circular" (gold and silver coins bimetal standard) and began to deposit money in state-chartered banks.

Unfortunately, the move to gold and silver coins did not allow for any expansion of the banking system. Consequently, when individual banks needed credit to cover land transactions, there was no institution to loan them the funds. This put banks in a huge dilemma. To counter the problem, the state banks actually exacerbated the situation by lending in "paper," or "kiting" their own notes to cover the land speculation. The thirst for "King Cotton" in Europe was thought to be unquenchable. Conversely, with inflation on the rise, signs of darkness started to emerge in late 1835. Cotton prices doubled and it fetched nearly 20 cents a pound, and inflation was headed toward double digits.

In 1836, Britain forced new and punitive trade agreements on the United States, and greatly reduced exporting and importing with America. For any trade that did take place, the British demanded payment in hard currency, not cotton. As it turned out, the demand for cotton was not infinite. By the winter of 1837, rising inflation led to social unrest. On February 14, a large assembly of angry men met in New York City to demand that the government curb exploding prices. When their demands for lower prices fell on deaf ears, the meeting turned ugly. The assembly turned into a mob and took to the street with torches. The military was called out to quell the violence, but before peace could be restored, several warehouses filled with grain were burnt to the ground. One of the unfortunate flour merchants noted with sarcasm that "burning the goods would not have a tendency to lower price."

Commencing in April, a number of large dry-goods companies went under. These companies were the nineteenth-century equivalent of Walmart, and their demise shook the foundations of American finance. The price of cotton began to collapse; in less than six weeks, it lost 50 percent of its value. By the first week in May, the banking system was in a state of panic. On May 10, 1837, with cotton and land prices collapsing and with nowhere to turn for "a lender of last resort," all banks in New York City stopped paying in Specie. Within two months of the New York

Bank failure, 40 percent of the banks in the United States went broke. Interest rates turned negative as the ensuing panic drove the country into a financial depression.

Although not as famous as the Great Depression of the 1930s, the collapse of the banking system in 1837 led to six years of "unprecedented misery" in the United States. By some estimates, in the industrial areas of the Northeast unemployment reached a staggering 30 percent. It took another war to pull the nation out of the funk.

■ The Panic of 1893: Railroads Have No Upper Limit

Railroads had been a reliable form of transportation for nearly a quarter of a century in Europe before they arrived in America in the late 1820s. Between 1830 and 1860, America saw a great period of expansion when the country more than doubled in size. The nation needed a way to move goods and people to new markets quickly, and the railroad was the perfect vehicle. It combined the ability to move bulk goods, as the river and canal system had, and it added the value of speed. It could move goods up to 400 miles a day; a trip that used to take weeks could now be accomplished in a couple of days.

Prior to 1850, most of the railroads were short lines that joined with other short lines to form an irregular system. However, in 1850 the US Congress decided it was time to try and establish longer-haul routes that were contiguous and made available the first railroad land grants. During the next 20 years, legislators granted 170 million acres to roughly 85 railroad companies. Although substantial portions of the grants were never developed, the country still had enough track in place to circle the globe.

One of the problems that Congress had not foreseen was the standardization of track. There was no Bill Gates to figure out that if one railroad had a different width of track than the next, it could create a problem, and, unfortunately, it created a massive one. With hundreds of railroads across the land and several different gauges, it became increasingly difficult to move goods over large areas without transferring to a new railroad each time the track size changed.

The problem gradually resolved itself in the decades after the Civil War as the standardization of track took place and Congress continued to extend free land to the railroads in an attempt to connect the West to the rest of the country. As with any new technology, it seemed that this time was different and the market for railroads had no limit. It allowed for both a revolution in commerce as well as a social revolution. By 1880, you could travel from New York to San Francisco in less time than it took to go from New York to Washington, D.C., 50 years earlier.

With innovation came the need for financing the next project, and who was better suited for that than Wall Street? By 1890, there was more than $12 billion (nearly $300 billion in 2014 dollars) invested in the industry. As with any successful product, competition came into play. Within 10 years of Leland Stanford driving the "golden spike" that completed the transcontinental railroad on May 10, 1869, at Promontory Summit in the Utah Territory, there were four competing railroads carrying passengers and goods across the country. Revenues began to shrink, but the cost of infrastructure continued to climb, latecomers started to have troubles, and some smaller railroads went under.

On February 23, 1893, a major carrier, the Philadelphia and Reading Railroad, declared bankruptcy. This created a crisis of confidence (Lehman Brothers?), and investors began to panic and withdraw their money from the banking system. The federal government sought to stop the run by repealing legislation that tied the price of silver to the dollar, but that effort failed when more major railroads ceased to do business.

The final result was that hundreds of railroads went broke; over 500 banks, the majority of them in the West, closed; and 15,000 other businesses went under. Unemployment in major manufacturing cities moved above 18 percent at the peak of the depression in 1894 and remained in double digits until the recovery began in 1897 with the Klondike Gold Rush.

■ September 11, 2001: Price Can Never Go Up Again

Although the three bubbles that we have observed were from different times and different places, they all had a common origin: speculation fueled the bubble. In each case, the perceived opportunity overcame rational thought. Even one of the most brilliant men in recorded history fell victim to the mass hysteria. So now the question must be asked: Is it possible to have a deflationary bubble?

Could the price of an asset class be deflated with the same logic that causes the inflationary bubble?

Consider Tuesday, September 11, 2001.

I doubt that any living American will ever forget that morning. The impossible had happened; terrorists were able to take down American financial icons, the World Trade Centers in New York City. The markets reacted swiftly and viciously. If you were not lucky enough to close your positions, there was no way to reach financial safety.

Within minutes of the second tower being hit, the exchanges were forced to close. The infrastructure damage was immense, and it would take a full week before they could reopen. Although authorities pleaded for calm, as a professional trader you sensed the result before the markets reopened: panic.

When the markets resumed trading on Monday, September 17, the financial devastation of the attack was immediately apparent. The DJIA plummeted more than 4 percent on the opening bell. When the carnage stopped at 4:00, the Dow was down more than 7 percent.

Rumors on the street flourished. Bin Laden was not only the mastermind of the attack but he had purchased millions of dollars of puts on the OEX. New attacks were on the way. The economies of the Western Allies had lost hundreds of billions, and it would take decades to recover. The rest of week was even worse. Every day, the decline accelerated. Investors refused buy any US asset. Treasury Bonds, which had been used as a "flight to quality" for more than 80 years, joined the rout.

Friday morning, September 21, the economic news was horrible. There was no tomorrow; in a single stroke of violence, Bin Laden had realized his dream to bring the decadent Western world to its knees. The market opened down almost 5 percent from Thursday's close. The worst week in over 140 years was in the making. The futures markets were locked limit down. Economic Armageddon had arrived, and this time there was no bottom!

And then it stopped.

Some anonymous investor stepped up to the plate and bought. The market rallied the rest of the day to finish marginally lower; by December 31, 2001, it had rallied 23 percent from the bottom. Bin Laden did not accomplish his goal.

The United States not only survived but continues to flourish. The masterminds of the plot are either dead or in captivity.

■ The Commodity Bubble of 2008: Price Can Never Go Down Again

The housing bubble has gotten extensive coverage in all forms of media, so it will not be discussed here. But one of the largest meltdowns in world history was in the works in a parallel universe, the commodity bust of 2008.

The commodity panic was not limited to a specific country or a specific product. Modern trade and the speed of information allowed the panic to spread quickly across the world. The list of culprits is long. Evil speculators, farmers who overplanted fields, hoarders who withheld goods from the market, consumers who raced each other for more goods than they could possible use, and, of course, the pigs on Wall Street. Rather than take the time to go over each individual market, the focus of this story will be placed on the biggest commodity market in the world—crude oil.

Crude oil has been a major source of energy for more than 150 years. Fortunes have been made and lost acquiring it. Nations have been built on its back. Nations have gone to war to acquire it. It is a god of wealth to some and the devil for others, but one thing is clear: Twenty-first-century society needs crude oil.

The bubble in crude oil started as countless panics that preceded it, with a gradual inflation of price. Less than 10 years before the bubble burst, the price of crude oil was $17 a barrel.

Iraq was selling as much as it could produce to cover its costly mistake with Kuwait and the resulting war with the US-led coalition. In addition, financial problems in the Far East reduced the demand, making it unprofitable to recover crude from marginal fields.

Demand was not suppressed for long, though, and crude oil prices reached $60 a barrel in June 2005. By the summer of 2006, crude oil futures at the NYMEX peaked at $77 a barrel. After the summer surge, prices retreated and closed on New Year's Eve at $63. However, the uptrend did not halt for long. In September 2007, crude took out the previous year's high and closed at over $80 a barrel.

Multiple factors were cited for the increase in price.

US oil reserves had fallen to dangerous levels, OPEC was reducing production, leftist rebels had attacked and destroyed pipelines in Mexico, an El Nino was predicted, the US dollar was getting pummeled, there was social unrest in Turkey, and Elvis had been sighted in Reno. In November 2007, oil hit $90 a barrel on fears of social unrest in Turkey; the US dollar was getting pummeled. Every bit of news, no matter how bizarre and unrelated, was a reason to buy oil.

On January 2, 2008, crude hit the magic $100 a barrel level. Prices continued to skyrocket throughout the spring and early summer. Finally, on July 11, 2008, oil peaked at $148 a barrel. Now under extreme pressure from the public, President George W. Bush issued an executive order on July 14 removing the ban on offshore drilling that had been in place since 1990. This was largely a political tool, as it did not change production or distribution capacity. By the end of July, oil had retreated to $125. It appeared that the worldwide demand for oil, which six months before could never be satisfied, was now overwhelmed by supply. The global meltdown in housing prices further reduced the amount petroleum by-products needed in construction.

Throughout the fall, oil prices continued to collapse, as the global stock markets plummeted and cash was poured into US Treasury Bonds. The world didn't seem to care that the yield on the 30-year investment was less than 3 percent, the lowest return in 80 years. The cash price of West Texas crude oil bottomed at $38 a barrel on December 21, 2008. In less than six months, the price had fallen by 75 percent, and trillions of dollars had been lost.

Who was to blame for this unprecedented implosion?

Well, according to testimony before congressional committees, the government claimed that there was a single source—the usual suspects, the greed on Wall Street. On June 3, 2009, testimony before the Senate Committee on Commerce, Science, and Transportation, former director of the CFTC Division of Trading & Markets Michael Greenberger fingered the Atlanta-based Intercontinental Exchange founded by Goldman Sachs, Morgan Stanley, and British Petroleum as the agency playing a key role in the speculative run-up of oil futures prices traded off of the regulated futures exchanges in London and New York. In January 2011, crude oil reached the $100 a barrel mark once again.

Bitcoin 2009 to Present: Crypto-Currency Meets Greed

The last bubble we will examine is one that is current, and the final results are not in. Proponents claim that this is the techno-currency of the future; detractors claim it is a way for criminals to hide transactions and is most likely a Ponzi scheme.

Look at the results thus far and you can be the judge.

Bitcoin first appeared in a scientific paper and is credited to the name Satoshi Nakamoto. Since no one has come forward to claim its authorship, it is difficult to determine if it is a pen name or simply an individual or a group that wants to remain anonymous.

Bitcoin is a digital currency that doesn't have any ties to a central bank. The point-to-point payment system allows for transactions to be made in complete anonymity. The coin is created by a complex set of computer codes that create the currency through a process called *mining*. Unlike central bank–issued currency, which can expand and contract the money supply, bitcoins have a finite number, and once the final coin is mined, it is a closed environment. In addition to being untraceable, the value of the currency is not being manipulated by a central bank. Proponents claim that in the long run, it will allow for a stable market and that supply and demand will establish its value. Opponents claim the opposite—that this trait gives it all of the features that promote extreme price manipulation and can give seeds to a massive Ponzi scheme.

The price history of Bitcoin suggests that the opponents' view is hard to argue.

In 2011, the price of a single Bitcoin fluctuated from a low of 30 cents per US dollar to as high of $32 before crashing back to $2. If this is supposed to be a way to put stability in a currency system the initial result seems to indicate the opposite. In March 2013, the Bitcoin exchange known as Mt. Gox had a software meltdown and triggered another massive selloff in the crypto-currency, as prices plunged by 70 percent in less than three hours. The market recovered and rallied back to over $1,100 a Bitcoin before a selloff in January of 2014 saw the price go down to $500 in less than a month. A rally in February of 2014 took the price back to $1,000 until money laundering and Internet scandals involving one of its strongest proponents rocked the currency. Later in February, Mt. Gox was again the victim of a computer glitch and suspended withdrawals. This time, the exchange closed and admitted that $350 million worth of Bitcoin was missing from its vaults. The victims of the loss are currently looking for a legal jurisdiction to pursue criminal action. The irony of this is that the traders who are searching for their money ($) were using the Bitcoin to avoid legal detection, and were manipulating the crypto-currency for profit; they are now complaining that they were scammed!

Isn't this the same defense that Bernie Madoff's minions used to defend the millions that they helped to steal off of investors? They also claimed that they were the victims because they took the stolen money and invested it with Mr. Madoff!

As of this writing, the Bitcoin is trading around $350, a drawdown of over 70 percent from its peak value during the height of the mania in December of 2013. Whether it will turn out to be a highly speculative investment or just another Ponzi scheme can't be determined at this point, but one thing is certain—it has not proven to be anywhere near as effective as advertised in combating the weakness of central bank–issued currency. In fact, it has multiplied any of their shortcomings many times over!

■ Lessons to Be Learned

Six famous markets have been examined. The time frame stretches for almost 300 years. Four of these markets resulted in bubble tops, one ended in an implosive bottom, and one is not a final score. Various reasons were given in order to justify the price action. Various underlying assets were involved in the bubbles.

Can we find a common thread?

■ *At market extremes, emotions drive the markets, not rational thought!*

When the markets were rallying, it was not the value of the underlying asset that drove the market higher; it was the mind-set of the investors.

■ *Investors become overwhelmed by greed.*

When it seemed that anyone could get rich in the South Sea Company, no one wanted to miss that ship.

■ *Investors become paralyzed by fear.*

In the case of the implosion after the 2001 terrorist attacks, fear drove investors to unload their stocks in a hurry.

■ *All market extremes are driven by two forces—fear and greed.*

Markets might generally pay attention to asset value, earnings, and global trends, but when emotion starts driving price, it can take over in a hurry.

You might be wondering why a book on how to trade weekly options would start with a chapter about economic history. I believe in order to be successful trading in the markets, you must be able to understand how the price got to certain levels and how to control your emotions when everyone around you is losing control of theirs.

Without an understanding of market psychology, it is almost impossible to be successful. You have to know what the *other side of the trade* is thinking and how they are reacting.

After each chapter, there will a brief quiz. Take it and check your responses in the answer section in the back of the book. The questions will be multiple choice, and the number of points you can earn on a question will vary from one to three.

If you can score 90 percent on any of the tests, you are ready to go to the next chapter. If you struggle with the quiz, please reread the material before going to the next section. This book is a building-block system to approaching the markets, and, therefore, if you don't build a solid foundation, the whole structure can come crumbling down.

■ Chapter 1 Quiz

1) The South Sea Company was set up to:
   a) take advantage of new trade routes to the South Seas
   b) be the world's first franchise
   c) fund the Crown's debt from the Spanish War of Succession
   d) do all of the above

2) Who funded the South Sea Company?
   a) investment bankers
   b) the British Crown
   c) individual investors
   d) all of the above

3) Why did Sir Isaac Newton lose his fortune in the South Sea bubble?
   a) The South Sea stock was allowed to trade freely.
   b) The Crown lost a great deal of money developing the trade routes to the South Seas.
   c) Land companies drove up the price of the trade routes.
   d) He was greedy.

4) What caused the Cotton Panic of 1837?
   a) Andrew Jackson's feud with Nicholas Biddle
   b) the move to a bimetal system to back the dollar
   c) the expansion to the Western territories
   d) none of the above

5) The lack of a lender of last resort in the 1837 Cotton Panic:
   a) had little to do with the panic; greed was the villain
   b) was accomplished by state banks
   c) created a panic in the cotton market
   d) caused the price of cotton to collapse

6) The 1836 British tariff on cotton:
   a) caused cotton prices to collapse
   b) caused land prices to collapse in the Mississippi delta
   c) caused inflation
   d) had little to do with the panic

7) What caused the railroad panic of 1893?
   a) Congress allowed too many free acres for railroad construction.
   b) There was competition among railroads.
   c) Wall Street's greed led it to finance unneeded infrastructure.
   d) Demand for coast-to-coast travel declined.

8) The stock market crash of 2001 was primarily caused by:
   a) the terrorist attacks in New York City
   b) an inflated market that was primed for a selloff
   c) the Federal Reserve's lack of response to the crisis
   d) the fear created by the attack

9) What was the Bitcoin bubble of 2014?
   a) a classic example of a new technology that had no upper limit
   b) an event caused by the collapse of the Mt. Gox Exchange
   c) an event caused by government corruption
   d) a classic example of greed

10) All the bubbles reviewed had which of the following common characteristics?
   a) Technology had produced a product that had no upper limit.
   b) Government regulations contributed to the problem.
   c) Inflation caused the markets to collapse.
   d) Greed or fear overwhelmed reason.

If you scored 90 percent or better, congratulations! If not, please reread the chapter to make sure that the first block of the foundation is in place.

Modern Markets

In this chapter, we are going to look at the major markets that we will be trading weekly options on, and compare their similarities and differences. Before you can attempt to trade any market you must have a thorough understanding of how it functions. All markets are not the same, and it is a mistake to try and trade them if you are not familiar with the way that they trade.

Twenty-first-century financial markets no longer rely on face-to-face barter, as they had for centuries; they are conducted through electronic transfers. The markets we will be concerned with are highly sophisticated, and will always result in the exchange of funds. Almost all thriving markets rely on a form of auction. The party who wants to buy something will place a bid. The counterparty will place an offer. If no one is willing to yield, the market does not trade. When a trade does occur, it is called **price discovery**. This is one of the most important terms you will learn in trading. It is the market mechanism that allows the transfer of value.

Equity Markets

Most investors refer to the equity markets as stock markets. Equity markets are the most famous investing venues, but they are relatively small when compared to debt and currency markets. This chapter will begin by looking at the US stock markets.

There are many ways to get equity in a company, and one is to buy stock. However, not all stock markets are the same. You have the very liquid big capitalization stocks that are traded on a variety of platforms, and exchanges, and you have over-the-counter stocks (OTC) that can vary from Pink Sheets to penny stocks. Our discussion will only be about securities that are traded on the major exchanges.

Who Do I Buy Stock From?

When you buy a stock, who actually sells it to you?

Is it your broker?

Is it the underwriter?

Is it the mysterious short seller?

The answer may surprise you. It is the company that issued the stock! This is very significant, and it will help you to understand the "flow of funds" we will discuss later.

When a company decides to offer stock to the public, it goes through a series of steps that will result in an underwriting and an IPO (initial public offering). If it is a small offering, it will be conducted in the OTC market, or even a smaller stock market known as "penny" stock. No matter which market the firm uses, when it offers stock the originator's interest will become **diluted**.

Suppose you come up with an idea for a new Internet company. You put together some funds, and start your business. It grows, and in a couple of years you need more capital. You meet with an investment banker and they go through a process called **due diligence** to arrive at a reasonable estimate of your company's net worth. They then calculate what portion of the company you will need to sell in order to bring in outside capital from investors. The portion that you give up is put on the public market and is generally referred to as the **float**. It is the portion that is available to be bought and sold by the public. Depending on market conditions, the price of the float may be higher or lower. However, unless you issue more stock, **the float will always be the same**. It is a finite number of shares available for trading.

If someone tries to accumulate this float, the price of shares should go up. The buyers in a rising market are referred to as the **strong hands**; the countertrend traders are called the **weak hands**. If the market reverses, the buyers would now become the weak hands, and vice versa. If the strong hands acquire enough shares over a short period of time, the price may explode; this is called a **short squeeze**. If weak hands think they can overwhelm the strong hands, they may borrow shares and **sell short** in an attempt to drive the price down and buy their shares back at a discounted value. No matter which party is the other side of your individual transaction, in effect you are buying your shares from the diluted shares the company originally issued. Stocks have no specific time for redemption, and will remain on the market until (1) the company does a **buyback**, (2) the stock is taken over by another company, or (3) the company ceases to exist.

■ Liquidity

The size of the float, or **open interest**, in the case of futures or options, is extremely important, as it will be the major factor in determining **liquidity**. *Liquidity for our purposes will be defined as the ability to move seamlessly in and out of a market.*

The **bid–offer spread** and **commissions** are vital components when choosing which stock or commodity to trade. In penny stocks, you may find a quote of "**20c@24c.**" Conventional wisdom implies that a 4-cent spread is immaterial. If you are trading in this market, you are in it for big gains. If I buy the offer, it will cost me 4 cents, no big deal.

That is the logic that unscrupulous brokers use—the markup on this stock is only 4 cents a share, or commissions on this stock are only 1 cent a share. What are they really telling you?

If you buy the stock, it needs to go up by **20 percent just to break even. Add in a commission and the stock must rise by 25 percent!** If there isn't enough float, the stock can easily be manipulated by **strong hands**. The **weak hands** will be overpowered and, in most cases, take a large drawdown on their investment. This power play can happen in any market, but it is particularly rampant in the OTC and penny markets. **Illiquid markets should always be avoided**.

Think about what happened in the meltdown of 2008. How did Wall Street bust out? It was overleveraging, and the liquidity of the market dried up. The major players knew what to do, but when there was no **other side of the trade**, the big players were forced to throw in the towel.

■ Flow of Funds

We have already learned that when we have price discovery, the market is in equilibrium. We know that, because a buyer and seller agreed on the price, and a trade took place. Stability may only exist for a split-second before price moves on, but at that point in time the market was in balance.

What causes the market to move?

If price is rallying, are there more buyers than sellers?

If it is breaking, are there more sellers than buyers?

Conventional wisdom is that an imbalance of buyers and sellers is what causes the market to move.

Conventional wisdom is wrong!

Remember, we are in an auction market. Price can only move higher or lower when we have new price discovery. The real answer is, in order to move price, there must be more **aggressive buyers and sellers**. If the market is rallying, buyers are willing to pay more for each purchase; however, they must still find a seller. If they cannot find a seller at the next price level, they must continue to bid until price discovery finds a new level. In extreme cases, the market **prices**—there are no buyers/sellers at the next level. The market **gaps** until more buyers/sellers can be found, and there is a new price discovery.

This flow of funds leaves a **technical footprint**, and in later chapters we will learn how to use this information to make logical trading decisions.

Many terms were introduced; some them may be new to you. You will need to become skilled at using my definitions for market behavior. You will see these terms constantly when I am referring to market action. If you can't read the map, you are going to have problems getting to your destination.

Futures Markets: Origins

The modern era of regulated future trading in the United States began with the Chicago Board of Trade (CBOT) in 1848. A serious concern for the credit risk in OTC grain contracts led to a private, centralized location where buyers and sellers could negotiate and formalize forward contracts. By 1864, the exchange had the first exchange traded forward contracts in place. In 1919, a group of members split off to form the Chicago Butter and Egg Board, which eventually became the Chicago Mercantile Exchange (CME).

Trading at the exchanges remained fairly backwater until the late 1970s. During this period, it became obvious that the Bretton Woods Agreement, which set the price for foreign exchange, was failing. The CME introduced the initial currency contracts in 1979. For the first time, rates of foreign exchange could be traded. This was quickly followed by the CBOT introducing contracts on US Treasury products. In 2007, the CBOT merged with the CME to become the CME Group, which is the largest futures exchange in the world. Today futures contracts are traded on hundreds of exchanges throughout the world. Many of them are totally electronic; others still use **open outcry** as a means of price discovery. Thousands of products are in place to offset producer and consumer risk.

Futures contracts differ from stock in several ways. First of all, stock has no expiration and can only be removed from the market in the ways mentioned earlier in this chapter. Futures are always for a specific period of time. The contract calls for the seller to deliver to the buyer the underlying goods at the time of expiration unless the seller buys the contract back before its expiration, known as the **delivery date**. The second major difference is that the contracts are not standardized, as is the equity market. The size will vary greatly, depending on the product that you are trading, and you must learn to read the terms of the contract. This can be done by contacting the exchange and requesting a list of contracts specs.

Calculating Futures Contract Values

If you buy 100 shares of stock at $10 per share, the cost is $1,000. This is not the case with futures contracts. If you are trying to decide which contract to trade, it is important to understand the amount of money you are dealing with. The size of the contract will be listed at the exchange where you are trading. The dollar amount will usually be quoted as **the size of the contract x the point value**. This computation can be tricky, so we will do a few calculations.

It is the spring and you think that this year's corn prices are going higher. You check the *Wall Street Journal* (WSJ) and find that corn for July delivery is quoted at **5,000 bu; cents per bu**. The market closed yesterday at 598 and it was down 8c. From this information, you should be able to tell the dollar size of the contract and what the price change in cents translates into in dollars. We are trading 5000 bu and the price closed at 598c per bushel. In **dollars**, it would be 598c, or $5.98 \times 5000 = \$29,900$. If you were long one July corn contract, you lost $(5000 \text{ bu}/100 \text{ c} \times 8 \text{ c}) = \$400$.

Let's try another one. You think that oil has fallen far enough over the last eight months, so you decide to buy a June oil contract. The WSJ quotes the price of the June contract as **1,000 bbls; $ per bbl**. If the contact closed at 94.47, up 1.27, and you owned one contract, which of the following would be true?

a) You made $127.
b) The value of the contract at the close was $944,700.
c) The point value of this contract is $100.
d) All of the above.
e) None of the above.

The correct answer is e, none of the above. The value of the contract is $94,470, you made $1,270, and the point value is $10.

Contract value in dollars multiplied by point value equals gain or loss for the day. If you had trouble with the math, please review it again. It is important to know what the dollar value is of the contract that you are trading. **When calculating risk in the futures market, a misplaced decimal point can cause some very serious heartburn.**

■ Tick Size

Tick size is a measure of liquidity and will be defined as the **minimum price fluctuation; this may or may not be the point value**. I know this can be confusing, so we will study a few examples.

Let's use the two contracts from the previous example.

Corn has a point value of $50, but the tick size is $\frac{1}{4}$c, or $12.50.

Oil has a point value of $10; it also has a tick size of $10.

How do I know the difference between the two numbers?

The simplest way to find out the difference between the point value and the tick size, if any, is to ask your clearinghouse. It will be glad to give you the information you need.

■ Margin

Margin on futures contracts is quite a bit different from margin on stock.

Margin on stock for individual investors is usually calculated using **Reg T of the Securities and Exchange Commission (SEC)**. Reg T requires approximately 50 percent cash deposit and must be maintained for the **current market** value of the stock. If the stock falls dramatically in price, the margin money must be increased. This is a **margin call**. If the stock price rises dramatically, more stock can be purchased with the margin or cash can be removed from the account.

In the futures market, margin is a **good-faith deposit** required by the exchange, before a contract can be bought or sold. If the price or the volatility of the market changes, the exchange has the right to call for any margin amount that it feels is appropriate to protect all of the market participants.

The major difference between the margin for stock and the margin for a futures contract is that the price of the futures contract does not have to change in order for the exchange to raise or lower the margin.

■ Stock Index Futures

In the fall of 1982, the CME received permission from the CFTC to begin trading the S&P 500 Index futures. The futures index mirrors the Standard and Poor's 500 cash index. The difference in price between the futures contract and the cash is referred to as the **basis** or **cost of carry**; it is a function of interest rates. At expiration, the cash index and the futures index converge and are settled in cash.

The index is calculated by multiplying the value of the contract × point value. If the point value for the S&P is $250 and the index is trading at 1800, the dollar value of the contract is $450,000 (1800 × $250). If you were to buy a standard S&P contract, you would control $450,000 worth of the underlying stock index.

In order to encourage trading by smaller investors and provide more liquidity, the CME Group offers **e-mini contracts**. The e-mini contract has a point value of $50 and is worth one-fifth of the full contract. E-mini contracts are traded electronically, and are also settled in cash.

Large investment banking firms use the futures contract to **arbitrage** their cash holdings. This is done by either buying or selling a futures contract against their

basket of stocks that they hold in the cash market. A bank tries to capitalize on the difference in the bid–offer spread on the stock. If the gap is large enough to cover operating costs and produce a small profit, the trade is executed. This type of trading is very sophisticated and requires large amounts of capital. It is not recommend for retail traders.

■ Index Futures versus Stock

Index futures have certain inherent advantages to trading stock outright. Many risks of an individual stock do not exist in the index futures market. When you own stock outright, you always run the risk that some adverse event will happen that will cause a precipitous decline in the value of the stock. In some cases, the stock could become worthless.

This could only happen in the index futures if the entire economy was wiped out. A comet hits Earth, Yellowstone Park explodes, and a tsunami destroys the East Coast. Hollywood loves to prey on these fears, but for practical purposes, we will not worry about these unlikely occurrences. As a rule, your money is much more insulated from adverse economic events when you use index futures. That is not to say that your investment would be safe in tough times, but you would be sheltered from the takeover or bankruptcy of any one company.

Stocks have risks as to dividends. You don't need to worry about "x-div" dates. The index futures have that information built into the price.

Technically, you feel that the market is due for a rally. If you buy an individual stock, it might not rally with the market because it doesn't have a very positive correlation. The term in the industry for the correlation between an individual stock and the underlying index is **beta**. In this case, it would have a negative beta correlation. If you use the same funds and trade the e-mini, you are guaranteed to be rewarded if you are correct in your prediction of price.

The "e-minis" are much more liquid than any stock. You can control a $50,000 position for as little as a $5 bid–ask spread (.0001). This type of liquidity guarantees the kind of seamless entry/exit that is necessary for you to operate, if you want to trade short term. As with any assets, liquidity is key—the same with the stock indexes. You want to only trade the front month, as it is very liquid. If your view is long term, don't use the deferred month, as it will probably be very illiquid. The solution is to roll back your contract when the front month expires.

Index futures have all of the positives of buying stock without many of the negatives. True, the index will not double or triple in a few weeks as an individual stock may do, but it will not lose 100 percent of its value overnight! You can be sure that you will be around to trade another day.

■ Forex: Currencies

Let's go onto another massive market. The market for currencies, the foreign exchange market **(Forex, or FX)**, is where large-scale currency trading takes place. The market had its origins in the early 1970s with the collapse of the Bretton Woods system of fixed currency price. For many years until 1971, all liquid foreign currencies had been pegged to the US dollar and were set for a specific period of time. Traders convinced economists that the Bretton Woods Agreement was flawed and that currencies were no different than any other commodity. The market has grown dramatically in the past 35 years, and today it is estimated that daily volume is over $5 trillion.

The currencies are traded in **spot** as well as **forward contracts**. The forward contracts are standardized as 100,000 units of the base currency; this is referred to as a **lot**. The spread between the bid and offer is referred to as the **pip**. Unlike the futures markets, there is no central clearinghouse, and major financial institutions clear each other's trades. This could become dangerous, as failure of a large commercial institution could cause a panic if central banks do not step in as lender of last resort.

Dissimilar to futures trading, not all players are considered equal. The large commercial interests and central banks are permitted to negotiate price. The size of one's "line" (cash position) determines who can participate in the negotiated trading. This market is not available to the average trader. The normal trader must pay a three- to five-pip spread to compete in the market. Although not technically a pure auction market, the large players are kept in line by arbitragers that can immediately take advantage of any price fluctuations that are outside the current retail bid–offer spread. The FX market is subject to the same squeeze conditions that are inherent in all markets. Enormous open interest in the forward contracts keeps this market very transparent.

■ Options

Now we will look at the final category of markets, and the one we will specialize in trading—**options**. They are definitely the most misunderstood part of the financial puzzle. They are not a mystery once you understand the basic concept and learn the terminology. They are far and away the most useful of all financial products.

Let's look at how they evolved.

It is difficult to say when options first started to trade, but it appears that they have been trading in one form or another for over 3,000 years. From archives, we are certain that the Phoenicians and Greeks benefited from them to hedge shipping risk. The option was used as a primitive form of insurance. One merchant would receive a premium for taking some of the risk, and the other would be willing to give up a piece of his profit for bearing less risk on his cargo.

Options were also traded in Europe starting in the 1600s. They played a major role in one of the greatest financial panics (or allegories concerning greed) of all time, the infamous **tulip frenzy**. The issuing of unregulated options allowed speculators to drive the price of tulips to farcical price levels; the subsequent fallout almost destroyed the national economy of Holland.

In North America, grain options traded as early as the eighteenth century. Many scandals arose from sellers being unable to meet their guarantees. The first **exchange-traded** products appeared with the formation of the Chicago Board of Trade in 1848. The CBOT regulated the contracts in size and term, demanding payment of margin from both the seller and buyer. With these regulated option contracts many of the abuses that had led to scandals in previous years were eliminated.

Options continued to trade in many forms over the next 130 years. In the late 1970s, the Chicago Mercantile Exchange introduced the first financial futures. As an offshoot, the CFTC allowed the trading of options on financial futures in the early 1980s. Today, options are a mainstay in the liquidity of the global economy, and they are one of the largest financial products in the world.

Options on stock are uniform; each contract represents 100 shares of stock. The value of the contract is $ price of the x 100. Options on commodities, indexes, and currencies are also uniform, but the dollar amount will vary with each individual contract. Before you attempt to trade options, you must know the size of the individual contract. That will determine the dollar volume of each option.

◾ Summary

In this chapter, we learned the difference between stock, futures, and stock indexes. The giant Forex market was defined, and a view of the option market was introduced. It is important to understand the fundamental difference between these markets. Futures and indexes will offer many advantages that stocks cannot, with few of the risks of individual stocks. Options can be traded on the indexes and that will be one of our biggest trading opportunities, but it is imperative to recognize the individual specifications and contract size that can place some of the large markets outside of many retail traders' capital limitations.

◾ Chapter 2 Quiz

1) Price discovery is:
   a) where value changes hands
   b) where price is in equilibrium

c) not recognized by fundamental traders

d) both a and b

2) Float in an equity market is:
   a) the amount of stock available for trading
   b) the originator's interest in the company
   c) not a real term used in equity markets
   d) never varies after the IPO

3) Liquidity is characterized by:
   a) high volume
   b) a large float or open interest
   c) tight bid–offer spreads
   d) all of the above

4) A rally in the market is caused by:
   a) a lack of sellers
   b) no strong hands to fight the buyers
   c) more buyers than sellers
   d) aggressive buyers

5) A market selloff is caused by:
   a) a lack of buyers in the market
   b) no strong hands to fight the sellers
   c) more sellers than buyers
   d) aggressive sellers

6) In a selloff, the weak hands are:
   a) aggressive sellers
   b) aggressive buyers
   c) countertrend traders
   d) both b and c

7) Price gaps are created when:
   a) buyers are active in the market
   b) sellers are active in the market
   c) there are no sellers to meet buyer demand
   d) overnight geopolitical news is negative

8) Futures markets are characterized by:
   a) different-sized contracts for each product
   b) an expiration date for trading
   c) good-faith margin deposits
   d) all of the above

9) Stock index futures:
   a) are a safe investment
   b) mirror the underlying index
   c) are settled in stock from the index
   d) have no specific expiration date

10) The Forex market:
   a) is guaranteed by the Forex currency exchange
   b) is dominated by large banks
   c) has fixed expiration dates
   d) is liquid for small traders

Technical versus Fundamental Price Analysis

This chapter will focus on the ways that markets can be priced. Some analysts believe that the only way to price a market is to look at the fundamental reports of a company, compare those results to other companies in the same market, and project the price from there. Others think that the current price tells us everything we need to know, so watch the direction of price and follow it.

There are countless ways to trade the markets, but almost all creditable teachers believe that only two ways work in the long run. One tries to *predict* where price will go based on certain economic data and geopolitical events. They believe that all long-term market trends are resolved through those fundamental political and economic changes to the market. They may combine the fundamental economic news with some statistical data, but they try to predict future price.

The interesting thing about fundamental numbers is that it all depends who looks at them. They are always subject to interpretation—hence the anguish that often occurs after major numbers are released. Fundamentalists only care about current price as to how it should relate to future price. The numbers are a fact; the way they are interpreted by the investor will determine whether they are bullish or bearish in the marketplace. The exact same number that was bullish 15 minutes ago will now be viewed as bearish. A different set of experts will interpret what the number says in relation to last month's number, and the market will spin off on its merry way.

Has this ever happened to you?

- It is the first Friday of any month; you are watching the market and the monthly unemployment figures come out. They are horrendous. Nonfarm payroll has fallen by 3 percent and total unemployment is now at 8.2 percent. On the financial news networks, anchors are fueling the flames. The market starts to break; this is going to be ugly. You sell an S&P 500 index contract, and after a brief but violent selloff, the market hits a bottom. It suddenly reverses and rallies for the rest of the day.

- You own stock in a major tech company. You have been trying to decide what to do with a fairly large position (for you) that you hold in the company. You feel that if the earnings are good, you want to increase your position. If they are poor, you will take your profit and look for a new stock. The earnings are released and the company shows record profits for the last quarter. The stock immediately rallies 4 percent. You decide that this is the signal you needed. You double your position in the market. Over the next three days the stock price declines by 13 percent.

It is a phenomenon called **market expectation**.

In the first case, after the massive selloff the market decided that the unemployment news probably wasn't as bad as was anticipated—in fact, it might even be good news. In the second case, although the earnings were a record, "upon further review" the Street decided that they were so good there was probably very little upside left in the stock price in the near future, and, hence, they let the air out of the balloon. Predictive traders took their stance and got run over.

In the case of the unemployment number, they would have reacted by selling the market. After it reached a bottom and the buyers became the strong hands, they would have abandoned their short position and joined the rally. They would have also reacted to the earnings number by joining the buyers to start the day, but when the sellers took over, they would be more than happy to join them with the rout.

The second group ignores fundamental data. They don't care why the price is moving up or down; they don't try to predict the direction it will be taking. They *react* to the price movement. If the market is going higher, they want to be long. If the market is going lower, they want to be short. They believe it is not important whether it is fundamental economic data that is driving the market or some technical aspect—all they are concerned with is reacting to the change in market conditions.

Our trades will always be **reactive in nature**; we are not going to try and predict market price action. We have already learned that when we have **price discovery**, the market is in equilibrium. We know this is true, because a buyer and seller have agreed on the price and an exchange of value took place. Stability may only exist for a split-second before price moves on, but at that point in time the market was in balance.

Fundamentalists would lead you to believe that it is a balance sheet, or P/E ratios, or inventories, or the producer price index. They believe that future price can be **predicted** from this information. Current price is just a function of buyers and sellers meeting temporally: *"It is technical,"* but *has no effect on the longer-term direction of price action.* Some technicians join fundamental traders and believe that they can predict future price movement more than can be expected by chance—and they are probably correct, but we will not be part of that school. All of our trades will be reactive in nature. We discount the fundamentals as being baked in the price.

I believe the market is always right; it is never tired, never sick, and is not forgiving when you are wrong.

In the next chapter, we will start to deal with technical market theory. You do not have to be a mathematician to understand the models, but you must be able to follow logic. You will see that the markets will repeat the same pattern time and time again. It will be proven that time and price are linked, and we will take those patterns to find profitable trading opportunities. But first, we will have a little test to see how much you have retained from this chapter. You will have 10 questions; 8 right is enough to pass. Make sure you understand all the terms before you go to chapter 3.

▉ Summary

Two observers looking at the same set of facts can come up with opposite conclusions. No one way of pricing a market is either correct or incorrect. Many factors go into market pricing, and we need to look at the ways "the other side of the trade" may be pricing their models.

▉ Chapter 3 Quiz

1) A stock collapsing on better-than-expected earnings:
   a) is very unusual and is generally a buying opportunity
   b) is caused by high-frequency traders
   c) is called market expectation
   d) all of the above

2) Stock indexes rallying after a bad unemployment number is:
   a) highly unusual and is generally a selling opportunity
   b) caused by high-frequency traders
   c) called market expectation
   d) all of the above

3) Fundamental traders generally:
   a) only look at supply and demand for a stock
   b) are predictive in nature

c) are reactive in nature

d) never consider technical factors

4) Fundamental traders:

    a) examine balance sheets

    b) watch EPS levels

    c) watch inventory levels

    d) all of the above

5) Fundamental traders never take into consideration:

    a) overbought over sold indicators

    b) high-frequency trading volume

    c) moving averages

    d) none of the above

6) Technical traders never take into consideration:

    a) P/E ratios of stocks they are looking to buy

    b) overbought or oversold conditions

    c) price retracement levels

    d) media buying or selling advice

7) Technical traders always:

    a) follow the trend

    b) look at key levels to trade

    c) countertrend trade media advice

    d) take profits too early

8) Technical traders usually buy:

    a) double bottoms

    b) breakouts from congestion

    c) blowoff bottoms

    d) all of the above

9) Technical traders believe that when price discovery occurs:

    a) the market is in equilibrium

    b) that value has been exchanged

    c) high-frequency traders are causing the price discovery

    d) both a and b

10) Which of the following do technical traders believe?

    a) retracement numbers are almost always correct.

    b) Liquid markets offer the best chance for profit.

    c) High-frequency traders are rigging the markets.

    d) Selling large rallies rarely fails.

Phases of the Market

This chapter will explore the price patterns that constantly reappear in the marketplace and discuss the participants that create the patterns. It deal with not only the patterns themselves but the psychology of the market participants and why the action of the traders reveals itself in the constantly repeating patterns.

We know mathematically that when a trade occurs, the market must be in equilibrium. Once the trade occurs, price can go anywhere. What this chapter is going to do is to put the market into phases. It will be a simple concept that can be used in any *liquid* market. The terms here are not universal but are unique to this study. Some teachers have different names for them, but for our purposes we will use the definitions described below.

■ Congestion

I believe that all **liquid** markets have the same cycle. It doesn't matter what the underlying asset is that is going to be traded, it will go through a cycle. I believe that the initial stage of any market is congestion.

Congestion is the segment of the cycle when the participants are confused by the current price action. The long and the short traders will exchange positions as the strong hands continually change. If you are a short-term trader, this can occur as many as five or six times during a session. Unless you are a countertrend trader (selling as price advances and buying when it declines, also known as the weak hands), trading in this type of market can be frustrating. You may buy a number of tops and sell a number of bottoms. This is known as getting *whipsawed,* and it is one of the problems of being a reactive trader. Another name for reactive traders is *trend following*. They look for the direction that price is moving and then use technical analysis to "follow the trend." I am not a strict trend trader but, rather, react to the current market phase.

Unfortunately, when the market begins to whipsaw, I always lose money on the first set of trades. However, once I recognize that the market is in congestion, I shift gears and take advantage of the opportunities that congestion creates. The congestion phase is marked initially by imaginary boundaries known as **support** and **resistance**. It might help to think of support as the floor of the market and that resistance is the ceiling.

Support is where the weak hands will **average down** and buy extra shares of stock or contracts to lower their average cost. It is also the position where traders who have been observing the current market will make a buy. If the support holds, the long traders will become the strong hands and the shorts (weak hands) will be forced to either take profit or begin to cover their loss and look for a new spot to enter. If the new buyers are strong enough, they will push the market to the other side and it will begin to find some resistance.

Resistance will bring sellers back to the market, countertrend traders will "average up," and the shorts sell extra shares or contracts in an attempt to raise their average sale. The resistance will also bring back traders who have been observing, and they will begin to sell. If the resistance holds, the short traders will become the strong hands and the market will force the long traders (now the weak hands) either to take profit or lock in their loss. If the sellers are strong enough, they will push the market back to test the support a second time.

This test is known as a **double bottom**. It is significant, as it will be one of the most profitable trades that you make in weekly options. If the double bottom holds, it will bring more buyers into the market, and the sellers will begin to take profit or lock in loss. The strong hands will now be the buyers, and they will take the price back to the previous resistance. If that point holds, it will become a **double top,** and it is very significant as the congestion area will now be defined.

As long as the market remains in the congestion pattern, it will be traded the same—buying the double bottoms and selling the double tops. Congestion can last for a very long time. If you trade on a daily basis, it might last for months, even longer. If you are a day trader or a swing trader, it could last several days or weeks. Most technicians believe that that market is in congestion more than 60 percent of the time. When we get into the chapters on option pricing, I will explain mathematically why we are in congestion for such long periods of time.

Figure 4.1 shows a market that started when the previous price pattern entered from the upside. It could have been a downside blowoff or a trend that ended with a move into congestion. What the pattern was that started the congestion phase is not important; the fact that you were able to identify that the market condition had changed is all that matters. Eventually, the congestion pattern resolved itself when the price broke out in an uptrend. Not all double tops and bottoms are perfect, In

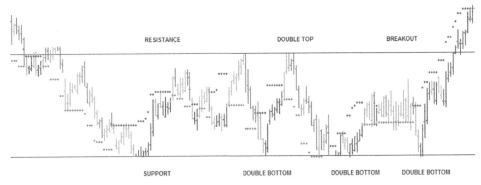

FIGURE 4.1 Congestion, Showing Support, Resistance, Tops, and Bottoms

this example, they hit on the exact top and bottom. Fundamentalists say that this pattern is self-fulfilling prophecy; technicians say that traders recognize this pattern and adapt their trading style to take advantage of it. Obviously, I agree with the technicians. The breakout occurred when the long traders from the third double bottom (triple quadruple; I always use double) in a row held and they forced the sellers out at the next double top.

■ Breakout to the Trend

The breakout to the trend will begin when the previous support and resistance levels fail to hold. The double top and double bottom sellers will begin to feel pressure when their levels are violated; they know that breakout and trend traders will be coming into the market as new money. This imbalance will start to bring in more buyers or sellers, forcing the countertrend traders to abandon positions. If they also believe that a new trend has started, they may join in with their former adversaries and go with the flow. The culmination of the buying or selling will occur when the market makes its first higher high or lower low. Profit takers will enter the market, and they may be joined by a wave of countertrend traders that could force the price below/above the old support or resistance levels. If that occurs, it would be titled a **false breakout.** Figure 4.2 shows a false breakout to the downside. After the low was made, the market reversed and made a series of lower highs and higher lows. Price eventually rallied back into the congestion phase and broke out to the trend on the upside when the double top failed to hold.

When the profit taking subsides, if a higher low or a lower high holds the trend is confirmed. Figure 4.3 reflects that pattern. The market never goes in one direction forever; even in a trend there will be some price movement to the other side of the trending market as profit taking and countertrend traders will continue to try and move price in their favor. The upward or downward angle at which the trend

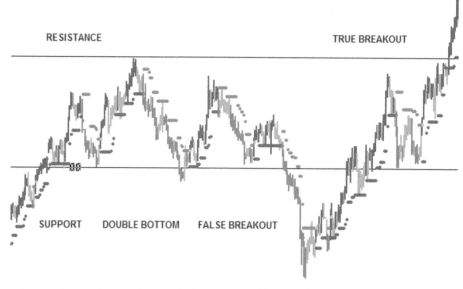

RESISTANCE   TRUE BREAKOUT

SUPPORT   DOUBLE BOTTOM   FALSE BREAKOUT

FIGURE 4.2   Breakout to the Trend, Showing Both False and True Breakouts

45 DEGREE BULL MARKET

FIGURE 4.3   45-Degree Bull Market

advances or declines will have a great deal to do with how long it will persist. The majority of trending markets cannot sustain a price rise/fall on an angle of over 45 degrees. As you can observe, the price meanders around the mean as profit taking and countertrend traders take their piece out of the pie.

Eventually, the market will make a high/low that has lower high or higher low follow it on the next price swing. This is the first sign that the trend may be reversing, as shown in Figure 4.4. Initially, it will be very difficult to determine if this pattern is a market pausing before it is resumes its trend or the current trend may be ending. The strong hands that had been controlling the market will become the weak hands,

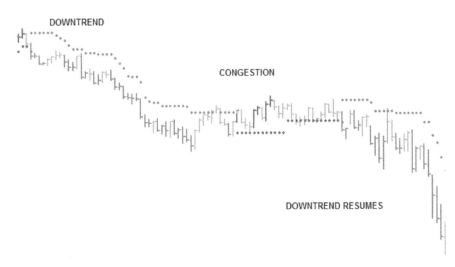

FIGURE 4.4 Downtrend Resumption after Congestion

and when this happens it will reenter the congestion phase. The new congestion may be a breather, and the battle between the strong hands and the weak hands may resolve itself in a breakout back to the previous major trend. If the market is making a rounding top or bottom, the new congestion phase will lead to a breakout to the opposite side of the current trend and a new trending phase will commence to the reverse side of the current market.

■ Blowoff

If the current trend doesn't resolve itself in a rounding top/bottom and prices begin to accelerate at a much steeper angle than the sustainable 45-degree rate, the market will most likely end in a blowoff, represented by Figure 4.5. The blowoff phase of the market is always the least amount of time in any of the three phases, but may result in the most absolute price movement. The blowoff occurs when the weak hands get squeezed to the limit. They can no longer fight the trend and they are forced to cover, most likely through lack of capital or margin calls that must be met. During the blowoff phase, price and time may become infinite, meaning price reaches a vertical move of 90 degrees. Every tick is either higher or lower, the weak hands become price insensitive, and the only thing they are concerned with is obtaining enough quantity to end the pain. The extent of the blowoff attracts new money to the old, weak hands' now-vacated position. The strong hands begin to take profit. They may also join the new money in changing directions. When this happens, the classic V pattern is formed in the market. Eventually, the market returns to equilibrium, and a new market pattern begins.

FIGURE 4.5 Classic Blowoff Pattern

This simple explanation of price movement works very effectively with the weekly option strategies that will be presented in later chapters. Of course, markets can go straight from congestion to a blowoff, or a blowoff can be followed by another blowoff triggering a W pattern, such as in Figure 4.6, or a blowoff can go to congestion triggering a hanging-branch pattern, as in Figure 4.7. A congestion pattern could also resolve itself in a triangle breakout, as depicted in Figure 4.8.

FIGURE 4.6 W Blowoff Pattern

FIGURE 4.7 Blowoff Hanging Branch

FIGURE 4.8 Triangle Breakout to a Trend

■ Summary

The essential concept presented is that in a liquid market, the major price patterns presented in this section can be counted on to repeat with regular frequency. They may have components linked, as in the examples of a blowoff leading to another blowoff, but the one thing they have in common is that they are mathematically guaranteed to repeat. Later on in the book, a complete chapter will be devoted to this mathematical approach.

■ Chapter 4 Quiz

1) All liquid markets:
   a) go through phases
   b) constantly repeat
   c) cannot be predicted with total accuracy
   d) all of the above

2) The most likely phase for a market to be in is:
   a) congestion
   b) trending
   c) blowoff
   d) none of the above

3) Congestion is marked by an invisible upper boundaries known as:
   a) support
   b) resistance
   c) double top
   d) both a and b

4) Double tops occur when:
   a) the weak hands turn strong
   b) the strong hands take profit
   c) new money enters the market
   d) all of the above

5) Congestion markets can extend for how long?
   a) Never more than six months; they then are known as a trend.
   b) Until they breakout to a trend.
   c) There is no time limit.
   d) All of the above.

6) What happens once a market breaks out from congestion?
   a) A trending market has begun.
   b) It can go back into congestion.
   c) A double top must have been violated.
   d) High-frequency traders will be scrambling for cover.

7) When is a trending market confirmed?
   a) The double top or double bottom is violated.
   b) The market makes a new higher high and a higher low.
   c) The market has a 45-degree downtrend confirmed.
   d) New money enters the market.

8) What happens when a false breakout occurs?
   a) The market goes back to congestion.
   b) It fails to make new higher highs or lower lows.
   c) The strong hands trade places with the weak hands.
   d) All of the above.

9) Even in a bull market of 45 degrees:
   a) the weak hands will push the market down
   b) there can be a congestion phase

c) the strong hands can become the weak hands

d) all of the above

10) All bear trending markets are controlled by:

    a) the weak hands

    b) the strong hands

    c) new money

    d) none of the above

11) All bull markets have which characteristic(s)?

    a) They are controlled by the strong hands.

    b) Stubborn weak hands will be hurt financially.

    c) It will make a series of higher highs.

    d) All of the above.

12) What happens when the angle of the bull market approaches 60 degrees?

    a) The last of the weak hands will be getting forced out.

    b) Longs will be the strong hands.

    c) New money will come in on the long side of the market.

    d) None of the above.

13) What happens during the blowoff phase?

    a) The weak hands become price insensitive.

    b) The weak hands are forced out.

    c) New money joins the market.

    d) All of the above.

14) What causes a blowoff?

    a) unexpected news

    b) change in market sentiment

    c) the strong hands and weak hands both lose money

    d) fear or greed

15) A blowoff is characterized by:

    a) the weak hands capitulating

    b) new money entering and forcing the market in the other direction

    c) strong hands reversing their position

    d) all of the above

The Relationship of Time and Price

In the first four chapters, we dealt with the psychology of the market—why this time won't be different. We addressed how markets have evolved, why we need liquid markets in order to compete with Wall Street, the different ways to analyze markets, and how traders and investors decide which markets to trade. Also, we presented a case for using market patterns to help us decide when we should initiate certain types of trades, and explained why those patterns constantly repeat.

This chapter will focus on the relationship of time and price and will prove that in liquid markets, all time frames that are observed share similar characteristics. It has a couple of corollaries, the first of which applies if you are observing a market:

Without both time and price axes as reference points, all liquid assets appear the same and it is impossible to tell what time frame or asset that you are trading.

I like to give my students an example using a sailor.

He has a small sailboat and decides to go on a day trip from Newport Beach to Catalina Island. Unfortunately, the weather turns bad, and during the storm he drifts beyond the sight of land. He knows he needs to get back to port but he can no longer see land, and to make matters worse, the sun set during the storm and he is now completely adrift on an overcast night. He has four choices. Three of them will take him away from land, one to the north, one to the west, and one to the south, all of which might cause him to be permanently lost at sea; only going to the east will save him.

Can he solve this problem, given these facts?

The answer is no, but he can get lucky and guess the right direction once in four times. The other three may result in disaster, which are not very good odds of succeeding.

As he is contemplating his fate, a helicopter flies overhead. From the pilot's vantage point, he can see that land is very close—in fact, it is only a little over 12 miles away, just out of the sailor's range of vision. Unfortunately, the pilot can't see the sailor's boat. If the pilot could see and contact the sailor, he could change his odds of success from 25 percent to 100 percent.

Look at Figures 5.1 and 5.2. They are the exact same market but with a different perspective. Figure 5.1 has no time and price axes (the sailor). Figure 5.2 shows the

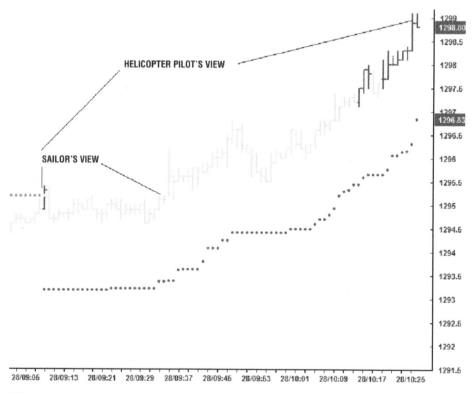

FIGURE 5.1   Congestion with No Points of Reference

FIGURE 5.2   Two-Time-Frame Observation: Sailor's and Pilot's Points of View

IS THIS A CHART OF AAPL?

FIGURE 5.3   Is This (AAPL) Apple?

same chart from a different point of view (time frame), and it includes the time and price axis labels (the pilot). As you can see, if you were to attempt to trade off of Figure 5.1, not only would you have no idea what you are trading, you would have no idea where you are in the market. Figure 5.2 clearly shows that you are in a bull market and should be long.

Let's look at another example of how a distortion of time and price can fool you. Figure 5.3 is another chart where the time and price labels have been removed. Are you looking at AAPL? The answer should be that it is impossible to tell what chart you are looking at, but students have often informed me that they can tell it is AAPL!

In fact, it is the same chart as Figure 5.2 in an extended time frame, with the time and price labels removed. The whole point of this is that if you don't have a logical view of the market, there is no chance to beat it in the long run. It is a puzzle, and by now you should have started to figure out that *it is impossible to predict or react to price action with 100 percent accuracy or anywhere near that.* The best you can do is try to put yourself in a mathematical position that gives you the best chance to win!

One more puzzle, and then we will go on to the second corollary.

Figure 5.4 gives a little more information about the relationship of price and time. It asks you to see if you can identify a stock with the clues that are revealed.

Can you guess if one chart is GOOGLE? A clue: It is not the one labeled AAPL. Can you guess if one of the charts is NFLX? A clue: It is not the one labeled AMZN. The chart labeled AAPL is Apple. Given this information, can you identify the other three charts?

The answer is in Figure 5.5.

The correct answer—it was almost impossible to figure out the puzzle unless you are Carnac the Magnificent. All of the charts were different time frames of AAPL on April 28, 2014!

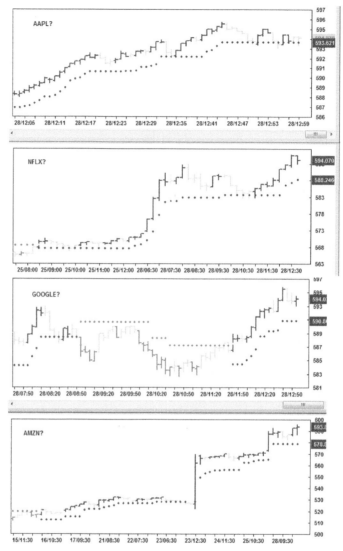

FIGURE 5.4 What Chart Are You Observing?

I tricked you by insinuating that they could all be different stocks, but I only told you that one was AAPL. I never said any of the others were GOOGLE, AMZN, or NFLX; I only informed you that they weren't AAPL. It is a silly puzzle, but the market likes to do this to you. It gives you a few clues and then you try to make a decision. The whole point of this exercise is to show you how tough your opponent is, and that you will never be able to figure out the puzzle entirely. No one can, no matter what they tell you, so don't feel alone!

FIGURE 5.5 Which Chart? The Answer

The second corollary of the relationship of time and price is this:

The sum of all shorter time frames will equal the longest time frame.

This should be fairly obvious, but most students don't realize this. If the market has been in an uptrend for a year, all of the shorter time frames will also be in an uptrend. That doesn't mean that they will always be going up at the same rate, but if you add the pluses and minuses together, they will be positive and will approach the long-term trend. If the market has been in congestion for a few weeks, all of the shorter time frames will be in congestion. If the market is blowing off, all of the shorter times frames will be blowing off. Figure 5.6 shows AAPL over a period of time from a 1-minute to a 60-minute time frame. You will notice that all of the time frames from 1 minute to 60 minutes are positive, but at various points in the day, some of the time frames are actually going down. This is quite common and will afford us trading opportunities when we get to the weekly options.

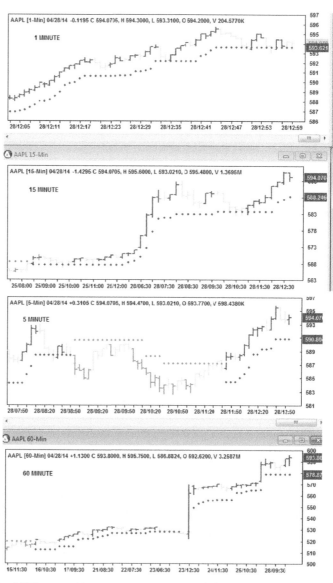

FIGURE 5.6 AAPL over a 60-Minute Time Frame, including Shorter Time Frames

A final note: Figure 5.6 is Figure 5.5 with the time and price axis labels added. As you can see, it is a composite chart ending April 28, 2014. Does that mean it was impossible to make money selling AAPL during that period? No, and the weak hands had chances, too—in fact, the 5-minute chart had a $700 drawdown before it took off. However, it is much easier to make money in those conditions by buying when the shorter time frames got a signal to buy; we put ourselves in the best mathematical position to win!

The final corollary regards the use of time frames.

The longest time frame you are observing will always be the guiding chart; the shortest is the execution time frame.

This is another pretty simple concept, but one that many traders don't use to set up their entries. Using more than one time frame will always improve your trading, as it gives you an additional market perspective (the pilot). Your longest time frame sets up the trade and the shortest time frame is where you execute it. When the market is trending you can use one time frame, but you will get better results when you use two. If the market is in congestion, it is essential to use two time frames, and the only way you can trade a blowoff is to use two, unless you can catch the falling knife or stop the rocket ship.

■ Summary

This marks the last chapter that will be used to introduce you to the various markets that can be successfully traded. All of the building blocks to help you recognize market psychology, how the markets are organized, and how the various markets trade have now been introduced.

The trading principles that I believe in should be obvious by now, the most important being that you can only make money in a liquid market. That point has been stressed many times but it can't be emphasized enough: **It is impossible to make money in illiquid markets as a retail option trader**. The dual problems of overcoming the bid–offer spread and commissions will eventually wear you down and you will lose money.

Illiquid markets are characterized by low volume and small open interest. Open interest is the number of outstanding option contracts in the serial month by strike. Liquid markets are characterized by tight bid–offer spreads and big volume. The final key to the weekly option market is that you must have reasonable commission rates. You can't pay $20 a round turn and have any hope of being successful. There are many option brokers that offer reasonable rates as low as $1.50 a round turn. Before you start to trade, make sure that you know the total commission rate plus any fees that must be paid.

■ Chapter 5 Quiz

1) The relationship of price and time:
   a) is constant in all time frames
   b) is different for various asset classes
   c) cannot be predicted with great accuracy
   d) a and b

2) Without time and price axes on a chart:
   a) it is impossible to identify the underlying asset
   b) you can tell the market trend
   c) the market can become uncertain
   d) none of the above

3) In the example in this chapter, why couldn't the sailor see land?
   a) His boat lost sight of his reference points.
   b) An unexpected storm carried him out to sea.
   c) The clouds covered the stars.
   d) All of the above.

4) In the example in this chapter, why could the helicopter pilot see land?
   a) He was flying high enough to see the horizon.
   b) He had reference points to know his position.
   c) He was flying under the clouds.
   d) None of the above.

5) The time and price axes allow traders to:
   a) have a directional compass
   b) sell the market without much risk
   c) guarantee winning trades
   d) all of the above

6) Markets can:
   a) be confidently predicted from time and price charts
   b) never be accurately predicted
   c) be beaten even if they are illiquid
   d) be rigged by high-frequency traders

7) The longest time frame is:
   a) not related to shorter time frames
   b) not valid if the market is blowing off
   c) the sum of all shorter time frames
   d) generally in congestion

8) Another name for the longest time frame is:
   a) the major trend that we are observing
   b) the strong hands running over the weak hands
   c) new money entering a bear market
   d) none of the above

9) What happens during a major downtrend?
   a) The strong hands are bullish.
   b) The weak hands can make money countertrend trading.
   c) The strong hands will overwhelm the weak hands.
   d) Both b and c.

10) In a bull market, the shorter time frames:
    a) are always bullish
    b) are not relevant
    c) can be bearish
    d) none of the above

Introduction to Options

Weekly options represent a great trading opportunity, but before you can trade them, you need to know the definitions that are standard in the industry. I don't want to flood you with complicated mathematical models and a 30-page vocabulary, but you must master some terms before you can attempt to trade. This chapter will deal with essential vocabulary; a complete glossary of terms is included in the back of the book. Once you have mastered the vocabulary you will be prepared to learn how the option model functions.

Basic Option Glossary

This list is in alphabetic order and refers to all serial options. It is not necessary that you have complete command of this list in order to trade the weekly options, but you should read it to familiarize yourself with general option terms.

ASK, ASKED PRICE: This is the price at which the trader is willing to sell an option or security.

ASSIGNMENT: The obligation an option writer has to deliver the underlying asset at the specific price and time. If it is a call, the writer must sell the buyer the underlying asset at the specific strike called for in the contract. If it is a put, the writer must buy from the buyer the asset at a specific strike price called for in the contract.

AT THE MONEY (ATM): An at-the-money option is one whose strike price is equal to (or, in practice, very close to) the current price of the underlying asset.

BID, BID PRICE: This is the price that the trader is willing to buy an option or security for.

BID–ASK SPREAD: The difference between the bid and ask prices of a security. The wider (i.e., larger) the spread is, the less liquid the market and the greater the slippage.

BROKER: The middleman who passes orders from investors to the floor dealers, screen traders, or market makers for execution.

CALL: This option contract conveys the right to buy a standard quantity of a specified asset at a fixed price per unit (the strike price) for a limited length of time (until expiration).

CLOSING TRANSACTION: To sell a previously purchased position or to buy back a previously purchased position, effectively canceling out the position.

CONTRACT SIZE: The number of units of an underlying specified in a contract. In stock options, the standard contract size is 100 shares of stock. In futures options, the contract size is one futures contract. In index options, the contract size is an amount of cash equal to parity times the multiplier. In the case of currency options it varies.

CREDIT: The amount of cash you receive for writing an option. This is the maximum amount that you can make on a trade; it is also known as selling a option naked.

DAY ORDER: An order to purchase or sell an asset or option, usually at a specified price, that is good for just the trading session on which it is given. It is automatically canceled on the close of the session if it is not executed.

DEBIT: The amount you pay for buying an option. It is your maximum risk.

DELTA: Measures the rate of change in an option's theoretical value for a one-unit change in the underlying asset expressed in percentage. Calls have positive deltas and puts have negative deltas.

EXERCISE: The act by which the holder of an option exercises his right to buy or sell the underlying asset at the designated strike price.

EXERCISE PRICE: The price at which the owner of a call option can buy the underlying asset. It is the price at which the owner of a put option contract can sell an underlying asset. See **STRIKE PRICE**.

EXPIRATION, EXPIRATION DATE, EXPIRATION MONTH: This is the date by which an option contract must be exercised or it becomes void and the holder of the option ceases to have any rights under the contract.

EXTRINSIC VALUE: The opposite of intrinsic value, it is the premium (air) that is an option at any strike. In a call, it is the price above the intrinsic value of a strike, and vice versa for a put.

FILL: When an order has been completely executed, it is described as filled.

GAMMA: Gamma expresses how fast delta changes with a one-point increase in the price of the underlying. Gamma is positive for call options, negative for put options.

GOOD 'TIL CANCELED (GTC) ORDER: A Good 'Til Canceled order is one that is effective until it is either filled by the broker or canceled by the investor. This order will automatically cancel at the options expiration.

GREEKS: The Greek letters used to describe various measures of the sensitivity of the value of an option with respect to different factors. They include delta, gamma, theta, rho, and Vega.

HISTORIC VOLATILITY: The measure of the actual price fluctuations of the underlying asset over a specific period of time, also known as *statistical volatility*.

IMPLIED VOLATILITY (IV): This is the volatility that the underlying would need to have for the pricing model to produce the same theoretical option price as the actual option price. The term *implied volatility* comes from the fact that options imply the volatility of their underlying, just by their price. A computer model starts with the actual market price of an option and measures **IV** by working the option fair value model backward, solving for volatility (normally an input) as if it were the unknown.

INDEX OPTION: An option that has an index as the underlying asset. These are usually cash-settled.

IN THE MONEY (ITM): Term used when the strike price of an option is less than the price of the underlying for a call option, or greater than the price of the underlying for a put option. In other words, the option has an intrinsic value greater than zero.

INTRINSIC VALUE: The value of the current market price minus the strike price, if the current price is less than the strike price for a call it has no intrinsic value, and vice versa for a put.

LAST TRADING DAY: The last business day prior to the options expiration during which purchases and sales of options can be made. For equity options, this is generally the third Friday of the expiration month.

LIMIT ORDER: An order placed with a brokerage to buy or sell a predetermined number of contracts (or shares of stock) at a specified price, or better than the specified price. Limit orders also allow an investor to limit the length of time an order can be outstanding before canceled. It can be placed as a day or **GTC** order. Limit orders typically cost slightly more than market orders but are often better to use, especially with options, because you will always purchase or sell securities at that price or better.

LONG: You are long if you have bought more than you have sold in any particular market, commodity, instrument, or contract. Also known as having a long position, you are purchasing a financial asset with the intention of selling it at some time in the future. An asset is purchased long with the expectation of an increase in its price.

OPENING TRANSACTION: An addition to, or creation of, an option trading position.

OPEN INTEREST: The cumulative total of all option contracts of a particular series sold, but not yet repurchased or exercised.

OPEN ORDER: An order that has been placed with the broker, but not yet executed or canceled.

OPTION CHAIN: The list of available options for a given underlying asset.

OUT OF THE MONEY (OTM): An out-of-the-money option is one whose strike price is unfavorable in comparison to the current price of the underlying. This means when the strike price of a call is greater than the price of the underlying, or the strike price of a put is less than the price of the underlying. An out-of-the-money option has no intrinsic value, only time value.

PREMIUM: This is the price of an option contract over the intrinsic value.

PUT: This option contract conveys the right to sell a standard quantity of a specified asset at a fixed price per unit (the strike price) for a limited length of time (until expiration).

RHO: The change in the value of an option with respect to a unit change in the risk-free rate.

ROUND TURN: When an option contract is bought and then sold (or sold and then bought). The second trade cancels the first, leaving only a profit or loss.

This process is referred to as a *round turn*. Brokerage charges are usually quoted on this basis.

SHORT: An obligation to purchase an asset at some time in the future. You are short if you have sold more than you have bought in any particular market, also known as having a short position. An asset is sold short with the expectation of a decline in its price. Can have almost unlimited risk. Uncovered short positions require margin.

STOP ORDER: Stop-Loss and **Stop-Limit** orders placed on options are activated when there is a trade at that price only on the specific exchange on which the order is located. They are orders to trade when its price falls to a particular point, often used to limit an investor's losses. It's an especially good idea to use a stop order if you will be unable to watch your positions for an extended period.

STRIKE PRICE: The price at which the holder of an option has the right to buy or sell the underlying. This is a fixed price per unit and is specified in the option contract.

THETA: The sensitivity of the value of an option with respect to the time remaining to expiration. It is the daily drop in dollar value of an option due to the effect of time alone. Theta is dollars lost per day, per contract. Negative theta signifies a long option position (or a debit spread); positive theta signifies a short option position (or a credit spread).

TICK: The smallest unit price change allowed in trading a specific security. This varies by security, and can also be dependent on the current price of the security.

TIME DECAY: Term used to describe how the theoretical value of an option "erodes" or reduces with the passage of time. Time decay is quantified by theta.

UNDERLYING: This is the asset specified in an option contract that is transferred when the option contract is exercised, unless cash-settled. With cash-settled options, only cash changes hands, based on the current price of the underlying.

VEGA: A measure of the sensitivity of the value of an option at a particular point in time to changes in volatility. Vega is the dollar amount of gain or loss you should theoretically experience if implied volatility goes up one percentage point.

VOLATILITY: Volatility is a measure of the amount by which an asset has fluctuated, or is expected to fluctuate, in a given period of time. Assets with greater volatility exhibit wider price swings, and their options are higher in price than less volatile assets. Volatility is not equivalent to **BETA**.

VOLUME: The quantity of trading in a market or security. It can be measured by dollars or units traded (i.e., number of contracts for options, or number of shares for stocks).

WRITE, WRITER: To sell an option that is not owned through an opening sale transaction. While this position remains open, the writer is obligated to fulfill the terms of that option contract if the option is assigned. An investor who sells an option is called the writer, regardless of whether the option is covered or uncovered.

■ Working Option Vocabulary

This section is not in alphabetical order, but it is listed in the order that you will be using to place orders. Some of the terms are unique to this book and will be used to initiate trades. It is important that you have a very good knowledge of these terms and how they apply to executing orders.

EXPIRATION: The date on which an option contract is terminated.

SERIAL: The specific group of options that have the same expiration date.

CONTRACT SIZE: All contracts for US stocks are for 100 shares times the $ price. If you were to buy one AAPL October 2014 500C @ 9.00, you would have the right to purchase 100 shares of APPL stock @ 500 a share anytime before the third Friday in October 2014. For this right, you would pay $900.

STRIKE PRICE: The price at which the holder of an option has the right to buy or sell the underlying. This is a fixed price per unit and is specified in the option contract.

CALL: It gives the buyer the right but not the obligation to buy stock at a specific price (strike price) for a specific time (expiration). As an example, if you were to buy the AAPL October 2014 500 call, you have the right to exercise the underlying stock any time before the third Friday of October 2014. Buying a call always gives you unlimited reward, with limited risk.

PUT: It gives the buyer the right but not the obligation to sell stock at a specific price (strike price) for a specific time (expiration). As an example, if you were to buy the AAPL October 500 put, it would define your contract. You have the right to sell the underlying stock anytime before the third Friday of October 2014. Buying a put always gives you unlimited reward (to zero) with limited risk.

BID–ASK PRICE: This is the price that you would be charged to buy or sell the option. If you want to buy an option, generally you must pay the asking price; if you want to sell you must "hit the bid." The **SPREAD** between these prices determines if the option is liquid. If the spread is too large, it is much harder to overcome commissions.

AT-THE-MONEY STRIKE (ATM): The strike price nearest to where the underlying stock is currently trading. It will always have the most premium. It is also the most liquid.

IN-THE-MONEY OPTION (ITM): An option that if the current market price were to hold would have value after expiration.

IRON CONDOR (IC): Two vertical credit spreads made up of a put and call spread. One must end up out of the money, and both can end up out of the money if the price expires in between the short strikes.

OUT-OF-THE-MONEY OPTION (OTM): An option, which if the current market price were to hold, would have no value after expiration.

PREMIUM (AIR): The supply and demand for a specific option.

DELTA: The percentage chance of the option to expire in the money with the current market price. If the option were currently at the money, it would have a 50 percent chance of expiring in the money, as it has no intrinsic value. It would therefore have a 50 delta.

GAMMA: The rate at which an options delta would change as price moves away from the **(ATM)** strike. Generally speaking, at the money will change the fastest as price moves.

VEGA: Is the amount of premium "air" in the option at any point in time. It is the supply and demand for the option. Generally speaking, deferred options have more VEGA, as there is more time to expiration and therefore more uncertainty.

THETA (TIME DECAY): The loss of premium "air" as time to expiration grows nearer.

LONG: The buyer of an option. Longs have limited risk and unlimited reward.

SHORT: The seller or writer of an option. Shorts have unlimited risk and limited reward.

ASSIGNMENT: The obligation an option writer has to deliver the underlying asset at the specific price and time. If it is a call, the writer must sell the buyer the underlying asset at the specific strike called for in the contract. If it is a put, the writer must buy from the buyer the asset at a specific strike price called for in the contract.

EXERCISE: The act by which the holder of an option exercises the right to buy or sell the underlying asset at the designated strike price.

VERTICAL SPREADS (CREDIT SPREADS): Allows the seller to take advantage of time decay and price movement without unlimited risk.

60/40 CREDIT SPREAD: A directional vertical credit spread that is created on a Vega neutral basis. It is initiated by selling one option that is slightly in the money and buying one that is slightly out of the money.

RISK REVERSALS / SYNTHETIC LONG / SHORT: These allow a trader to take a directional position in the market with limited risk and unlimited reward.

BACK SPREAD: Selling an option closer to the at-the-money strike and buying two at a strike further away from the at the money.

RISING / FALLING VOLATILITY ENVIROMENT: The implied volatility of the VIX in relation to the current market. If the VIX is rising above its 60-period moving average, it is a *rising volatility* environment. If it is below its 60-period moving average, it is a *declining volatility* market.

▓ Summary

Memorizing these basic terms will allow you to execute trades with confidence. Before you can go to the next section, you must have a thorough understanding of the basic option vocabulary. You can always go to the Glossary in the back of the book, which has the complete vocabulary, to look up specific terms.

▓ Chapter 6 Quiz

1) Assignment is:
   a) the right of an option buyer to exercise
   b) something that rarely happens to option buyers
   c) the obligation of an option seller to deliver the underlying asset
   d) none of the above

2) Selling a call:
   a) gives the seller all rights and no obligation
   b) gives the seller the obligation to deliver the asset to the buyer
   c) is always canceled at expiration
   d) gives the buyer the right to purchase the asset from the seller

3) What is a serial?
   a) another word for a near-term put
   b) the grouping of options that have the same expiration
   c) the order in which they are priced
   d) all of the above

4) What is the strike price?
   a) the value of a call at expiration
   b) the price at which a call must be delivered by the buyer
   c) the price at which the seller must buy or sell the underlying asset
   d) the at-the-money strike

5) A call gives:
   a) the seller an obligation to deliver the underlying security
   b) the buyer the right but not the obligation to take the underlying security
   c) the seller the right of assignment
   d) both a and b

6) A put gives:
   a) the seller the right of assignment
   b) the buyer the obligation to take assignment of the underlying security
   c) the seller an obligation to deliver the underlying security
   d) both b and c

7) An in-the-money option:
   a) has value at expiration if the current price holds
   b) has no value at expiration if price changes
   c) must be assigned to have any value
   d) none of the above

8) An out-of-the-money option:
   a) has no value at expiration
   b) can be in the money if the price changes
   c) gives the buyer the right to buy or sell the underlying asset
   d) all of the above

9) What is intrinsic value?
   a) the amount of premium in an option
   b) the opposite of extrinsic value
   c) the same as a credit
   d) none of the above

10) Buying long options can create which of the following positions?
    a) The trader owns a call.
    b) The trader owns a put.

c) The trader owns both a put and a call.

d) All of the above.

11) Selling or writing options has which of the following characteristics?

a) It gives the seller the right to exercise on or before expiration.

b) It gives the seller the obligation to deliver the underlying asset at expiration.

c) It gives the seller the right to assign options at expiration.

d) None of the above.

12) A large open interest and volume are generally synonymous with:

a) liquidity

b) open outcry

c) price discovery

d) all of the above

13) In terms of the markets, what is a tick?

a) a small insect

b) the smallest price change allowed in an option or underlying asset

c) an amount that varies from stock to stock

d) none of the above

14) The Greek letter theta best describes:

a) the loss of premium as options move closer to expiration

b) the increase of premium when there is more uncertainty in the market

c) the decrease of premium as uncertainty diminishes

d) none of the above; theta is not associated with options

15) An option that reaches parity is synonymous with:

a) an option that currently has no premium

b) an option that can be exercised

c) an option that can be assigned

d) all of the above

16) The standard contract size for all US exchange-traded stocks:

a) is 100 shares

b) is set by the SEC

c) expires on Friday after the close

d) all of the above

17) Vega is a Greek term that is used to describe:

a) the premium in an option

b) the current degree of uncertainty in the market

c) how fast a delta will change at the current price

d) none of the above

18) The at-the-money option always
   a) has the most amount of premium
   b) has the least amount of premium
   c) is closest to the underlying asset's current price
   d) both a and c

19) What is delta?
   a) the rate of change of the option to the underlying price of an asset
   b) a positive number for calls
   c) a negative number for puts
   d) all of the above

20) What is gamma?
   a) the change in premium as volatility increases
   b) a negative for calls
   c) the speed at which the delta changes for a one-point change in the underlying asset
   d) all of the above

The Option Model

This chapter will be an introduction of the option model. Too often, would-be option traders get confused by all of the complicated mathematical formulas used to describe option models. I am going to try and simplify the way you view an option model, by converting your observation to a single simple formula that will work with all liquid options.

Games of Chance

First a little background on the mathematical models that were used to create options. The first model was introduced in a paper published by Fischer Black and Myron Scholes in 1973. The math is quite complicated, but it basically describes a bell-shaped curve, Figure 7.1, in which the highest degree of uncertainty exists at the current market price; the ATM call and puts each have a 50 percent chance of being in the money at expiration. Therefore, the uncertainty decreases as price moves higher or lower from the current price. As options go deeper in the money, the probability that they will end up with a 1.00 delta continues to increase until it reaches a point at which there is no premium left in the option. That price is referred to as **parity**. At this time, the option will react to the underlying asset tick for tick to the upside (or downside for a put) and may be used as a surrogate for the underlying asset. If the market were to reverse, the option would eventually lose deltas and would not go down as quickly as the underlying asset. In fact, if the price were to fall/rise enough, it could lose all of its value and go out at a zero delta.

As options go further out of the money, they reach a point at which they no longer react to the underlying asset. In this case, their delta reaches zero and a maximum loss is established. This option is now classified as a **teenie**, and it will have a value of $1. It can have the opposite effect of the 1.00 delta option if price were to suddenly

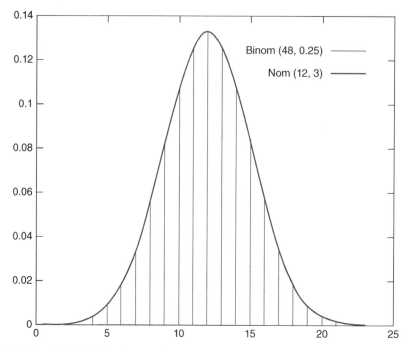

FIGURE 7.1 Black–Scholes Options Curve

change direction. This option will begin to pick up deltas, and if the price moves far enough to the other side of the model it could reach a delta of 1.00; it then could be substituted for the underlying asset again.

This conversion feature of options is what makes them attractive as investment vehicles, if properly used; you can always be sure that no matter what happens to the underlying asset, your risk is limited to the debit you paid for the option and your reward is unlimited.

I like to tell my students that if they have ever played a game involving chance that they have already been exposed to options. Any game that involves a combination of luck and skill is a form of playing the option game. Let's examine a few of the world's most popular games and see how they mesh with options.

Poker is one of the planet's most famous card games. Millions of people play it every day, and for good reason: It relies on a combination of skill and luck that makes it fascinating to people who enjoy participating in games. In the short run, the component of luck rather than skill can allow players to win making poor mathematical decisions against more skilled opponents. The game is divided into hands, and as each hand progresses, more cards are revealed and a round of betting ensues. Our opponent's play gives us information (or disinformation!) as to where the hidden cards may lie. When the hand moves closer to its conclusion, the value of a single card can have its delta quickly changed. It can go from almost a zero delta to a 1.00 delta, and vice versa, in a few seconds. In the end, either one player forces the other player(s) out of the hand and they win or they go to a showdown and the player with the best hand wins. In the long run, the player with the better combination of math and playing skills will defeat the inferior player, but in the short run anything can happen.

Backgammon is a slightly different game. It involves moving 15 checkers around a board that is defended by your opponents' checkers; the winner is the first one who removes all of their checkers from the opponent's side of the board. It also differs in the fact that you can see your opponent's position in advance of your turn to play. The moves that you are allowed to make are determined by a set of rules and the throw of two dice. The possible combinations of dice (36) can make the game change quickly. Your position can go from a near 1.00 delta of winning to almost a zero delta with one throw of the dice. Since the probability of rolling any number on the dice is equal for both players, the key is to know how to place your checkers in the best position to take advantage of the most likely combination of rolls. Generally, the player who has better knowledge of probabilities and playing strategy will win—however, long shots do hit, and in the short run an unskilled player can get a run of hot dice and defeat a much more accomplished opponent. In the long run, the better player always overcomes bad fortune and will win.

Blackjack is a game similar to poker in that cards are used and some of them are exposed to the players. The players make a decision based on a set of rules that are established by the house. In this game, the opponent is the casino, not the other players. Very skilled players can possibly beat the house if the rules are slightly in their favor and they have the ability to "count the deck," which is no easy task. The unskilled player has no chance to beat the house's edge, but can get a phenomenal hot streak and win for brief periods of time. Because of the rules, many times a single card that the dealer turns can send your hand from a very high delta to zero, and vice versa, in a matter of seconds. That is what brings the excitement into play; however, in the end the excitement wanes and the house always wins more than it loses.

Craps is probably the second most popular casino game; it is very similar to backgammon in that all of the information is revealed to the players. They must then make their bets based on a set of rules that favor the house. Craps allows the players to either bet on or against the dice, so at times it may appear that they are betting against the other players, but the truth is that in order to get into that position, they must pay the house a commission. The players are always against the house, no matter if they bet on or against the dice. Similar to other games of chance, a single throw of the dice can change the player's delta on a bet from very high to zero. Craps can produce wild winning streaks and occasionally a player will win a gigantic amount off of the casino, but in the long run, the casino's edge overcomes all luck and it will prevail.

The first two games, poker and backgammon, are examples of **favorable games**. They require skill, and the higher-skilled players win in the long run. The games played against the casino are examples of **unfavorable games** where no amount of skill can overcome their opponent's edge in the long run.

When you trade options, you want to be the skilled poker player or the skilled backgammon player—or better yet, you want to be the casino! You will learn when to make bets (trades) that give you the edge in the market, but you must also realize that crazy things happen and you must be prepared to take your medicine and move on to the next trade.

Turning back to the Black–Scholes model, it describes the exact thing that we looked at in the games of chance. It is showing you the information that the market participants are revealing *at a particular point in time*. It then puts that information into a mathematical model that allows you to make decisions. It is a **probability model** that is very accurate, and the longer you trade options, the more obvious that fact will become!

There are many option models that deal with binomial distributions and possible adverse events, and they may price certain strikes slightly differently than the Black–Scholes or the newer Cox–Rubinstein model. Don't worry about that; those slight variations in pricing will not affect your trading results. This is the reason that I use a simple method to explain option pricing, I let the supply and demand for the option give me my model, and then I combine that with my trading model to make decisions.

◼ Air in the Balloon

Options are priced differently than any other class of assets. The auction market is still the mechanism used to discover price; however, volatility (implied volatility) will determine the nominal price at any point in time. Other factors will contribute to the price, such as time to expiration and asset class, but volatility is the prime factor in determining the price of an option.

Imagine that the option model is a balloon that has air pumped into it at the at-the-money strike price (ATM, the current market price of the stock). As you pump air into the balloon, it expands equally in all directions. Figure 7.1 represents the balloon. Think of air going into the balloon as option *premium* (the Greek term for the air is Vega). This is the price that buyers are willing to pay over the intrinsic value, to own an option at a particular strike price. The at-the-money option (ATM) will always have the most air, as it is the point that has the greatest degree of uncertainty. That should become clear if you looked at the binomial distribution model earlier in the chapter. You have a good idea of the chance that an option will change from out of the money to in the money if we own an option at either extreme

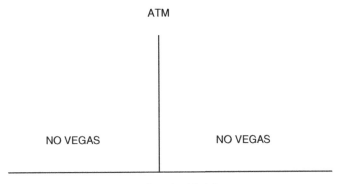

FIGURE 7.2 Expiration: No Premium Left in the Model

of the distribution curve. On one side of the curve, the chance is that it will have no value; on the other side of the distribution curve, we know that there is very little chance it will not have value at expiration. However, in the middle of the model (ATM), we have almost no idea if it will be in or out of the money at expiration; therefore, it is all premium and has no intrinsic value.

If we were to suck all the air out of the balloon, the option price would fall back to a specific "flat" cost relative to the underlying stock (current market price of our stock).

Figure 7.2 shows the option model at expiration. There is no longer any air in the model. All options are either worthless, as they finished out of the money (OTM), or they are intrinsic and finished in the money (ITM); in any case, there isn't any uncertainty, so no buyer is willing to pay a premium to own the rights to purchase or sell the underlying asset.

Summary

I have taught countless students how to use this simple method to understand the seemingly complex mathematics of the option model. In the next chapter, I will examine the option chain and demonstrate how the concept of the balloon looks when you observe it in a trading environment.

I have presented a lot of theory in this section; you might need to read through it a couple of times. Please don't go on to the next chapter until you have a firm grasp of the theory presented in this chapter.

Chapter 7 Quiz

1) The option model has the most uncertainty at:
   a) the current price of the underlying asset
   b) when an option reaches parity

c) when an option becomes a teenie

d) none of the above

2) An option model has the most certainty:

    a) at the point the calls reach parity and the puts become teenies

    b) at the point the puts reach parity and the calls become teenies

    c) at the at-the-money strike

    d) both a and b

3) The Black–Scholes option model:

    a) was the first option model

    b) has changed because of high-frequency traders

    c) is not reliable in volatile markets

    d) none of the above

4) How is poker similar to options?

    a) Some information concerning the market is revealed.

    b) Both rely on probability models to succeed.

    c) Luck can play a part in the short run.

    d) All of the above.

5) How is blackjack similar to options?

    a) Your opponent has unlimited capital.

    b) Both rely on probability models and skill to succeed.

    c) Luck can overcome your opponent in the short run.

    d) All of the above.

6) What happens when the at-the-money (ATM) call is exactly where the underlying asset is trading?

    a) It has a 50 percent chance of ending up in the money.

    b) It has less than a 50 percent chance if the market is in a bear trend.

    c) It is impossible to say what its chances are of ending up in the money.

    d) None of the above.

7) If the at-the-money (ATM) option has premium expanding, what is most likely true?

    a) The out-of-the-money options will have more air.

    b) The in-the-money options will have more air.

    c) Volatility of the underlying asset is probably greater.

    d) All of the above.

8) At expiration, which option will have the most premium?

    a) the at the money (ATM)

    b) the 40 delta put

c) the 40 delta call

d) none of the above

9) Once an option reaches parity, what will happen if the volatility doesn't change?

a) It will remain at parity.

b) It will mimic the underlying stock 100 percent.

c) It can never end up a teenie.

d) It is always at risk for market direction.

10) The amount of premium in the at-the-money option (ATM) is determined by:

a) the Black–Scholes model

b) the rate at which the underlying stock is moving

c) the supply and demand for the option in the specific expiration serial

d) all of the above

The Option Chain

The option chain is the parabolic curve presented in the form of prices. It is the vehicle that you will use to execute your trades, and you need a though understanding of how it works. This chapter will explain it in detail.

Let's review the basic premise of the last chapter before the option chain is presented.

The option model expands in all directions. The greatest volume of air (Vega) in the model will be at the spot that has the least degree of certainty, which will be the at-the-money (ATM) strike. As we move further away from the at-the-money (ATM) strike in either direction, the uncertainty will become less, and we will have more information to make our decision. The ATM option has no intrinsic value, and therefore it is all air. The more air that is pumped into the ATM, the more that spills into the other parts of the balloon, the other strike prices. Figure 8.1 and Figure 8.2 combine our first look at the option chain with the binomial distribution curve. The sample option chain is for Priceline Inc., one of the highest-priced stocks trading today. This particular option chain is a weekly chain that expired on Friday, April 25, 2014. The stock closed at exactly $1,230 a share on April 22, 2014. The Priceline option chain is located below the binomial distribution curve.

A couple of things should instantly stand out.

Since the underlying stock closed at exactly $1,230 per share, we can identify the ATM immediately—it has to be the 1230 strike. You will notice that it falls in line exactly with our binomial distribution curve from the previous chapter. The 1230 call settled at $12.00 and the 1230 put settled at $12.00. The 1230 straddle settled at $24.00.

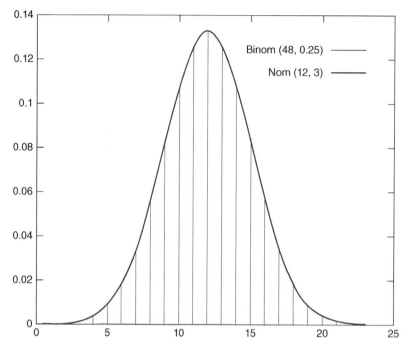

FIGURE 8.1 Binomial Distribution Curve

UNDERLYING								
Last X	Net Chng	Bid X	Ask X	Size	Volume	Open	High	Low
1230.00 D	+8.96	1229.50 P	1231.50 P	2 x 1	669,764	1222.01	1237.15	1220.15

TRADE GRID

OPTION CHAIN Spread: Single Layout: Last X, Net Change Exchange: Composite

	CALLS				Strikes: 14		PUTS		
Last X	Net Chng	Bid X	Ask X	Exp	Strike	Bid X	Ask X	Last X	Net Chng
APR4 14 (3) 100 (Weeklys)									25.17% (±24.635)
22.00 Q	+6.00	20.40 X	21.70 X	APR4 14	1215	5.60 X	6.40 W	6.10 Z	-6.10
20.00 C	+4.30	18.70 W	20.40 X	APR4 14	1217.5	6.30 X	7.20 X	6.61 C	-9.29
17.01 I	+2.91	17.10 W	18.30 X	APR4 14	1220	7.10 X	8.10 X	8.10 Z	-6.30
15.50 C	+3.15	15.60 I	16.80 X	APR4 14	1222.5	8.10 X	9.20 X	8.39 W	-9.81
15.00 Z	+3.70	14.10 X	15.00 I	APR4 14	1225	9.20 H	10.10 X	9.80 Z	-8.00
13.00 C	+2.60	12.80 X	13.60 X	APR4 14	1227.5	10.30 X	11.10 H	10.61 W	-8.79
12.00 Z	+2.70	11.50 X	12.50 W	APR4 14	1230	11.40 X	12.30 X	12.00 A	-10.20
11.00 X	+3.19	10.40 W	11.30 X	APR4 14	1232.5	12.80 X	13.60 X	13.40 A	-10.17
9.30 X	+1.50	9.30 W	10.10 X	APR4 14	1235	14.10 X	15.00 X	14.80 N	-7.80
8.50 Q	+1.75	8.30 X	9.10 X	APR4 14	1237.5	15.60 X	16.40 X	16.30 X	-13.90
7.30 Q	-1.30	7.30 X	8.00 Z	APR4 14	1240	17.10 X	18.00 X	17.70 N	-12.40
8.52 C	+3.52	6.50 X	7.20 X	APR4 14	1242.5	18.80 X	19.60 X	20.50 N	-10.60
6.20 Q	+1.10	5.70 X	6.20 Q	APR4 14	1245	20.50 X	21.30 X	21.50 Z	-16.30

FIGURE 8.2 (PCLN) Priceline Inc. Weekly Option Chain

POP QUIZ

How much of the 1230 straddle is air (Vega) and how much is intrinsic?

The answer is that since we are at the point of the greatest uncertainty and each option has a 50 percent chance of being in the money at expiration, the entire amount was air. If the price of PCLN is $1,230 a share on expiration day, Friday, April 25, 2014, both the 1230 call and the 1230 put would expire worthless!

If you did not get this pop quiz correct, please go back and reread the previous material, as you will not be able to follow the logic until you understand the principle of option premium!

Some more points should now be coming together. As the price moves further away from the ATM strike, the amount of air in the balloon decreases in the exact percentage of the distribution curve. As we move further away from the ATM, we get more information.

Remember the previous chapter where various games were discussed. All of the games had sections that were similar in that each new play disclosed more information. If you understood the game concept, then it should be clear that each play gave you more information and that data gives you a better opportunity to make the correct trading decision. The option chain is releasing the same information, as price moves up and down the option curve!

Each strike that is out of the money has less air (Vega) than the strike that is closer to the at-the-money option. As you can see, the out-of-the-money puts and the out-of-the-money calls have the same amount of premium (air) in them as their counterparts on the opposite side of the distribution curve. The slight differences in Vega are attributed to the way the exchange settles the various strike prices, but you should notice that each subsequent strike that is further away from the money has less air. Because PCLN has such a big distribution, the deltas change slowly and you need many strikes until you reach parity on one side and teenies on the other. Those numbers are too big to present in this example, but later, when we examine whether the Black–Scholes or any other model is universal, you will be able to see when the option reaches parity or becomes a teenie.

POP QUIZ

Once an option reaches parity or becomes a teenie, can it ever go to the other side of the distribution curve?

The answer is **yes**, it can, and many traders have been blown out when they didn't understand this principle. It is a long shot, but we saw earlier in the section on games of chance that long shots do hit. That is why we never take a trade that gives us limited reward and unlimited risk!

Do you know why?

The further that you move in any direction from the current price, the less chance you have to reach the higher or lower price on the other side of the distribution curve. Buyers can ascertain their chance of the price reversing to the other extreme price level before expiration by looking at the air in the ATM. As the volatility (Vega) increases (air going into the balloon), the chances of extreme price moves to the other side of the distribution curve increase in direct proportion to the additional amount of volatility.

Figure 8.2 is the binomial distribution of Figure 8.1 displayed as an option chain, and also from Priceline on April 22, 2014. The difference is that it is a later serial that will expire on May 9, 2014. There are a couple of things that should be noted. This is not as liquid as the first model that was expiring in three days, and therefore some of the option values are skewed because of the wider bid–offer spreads. Second, there is much more air in the balloon, and, therefore, the Vegas for all of the strikes are much larger. The ATM straddle is trading at $84, as opposed to $24 in the first example. Can you figure out why?

The answer is because there is more time until the expiration. Traders know that there is more uncertainty, and they demand a bigger premium to sell to investors. Everything else is exactly the same. If Priceline is trading @ $1,230 at the expiration on Friday, May 9, 2014, both the 1230 put and 1230 call will go out worthless, all of the other strikes will be either intrinsic or extrinsic, and the model will have no air, as there is no longer any uncertainty.

I want to visit Priceline one more time and look at an option chain that has an even longer time to its expiration. This is depicted in Figure 8.3, and this option chain doesn't expire until October 17, 2014. Because the chain is so large, the number of strikes that can be displayed is limited. However, enough is shown that you should be able to get the point. This market is very *illiquid, and a retail option trader cannot possibly get involved*. The bid–offer spreads are now $350 wide versus $30 wide in the first option chain. The 1230 strike is still the ATM, and the straddle is still all air and is trading at $2,200. Because the balloon has so much air in it and there is such a long time until expiration, there is little difference between the Vegas in the adjoining strikes. Not only does this make logical sense, but it also makes mathematical sense. If Priceline Inc. were to expire at 1230 on October 17, 2014, the 1230 call and puts

UNDERLYING

Last X	Net Chng	Bid X	Ask X	Size	Volume	Open	High	Low
1230.00 D	+8.96	1229.50 P	1231.50 P	2 x 1	669,764	1222.01	1237.15	1220.15

TRADE GRID

OPTION CHAIN Spread: Single Layout: Last X, Net Change Exchange: Composite

Strikes: 14

CALLS						PUTS			
Last X	Net Chng	Bid X	Ask X	Exp	Strike	Bid X	Ask X	Last X	Net Chng
APR4 14 (3) 100 (Weeklys)									25.18% (±24.642)
MAY1 14 (10) 100 (Weeklys)									29.64% (±49.679)
MAY2 14 (17) 100 (Weeklys)									42.35% (±91.602)
52.00 Q	+5.50	50.20 B	52.80 X	MAY2 14	1215	35.10 X	37.60 X	61.51 I	0
51.60 Z	+3.55	48.80 X	51.50 X	MAY2 14	1217.5	36.30 T	38.40 C	36.80 Z	N/A
50.40 Z	+5.40	47.10 C	50.10 X	MAY2 14	1220	37.40 X	39.50 C	41.15 Q	-22.85
50.90 H	+9.45	46.10 X	48.90 C	MAY2 14	1222.5	38.50 X	41.20 X	39.80 Z	N/A
47.40 Z	+6.40	44.80 X	47.60 C	MAY2 14	1225	39.60 C	42.30 C	44.00 C	-12.65
44.80 H	+4.85	43.30 X	46.40 X	MAY2 14	1227.5	40.80 X	43.80 X	45.00 C	N/A
46.00 Q	+20.00	41.90 C	45.10 X	MAY2 14	1230	42.10 X	44.40 C	42.31 C	-14.71
46.30 C	+25.90	41.30 B	43.70 X	MAY2 14	1232.5	43.30 M	46.50 X	N/A	N/A
40.50 Q	+4.33	39.60 X	42.60 X	MAY2 14	1235	44.60 C	47.70 C	54.60 Q	0
33.70 H	0	38.40 C	41.40 X	MAY2 14	1237.5	45.90 X	49.10 X	N/A	N/A
42.05 I	+5.85	37.10 C	40.20 X	MAY2 14	1240	47.00 C	50.00 X	48.61 C	-16.34
33.57 I	0	36.00 C	39.10 X	MAY2 14	1242.5	48.30 C	51.50 C	49.25 C	0
54.00 N	0	34.90 C	38.00 X	MAY2 14	1245	49.70 C	52.30 X	52.00 Q	-14.50
35.00 Z	+4.20	32.80 C	35.80 X	MAY2 14	1250	52.50 X	55.40 C	53.99 C	-19.43

FIGURE 8.3 (PCLN) Priceline Three-Week Option Chain

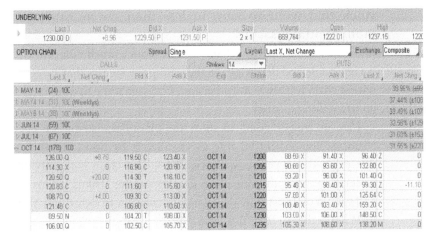

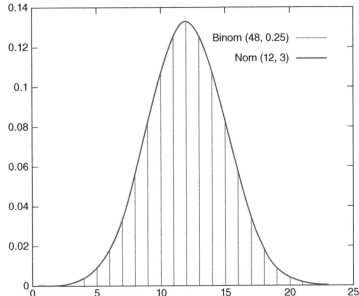

FIGURE 8.4 (PCLN) Priceline 178-Day Option Chain

would go out worthless, and all of the other options would either be at parity or worthless; nothing would change.

The reason that I used Priceline in this example is to show you how the option model changes as time expands in huge contracts. Priceline is not to be traded unless you have (1) a very large degree of risk tolerance and (2) a very large amount of risk capital.

If you were to buy the 1230 straddle in October and it were to expire worthless, it would be the equivalent of owning 100 shares of a $220

stock that went to zero in less than six months, and it would be a monumental disaster!

The next set of option chains will be from a much different type of stock, one that is very stable and doesn't have the wild price swings that Priceline does. The second option chain is from Caterpillar Inc. Let's see if the pricing model holds up when we go to a defensive stock.

I am no longer going to show the binomial distribution curve on every option chain, as you should be able to visualize it by now. Figure 8.5 is a weekly chain that expired on Friday, April 25, 2014. This chain is slightly different, because the underlying stock did not close exactly on the strike. It closed between strikes at $103.69. You must now do a small calculation to determine the ATM.

What is the ATM in this example?

You should be able to calculate that the ATM in this example is the 104 strike price; it is 31c from the 104 strike and 69c from the 103 strike. Because this stock is worth less than 10 percent of PCLN, we should expect to have an option chain with much less air in the balloon. And we do; the 104 call is priced @ 1.73 and the 103 put is trading @ 1.52. With the underlying stock trading at 103.69 the 104 call and the 103 put are all air (they are the ATM strangle). The 103 call and the 104 put have intrinsic value, but they also have the same amount of air as the 104 call and 103 put. In either case, as we move up and down they will become all air and the ATM straddle will be the sum of the 104 call and put plus the sum of the 103 call and put divided by two. This formula will work for any ATM that is currently between strikes!

This may seem complicated at first glance, but if you take a second to look at the numbers, you can see that the percentage of premium in the 104 call and the 103 put is the exact percentage of the difference between the strikes. As we roll up and down the option curve, the air will shift to the point that has the greatest

UNDERLYING								
Last X	Net Chng	Bid X	Ask X	Size	Volume	Open	High	Low
103.69 N	+1.05	103.52 P	103.69 P	4 x 3	4,533,140	102.78	104.1362	102.76

TRADE GRID

OPTION CHAIN — Spread: Single — Layout: Last X, Net Change — Exchange: Composite

	CALLS				Strikes: 14		PUTS			
Last X	Net Chng	Bid X	Ask X	Exp	Strike	Bid X	Ask X	Last X	Net Chng
APR4 14 (3) 100 (Weekly)									45.23% (±3.73%)
6.95 M	+.55	6.75 X	7.05 X	APR4 14	97	.19 Z	.23 C	.18 Z	-.05
5.31 C	0	5.90 X	6.25 X	APR4 14	98	.28 Q	.31 A	.27 C	-.07
5.17 B	+1.77	5.05 X	5.20 A	APR4 14	99	.41 Q	.44 A	.40 I	-.07
4.36 C	+1.21	4.25 A	4.40 X	APR4 14	100	.59 Q	.62 Q	.56 C	-.14
3.60 Q	+1.12	3.50 C	3.60 C	APR4 14	101	.83 Z	.87 A	.84 X	-.13
3.10 N	+1.15	2.82 Z	2.69 C	APR4 14	102	1.13 C	1.18 C	1.14 Z	-.24
2.39 I	+.99	2.21 M	2.28 C	APR4 14	103	1.52 X	1.55 A	1.53 A	-.36
1.77 N	+.82	1.68 Q	1.73 A	APR4 14	104	1.97 C	2.03 A	1.99 Q	-.87
1.28 I	+.63	1.23 I	1.26 Q	APR4 14	105	2.51 X	2.59 C	2.41 C	-1.39
.89 I	+.50	.87 C	.91 C	APR4 14	106	3.05 X	3.25 C	3.06 C	-.69
.72 Z	+.48	.59 C	.64 Q	APR4 14	107	3.55 X	4.00 C	3.55 A	N/A
.49 N	+.35	.39 I	.42 Q	APR4 14	108	4.40 X	4.80 X	4.62 C	N/A
.25 X	+.18	.25 Q	.27 H	APR4 14	109	5.15 X	5.65 X	5.40 X	N/A

FIGURE 8.5 (Cat) Caterpillar Inc. Three-Day Weekly Option Chain

UNDERLYING								
Last X	Net Chng	Bid X	Ask X	Size	Volume	Open	High	Low
103.69 N	+1.05	103.52 P	103.69 P	4 x 3	4,533,140	102.78	104.1362	102.76

TRADE GRID

OPTION CHAIN Spread: Single Layout: Last X, Net Change Exchange: Composite

CALLS					Strikes: 14	PUTS			
Last X	Net Chng	Bid X	Ask X	Exp	Strike	Bid X	Ask X	Last X	Net Chng
APR4 14 (3) 100 (Weeklys)								45.23% (±3.732)	
MAY1 14 (10) 100 (Weeklys)								30.09% (±4.261)	
MAY2 14 (17) 100 (Weeklys)								25.36% (±4.615)	
5.60 B	0	7.05 X	7.55 X	MAY2 14	97	.40 X	.44 A	.41 N	-.24
4.97 C	0	6.15 X	6.55 X	MAY2 14	98	.52 C	.57 C	.49 N	-.30
5.05 B	0	5.30 X	5.60 X	MAY2 14	99	.68 C	.73 X	.66 C	-.22
3.90 Q	0	4.55 X	4.75 X	MAY2 14	100	.88 C	.94 C	.87 Q	-.28
3.93 C	+1.17	3.80 C	4.00 X	MAY2 14	101	1.13 C	1.20 C	1.09 C	-.45
2.91 Z	+.73	3.15 C	3.30 X	MAY2 14	102	1.45 A	1.52 I	1.47 C	-.35
2.61 X	+.85	2.56 C	2.61 H	MAY2 14	103	1.84 C	1.91 C	1.77 Q	-.51
2.08 N	+.71	2.01 Z	2.08 C	MAY2 14	104	2.32 X	2.37 C	4.45 B	0
1.64 C	+.66	1.55 X	1.61 C	MAY2 14	105	2.82 C	2.91 C	3.40 T	0
1.19 T	+.46	1.17 C	1.23 C	MAY2 14	106	3.40 X	3.55 X	4.15 T	0
.75 M	-.09	.86 X	.91 A	MAY2 14	107	3.85 X	4.25 X	6.55 N	0
.67 A	+.34	.63 N	.67 C	MAY2 14	108	4.80 X	5.05 X	4.95 C	N/A
.65 Q	0	.45 N	.48 C	MAY2 14	109	5.45 X	5.85 X	N/A	N/A
.17 Q	0	.31 X	.34 X	MAY2 14	110	6.20 X	6.70 X	N/A	N/A

FIGURE 8.6 (CAT) Caterpillar 17-Week Option Chain

uncertainty, which is always the ATM. If price goes down, the air in the 104 call will shift in proportion to the 103 put, and if we go up, vice versa. In either case, the ATM will be worth 3.75 +/− a few cents. Being able to visualize the shift in premium is very helpful, and it should be second nature to you after studying it for a while. Since your trading will focus on the ATM +/− a few strikes, it is important that you learn this skill.

Figure 8.6 is CAT observed in a longer expiration serial. This particular chain is a weekly chain that expired on Friday, May 9, 2014. This chain is the same as the weekly chain that expired on April 25, 2014; the underlying stock closed between strikes at $103.69.

You should have known immediately that the ATM in this example is the 104 strike price; it is 31c from the 104 strike and 69 c from the 103 strike. Because we are looking at an option chain that has a longer time frame until expiration, you would assume that there would be more air in the balloon—and there is. The 104 call is priced @ 2.08 and the 103 put is trading @ 1.84; we can extrapolate this to know that if we go down to 103, that straddle will be trading 4.60 +/− a few pennies, and if we go to the 104 strike it will be trading 4.60 +/− a few pennies.

The ATM straddle will be the sum of the two out-of-the-money options + the sum of two in-the-money options ÷ 2. This formula will work for any ATM that is currently between strikes!

Figure 8.7 provides our final look at CAT. This is a serial that is set to expire November 2014 and will be the last serial for the stock in 2014. You should notice that everything is similar to the previous two chains except that the bid–offer spreads are wider and there is more air in the balloon. Other than that, the formula to calculate the ATM is exactly the same:

	CALLS						PUTS		
Last X	Net Chng	Bid X	Ask X	Exp	Strike	Bid X	Ask X	Last X	Net Chng

UNDERLYING

	Last X	Net Chng	Bid X	Ask X	Size	Volume	Open	High	L
	103.69 N	+1.05	103.52 P	103.69 P	4 x 3	4,533,140	102.78	104.1362	102.

OPTION CHAIN — Spread: Single — Strikes: 14 — Layout: Last X, Net Change — Exchange: Composite

Last X	Net Chng	Bid X	Ask X	Exp	Strike	Bid X	Ask X	Last X	Net Chng
MAY4 14 (31) 100 (Weeklys)									21.85% (±5.3
MAY5 14 (38) 100 (Weeklys)									20.90% (±5.8
JUN 14 (59) 100									20.32% (±6
JUL 14 (87) 100									16.72% (±6.7
AUG 14 (115) 100									20.66% (±9.6
NOV 14 (213) 100									21.37% (±13.8
22.30 Q	0	23.80 X	24.55 X	NOV14	80	.79 A	.85 H	.85 Q	-.17
18.75 N	0	19.35 X	19.90 X	NOV14	85	1.24 A	1.31 I	1.54 H	0
13.30 C	0	17.10 X	17.65 X	NOV14	87.5	1.58 A	1.65 I	1.81 B	0
13.75 Q	0	14.95 A	15.50 X	NOV14	90	1.98 A	2.06 I	2.00 Z	-.25
13.15 X	+1.35	12.95 A	13.45 X	NOV14	92.5	2.50 A	2.68 M	2.55 Q	-.25
11.23 C	+1.08	10.95 A	11.25 A	NOV14	95	3.15 A	3.25 C	3.16 C	-.39
8.42 X	0	9.25 A	9.40 C	NOV14	97.5	3.90 X	4.00 I	4.10 N	-.55
7.70 A	+.80	7.65 A	7.80 X	NOV14	100	4.85 A	4.95 C	4.80 Z	-.45
5.15 C	+.80	4.95 A	5.05 H	NOV14	105	7.20 A	7.35 C	7.20 Z	-1.00
3.10 C	+.45	3.00 A	3.10 I	NOV14	110	10.30 A	10.45 X	11.30 N	0
1.79 A	+.26	1.73 X	1.80 H	NOV14	115	14.00 A	14.35 A	14.76 A	0
1.00 N	+.08	.95 I	1.02 X	NOV14	120	17.85 X	18.55 X	N/A	N/A
.60 H	0	.49 I	.58 X	NOV14	125	22.10 X	23.20 I	25.81 C	0
N/A	N/A	.23 A	.32 A	NOV14	130	27.15 X	29.15 X	28.45 B	0

FIGURE 8.7 (CAT) Caterpillar 213-Day Option Chain

The ATM straddle will be the sum of the two out-of-the-money options + the sum of two in-the-money options ÷ 2. This formula will work for any ATM that is currently between strikes!

Before we leave the option chain and go on to the next section, I want to examine a couple of stocks that have an even lower price and see if the principles that we found in a large stock and a medium-priced stock hold when we get to much smaller stocks.

Figure 8.8 is a stock that has recently had an IPO, Twitter Inc. Its absolute price is less than half of CAT, and therefore we would expect that there would be less air

UNDERLYING

	Last X	Net Chng	Bid X	Ask X	Size	Volume	Open	High	Lo
	46.02 N	-.11	45.97 P	46.00 Q	1 x 1	6,997,216	46.23	47.09	45.8

TRADE GRID

OPTION CHAIN — Spread: Single — Strikes: 14 — Layout: Last X, Net Change — Exchange: Composite

	CALLS						PUTS		
Last X	Net Chng	Bid X	Ask X	Exp	Strike	Bid X	Ask X	Last X	Net Chng
APR4 14 (3) 100 (Weeklys)									85.52% (±2
3.20 H	-.28	3.00 X	3.40 X	APR4 14	43	.25 X	.30 H	.35 H	0
3.30 Z	+.30	2.60 X	2.95 X	APR4 14	43.5	.35 X	.45 X	.38 X	-.12
2.50 H	-.0	2.25 X	2.50 X	APR4 14	44	.45 X	.55 X	.45 C	-.05
2.10 A	-.05	1.95 X	2.15 X	APR4 14	44.5	.60 X	.70 X	.70 H	-.05
1.70 Q	-.20	1.60 X	1.75 Q	APR4 14	45	.75 X	.85 C	.90 C	+.10
1.55 C	-.05	1.30 X	1.50 X	APR4 14	45.5	.95 X	1.10 X	1.10 A	+.05
1.10 Q	-.25	1.05 X	1.15 H	APR4 14	46	1.20 H	1.30 H	1.30 X	0
.90 H	-.25	.85 X	1.00 X	APR4 14	46.5	1.45 X	1.60 X	1.50 A	-.05
.70 H	-.5	.65 X	.75 X	APR4 14	47	1.75 X	1.95 X	1.65 Q	-.20
.50 H	-.25	.50 X	.60 X	APR4 14	47.5	2.05 X	2.30 X	2.10 A	N/A
.35 C	-.20	.35 X	.45 X	APR4 14	48	2.40 X	2.75 X	2.00 I	-.75
.30 C	-.5	.25 C	.35 C	APR4 14	48.5	2.75 X	3.10 C	2.90 H	-.20
.20 Z	-.5	.15 X	.25 X	APR4 14	49	3.10 X	3.60 X	4.15 C	0
.10 A	-.25	.10 X	.20 X	APR4 14	49.5	3.50 X	4.00 X	2.95 H	-6.10

FIGURE 8.8 (Twtr) Twitter Inc. Three-Day Option Chain

	Last X	Net Chng	Bid X	Ask X	Size	Volume	Open	High	Lo
▸	15.24 N	+.29	15.20 K	15.21 Q	159 x 15	155,338,090	15.04	15.30	14.9

TRADE GRID

OPTION CHAIN Spread: Single Layout: Volume, Open Interest Exchange: Composite

		CALLS					PUTS			
Volume	Open Int	Bid X	Ask X	Exp	Strike	Bid X	Ask X	Volume	Open Int	

Strikes: 14

MAY1 14 (3) 100 (Weekly) 29.50% (±0.3%

Volume	Open Int	Bid X	Ask X	Exp	Strike	Bid X	Ask X	Volume	Open Int
5	5	3.15 C	3.25 Q	MAY1 14	12	0 B	.01 H	0	0
0	8	2.66 I	2.76 I	MAY1 14	12.5	0 T	.01 N	0	0
0	0	2.18 I	2.25 I	MAY1 14	13	0 B	.01 M	10	477
0	104	1.67 X	1.74 Q	MAY1 14	13.5	0 B	.01 X	0	5
268	346	1.23 Q	1.24 Q	MAY1 14	14	0 B	.01 M	93	2,542
2,891	4,104	.74 Q	.76 Q	MAY1 14	14.5	.01 Q	.02 M	5,620	6,315
10,708	17,346	.30 H	.31 Q	MAY1 14	15	.07 I	.08 C	9,590	14,633
19,555	15,249	.04 X	.05 Q	MAY1 14	15.5	.31 Q	.32 Q	5,115	6,586
771	12,984	0 B	.01 M	MAY1 14	16	.76 I	.77 Q	2,953	10,651
1,065	18,607	0 B	.01 X	MAY1 14	16.5	1.25 M	1.31 X	632	2,556
41	11,189	0 X	.01 X	MAY1 14	17	1.75 I	1.81 X	143	822
52	5,880	0 Z	.01 M	MAY1 14	17.5	2.25 I	2.31 I	24	282
10	8,683	0 Z	.01 M	MAY1 14	18	2.76 I	2.80 I	0	219
230	2,139	0 M	.01 M	MAY1 14	18.5	3.25 Q	3.35 Q	0	4

FIGURE 8.9   (Bac) Bank of America Three-Day Option Chain

in the balloon—and it does have considerably less. The ATM straddle is trading for about 2.30. The stock settled @ 46.02, so, in theory, the 46 call has .02 of intrinsic value. The settlement prices are disrupting the option pricing, but you can see that each strike that is further away from the ATM has less premium in the strike, so it would seem that our binomial distribution is holding no matter what the price of the underlying stock. I want to look at one final stock to see if we can still trade a smaller-value stock with the same principles.

Figure 8.9 is Bank of America, and it is one of the most active stocks in the market.

In Figure 8.9, I have also enclosed the open interest and volume figures, and at first glance by our definition of liquidity, it appears to meet all of the criteria—huge open interest and volume. You should also notice that no matter how small the stock's underlying price, you still have the binomial distribution curve—but you might detect something else. **There is very little air in the balloon. In fact, two strikes away from the ATM there is no air at all!**

This type of stock is not tradable for retail option traders; **there is not enough premium to cover your commission costs.** The trade in this stock comes from market makers that are paying no commission. In fact, they might collect a commission to trade this stock if they provide liquidity. If you trade this type of stock long enough, the commissions that you are paying to your broker will eventually wear you down and take away all of your profit potential. Remember, liquidity is a function of the bid–offer spread and the commissions that you must pay. Many wannabe traders think that if they trade small-priced stocks they will have less risk, but the opposite is true: **If the premium is too small, the stock becomes illiquid no matter how big the open interest and volume.**

Summary

The ability to grasp the relationship of the strikes in the option chain is vital to your trading success. The examples that were presented in this section should be reviewed until you have a thorough understanding of their relationship. In the next section, I will discuss the various types of options trades that are available, and how they react to an assortment of market conditions.

Chapter 8 Quiz

1) An option chain resembles:
   a) a standard bell-shaped curve
   b) a triangle breakout pattern
   c) a trending pattern
   d) none of the above

2) What is true about the 40 delta call and the 40 delta put?
   a) It is approximately the same premium.
   b) The 40 delta call will always have more premium.
   c) They have no correlation, as one is a put and the other a call.
   d) None of the above.

3) As air goes into the option chain (balloon):
   a) it will have the greatest increase in the ATM
   b) it will spill into all of the strikes
   c) it will have no effect on the way out-of-the-money strikes
   d) both a and b

4) The deferred serial will always have:
   a) more air in the balloon as it has more uncertainty
   b) more air in the out-of-the-money options
   c) parity options and teenies
   d) all of the above

5) What will happen if volatility doubles in the expiring month?
   a) The at-the-money options will double in price.
   b) The differed serial expirations will double.
   c) There will no longer be parity options.
   d) Volatility cannot double in the front month.

6) What is true about in-the-money options?
   a) They expire in the money.
   b) They will have no premium at expiration.

c) They have intrinsic value at expiration.

d) It cannot be determined from this information.

7) An expiring option can:

   a) never have more premium than a differed option at the same strike price

   b) always be exercised

   c) be assigned

   d) all of the above

8) A lower-priced stock can never have:

   a) more premium than a higher-priced stock

   b) more volatility than a higher-priced stock

   c) more price movement than a higher-priced stock

   d) none of the above

9) The Black–Scholes model is designed to:

   a) predict future price movement

   b) react to future price movement

   c) price supply and demand for options

   d) none of the above

10) What does the Black–Scholes model ensure?

   a) The underlying asset will be fairly priced.

   b) The option chain will have liquidity.

   c) The options will be fairly priced.

   d) The at-the-money option will have the most air.

Option Trading Strategies

This chapter is going to introduce various strategies that I use to make my weekly option trades. There are many strategies that can be used, but limiting yourself to a few choices will guarantee that you don't get a trading condition known as *paralysis by analysis*.

By now you should have a fairly good perception of the option model and how it is used to create the option chain. The option chain is our execution vehicle, so it is critically important that you are on familiar terms with what you are reading. If you don't have a full grasp, this chapter will help you to gain the confidence you need to begin to at least paper trade the concepts that will be presented.

The trades that you will use depend on a number of different conditions, both financial and emotional.

First and most important is your ability to handle risk.

If you are an aggressive trader and don't mind swings in your capital base, you will want to use aggressive trades that offer the best risk–reward opportunity. If you are more conservative and want to grind out small profits without subjecting yourself to potentially large capital swings, alternative trades will be suggested. All of the trades that I use have one thing in common: **They never have unlimited risk**.

Why Selling Naked Options Is Always Wrong!

The one universal trait that I find in unsuccessful option traders is that they use trades that contain unlimited risk and limited reward—in other words, they sell

naked options. It can be straddles, strangles, or calendars or some combination of them, or, worst of all, they sell teenies. Selling naked options is often successful and you may make money for long periods of time; however, eventually you will get caught in a disastrous trade and you will lose all of your profits. I personally know traders who have lost all of their capital and were out of the game.

The horror stories you read about banks and hedge funds blowing out are because they violated this rule.

In the past 20 years, at least two banks and a large hedge fund have blown out because they sold naked options, and another bank, J.P. Morgan, also lost over $5 billion on a single trade.

Look at this roster of greed and arrogance.

In 1995, Nick Leeson, a rogue trader for Barings Bank, the oldest investment bank in the United Kingdom, took the firm down when he sold naked straddles against the Tokyo stock exchange's Nikkei Index. Immediately after he sold the options, an earthquake hit the city of Kobe, Japan, and drove the index into a free fall. The bank collapsed when it couldn't meet the margin call of over $1.4 billion. Lesson was sent to prison for his unauthorized trades.

In 1998, Long-Term Capital Management of Greenwich, Connecticut, imploded when it sold naked puts during the Russian financial crisis. The company had been founded in 1994 by several highly successful Wall Street traders. Among its board of directors were Myron Scholes and Robert C. Merton. Scholes and Merton had won the Nobel Prize for Economics in 1997 for their "new method to determine the value of derivatives" (no, that is not a joke!).

The company's board of directors had countless PhDs in economics and statistics from the best business schools in the world monitoring the risk. Long-Term Capital had returned an average of 30 percent a year after fees in its first three years of existence by selling naked options.

It lost all of its capital—$4.6 billion—in less than four months. The Federal Reserve had to bail it out, and the fund was dissolved in 2000.

In 2008, AIG, the world's largest insurance firm, blew out for over $100 billion and had to be bailed out by the Federal Reserve because it sold more than $400 billion of credit default swaps on the collateral debt obligations to the other major investment banks.

These insurance policies were actually **naked options** that AIG collected in the form of a premium. It also had a staff of rocket scientists that the world has rarely seen monitoring the risk.

In 2012, the "London whale" trading for J.P. Morgan initiated a trade in the credit default swaps market in which he sold billions of dollars' worth of premium as a "hedge" for the bank's credit risk. The trade became so large that other units of J.P. Morgan took the other side of the trade! By the time it was over, it cost Morgan more than $5 billion, and the final tally is not in, as various securities agencies are still pursuing litigation.

What was the common thread of these debacles?

How can the best and brightest financial minds in the world possibly get it so wrong?

The answer is simple: Greed and arrogance to an extent that is hard to fathom!

The public sees these trades and blames the derivatives as being the danger, when nothing could be further from the truth: **It was the selling of unlimited risk that caused the loss, not the options!** Legislators constantly rail about the danger of options, and some radicals go as far as initiating legislation that would outlaw them. This is as silly as banning automobiles because more than 1,000,000 people die in them each year. Generally the car is safe; it is the way it is operated that can't be controlled.

In the first chapter we talked about financial panics and the role of greed and fear in trading. Once again, I am reinforcing the fact that if you allow yourself to become greedy and arrogant, you are going to suffer the same fate as the above mentioned banks and hedge funds. The only difference is that your blowout won't make headlines!

■ Suitable Option Trades

Jack Nicklaus, the best golfer of the twentieth century, was asked how he was so successful for such an extended period of time. His reply was that he "made the same swing every time; he just used a different club depending on the distance." Before you can make money trading weekly options, you must know what club you are going to use and how far you need to hit the ball. In this section, we are going to discuss the various methods that I use to trade the weekly options. There are literally hundreds of trades that can be made, but I only use a few. Believe it or not, the few trades that I am going to teach you will do as much as the millions of possible combinations that are available. They are designed to minimize commissions and allow you to play the game at whatever risk level you desire.

All of the trades in this section we will initiate using the prices of the option chain for **AAPL**, Figure 9.1 You can see two option chains are used—one for the expiring week and one for the next week if we need to "roll back" (selling the current serial and buying the next serial) a trade late in the week. Each trade that is discussed will reference the price and strike that is used in the option chain.

Outright Purchase of an Option

This is the most basic of option trades, the "opening" purchase of a call or put.

CALLS					Strikes: 12 ▼		PUTS				
Position	Last X	Net Chng	Bid X	Ask X	Exp	Strike	Bid X	Ask X	Position	Last X	Net Chng
2 14 (1) 100 (Weeklys)											16.03% (
	12.70 Q	.05	12.45 X	12.95 X	MAY2 14	580	.13 Q	.14 I		.14 Q	-.44
	9.65 M	.35	10.05 X	10.45 I	MAY2 14	582.5	.21 N	.22 Q		.19 C	-.86
	8.00 Z	+.30	7.70 X	8.10 I	MAY2 14	585	.40 N	.42 Z		.41 Q	-1.29
	5.75 A	+.40	5.70 A	5.90 N	MAY2 14	587.5	.77 Z	.81 N		.77 N	-2.00
	3.95 A	+.70	3.95 H	4.05 Q	MAY2 14	590	1.44 N	1.50 Q		1.51 A	-2.36
	2.58 C	+.38	2.51 M	2.58 N	MAY2 14	592.5	2.50 Q	2.54 Q		2.50 Q	-2.82
	1.42 N	+.12	1.41 H	1.46 N	MAY2 14	595	3.85 N	3.95 Q		3.95 A	-3.15
	.74 N	-.12	.73 N	.75 Q	MAY2 14	597.5	5.65 N	5.80 Q		5.70 Z	-3.35
	.34 I	-.21	.36 N	.38 N	MAY2 14	600	7.80 Q	8.00 C		7.85 C	-3.19
	.18 Q	-.17	.18 N	.19 I	MAY2 14	602.5	9.90 C	10.35 C		10.01 X	-3.38
	.08 I	-.16	.09 N	.10 Z	MAY2 14	605	12.30 X	12.75 X		13.20 Z	-2.55
	.06 X	-.11	.05 Z	.06 Q	MAY2 14	607.5	14.75 A	15.25 A		14.85 X	-4.65
Y 14 (8) 100											17.67% (±
	14.50 Q	+1.75	14.20 C	14.45 H	MAY 14	580	1.76 N	1.80 Z		1.76 I	-1.26
	12.30 B	N/A	12.30 C	12.50 M	MAY 14	582.5	2.31 N	2.36 Q		2.29 H	N/A
	10.50 Q	+1.49	10.50 A	10.65 A	MAY 14	585	2.99 Z	3.05 Q		2.94 Z	-1.64
	8.95 A	N/A	8.85 A	9.00 Q	MAY 14	587.5	3.80 N	3.90 C		3.90 C	N/A
	7.35 N	+1.15	7.35 A	7.50 N	MAY 14	590	4.80 Q	4.90 N		4.91 I	-2.09
	6.00 C	N/A	6.00 I	6.15 N	MAY 14	592.5	5.95 N	6.10 X		6.00 N	N/A
	4.90 Q	+.55	4.85 C	4.95 N	MAY 14	595	7.25 N	7.40 A		7.38 I	-2.42
	3.95 A	N/A	3.85 Z	3.95 C	MAY 14	597.5	8.75 N	8.90 C		8.75 X	N/A
	3.05 A	+.40	2.98 C	3.05 Q	MAY 14	600	10.35 Q	10.55 Q		10.40 N	-2.85
	2.34 Q	N/A	2.30 N	2.34 Q	MAY 14	602.5	12.20 N	12.45 C		12.60 A	N/A
	1.78 I	+.08	1.75 A	1.80 Q	MAY 14	605	14.10 N	14.35 N		14.85 M	-3.00

FIGURE 9.1   (AAPL) AAPL One-Day Option Chain

The buyer of a **call** has the right, but not the obligation, to "call the stock" from the seller at any time prior to expiration at the strike price that is underlying the call. You may sell the call at any time prior to expiration at the market price.

The buyer of a **put** has the right, but not the obligation, to "put the stock" to the seller at any time prior to expiration at the strike price that is underlying the put. You may sell the put at any time prior to expiration at the market price.

The purchase of a call or put always has limited risk and unlimited reward (call only). The maximum you can lose is the debit that you paid for the option. On the other hand, a call has unlimited reward to the upside. The put has its reward limited to the stock going to zero, but the loss is limited to the debit if the stock rallies.

Most software execution platforms have analyzers that calculate the profit or loss at expiration. **I do not use the analysis tools** because I find that they can be very deceptive in that the results that you get trading before expiration may be very different from what the analyzer tells you at expiration.

Example: Buying a Call to Open

Your technical analysis tells you it is time to get long AAPL and you decide to buy a call.

What call do you buy?

You have many choices, from those deep in the money to those that are currently teenies. Which one is right?

In options, there is no such thing as buying the absolute right option; that depends on your taste. But there is a wrong way to buy, and that is buying "cheap calls," those that are far out of the money and have a small delta. Those calls are not cheap—they are either fairly priced or they are expensive in relation to the ATM and ATM $+1/-1$ calls.

Here is why.

Although the absolute price is diminutive, the chance that it will ever be worth anything is also very small. Nothing is more frustrating as an option trader than to nail the price direction on the nose and end up losing money! It is the biggest complaint I hear from students.

"I don't like to trade options because of the premium decay." They are correct, the time decay (theta) is something that you must deal with, and you have to find ways to defeat the problem. When you buy a call, unless it is parity to begin with, you will be dealing with time decay.

Suppose you want to buy the May 2 14 590 call for 4.05. What needs to transpire in order make money at expiration?

The first thing you need to have happen is that the price must go in the direction that you have predicted. You notice I said "predicted." The reason is that even if you are reacting to technical analysis, it is now a prediction; if the price doesn't go higher, you will have a losing trade. This section answers some common questions.

How far does price have to advance to make money?

The math is very simple, and you don't need a computer. The underlying strike is the 590 and you paid a debit of 4.05 in order to figure your breakeven price at expiration; add the strike to the debit and you have the breakeven price.

$590 + 4.05 = 594.05$, so the stock must close above 594.05 to break even.

What is your risk in this trade?

The standard answer is the \$4.05 that you paid for the call, but this answer is not necessarily correct. If AAPL expires at the current price of around 592.65, your risk is only \$1.40, not \$ 4.05!

How can I know that to be true when if I can't see the underlying stock price?

I am going to teach you a little trick to price any stock through the options, It is called a conversion or reversal, and it is the way all market makers price a market!

If you remember the last chapter on pricing options, the ATM put and call are all air when the underlying stock settled exactly on a strike. *The amount of air is constant in the strike at all times until expiration.* What this means is the premium in the put and call will be constant. They can vary slightly because of the bid–offer spread, but they will be quickly put back into line by market makers doing conversions and reversals to capture the bid–offer spread that is out of line.

UNDERLYING

Last X	Net Chng	Bid X	Ask X	Size	Volume	Open	High	Low
1230.00 D	+8.96	1229.50 P	1231.50 P	2 x 1	669,764	1222.01	1237.15	1220.15

TRADE GRID

OPTION CHAIN — Spread: Single — Layout: Last X, Net Change — Exchange: Composite

Strikes: 14

CALLS						PUTS			
Last X	Net Chng	Bid X	Ask X	Exp	Strike	Bid X	Ask X	Last X	Net Chng
APR4 14 (3) 100 (Weeklys)									25.17% (±24.635)
22.00 Q	+5.00	20.40 X	21.70 X	APR4 14	1215	5.60 X	6.40 W	6.10 Z	-6.10
20.00 C	+4.30	18.70 W	20.40 X	APR4 14	1217.5	6.30 X	7.20 X	6.61 C	-9.29
17.01 I	+2.91	17.10 W	18.30 X	APR4 14	1220	7.10 X	8.10 X	8.10 Z	-6.30
15.50 C	+3.15	15.60 I	16.80 X	APR4 14	1222.5	8.10 X	9.20 X	8.39 W	-9.81
15.00 Z	+3.70	14.10 X	15.00 I	APR4 14	1225	9.20 H	10.10 X	9.80 Z	-8.00
13.00 C	+2.80	12.80 X	13.80 X	APR4 14	1227.5	10.30 X	11.10 H	10.61 W	-8.79
12.00 Z	+2.70	11.50 X	12.50 W	APR4 14	1230	11.40 X	12.30 X	12.00 A	-10.20
11.00 X	+3.19	10.40 W	11.30 X	APR4 14	1232.5	12.80 X	13.60 X	13.40 A	-10.17
9.30 X	+1.60	9.30 W	10.10 X	APR4 14	1235	14.10 X	15.00 X	14.80 N	-7.80
8.50 Q	+1.75	8.30 X	9.10 X	APR4 14	1237.5	15.60 X	16.40 X	16.30 X	-13.90
7.30 Q	+1.30	7.30 X	8.00 Z	APR4 14	1240	17.10 X	18.00 X	17.70 N	-12.40
8.52 C	+3.52	6.50 X	7.20 X	APR4 14	1242.5	18.80 X	19.60 X	20.50 N	-10.60
6.20 Q	+1.10	5.70 X	6.20 Q	APR4 14	1245	20.50 X	21.30 X	21.50 Z	-16.30

FIGURE 9.2 (PCLN) Priceline Inc. Three-Day Option Chain

To figure the premium in any strike, subtract the intrinsic value from the current price and it will give you the premium left in the strike. Both the put and call will have the exact premium, plus or minus the bid–offer spread.

Here is the exact process. Figure 9.2 revisits the PCLN option chain from Chapter 8.

In the PCLN option chain with the underlying stock trading at exactly at $1,230 a share, the premium for both the call and the put was $12.00, but they also had a bid–offer spread of $1.00. If the market maker can buy the bid or sell the offer in either the call or the put and buy or sell the stock at $1,230 they are guaranteed a profit no matter what happens to the stock! They are **converting or reversing** the option into the underlying stock. So if I can buy the put for $11.50 and sell the call for $12.00 and buy the stock for $1,230, then no matter what happens between now and expiration, I will make the spread of $50 minus commissions and fees.

If it is so easy to make money with this trade, why can't I just do these trades?

Two reasons: First, your commissions generally won't allow you to make this type of trade, and, second, the market maker's software is bidding and offering on thousands of puts and calls at the same time; they only execute when the market will allow them to take a small profit in a trade. However, you can always price any option market using this technique, so it is a little trick that will always come in handy.

If I hold the call to expiration, I know it will be worthless, but how can I tell if will have any value prior to the expiration?

I find this to be one of the hardest concepts for students to understand—why there is premium right up to expiration.

Remember the bell-shaped curve from Chapter 6? It showed that at expiration, there is no longer any doubt about the final price and the premium in all options is zero, but what about if the 590 strike is the ATM on expiration day?

Will the 590 call have no value, as the analyzer tells you?

The answer is no, it will still have a 50 delta and because there is uncertainty it will have premium left in it.

Days until Expiration is a composite of the most likely premium levels on any given day for the final 14 days of the 50 most liquid stocks that are priced over $50. I believe that this table is the only one to be printed, and it will give you the highest probability of premium levels on any given day. As you can see, even on expiration Friday of May2 14 AAPL 590 call will still be worth 2.90 (50 percent of the straddle) if it is at the money. Knowing this information will give you an edge against other traders. Figure 9.1 is the table for AAPL. To check other liquid stocks simply go to the appendix "Days until Expiration" and it will give you the most likely results.

This table can be constructed for any stock that you desire by following the ATM straddle for the final 14 days until expiration. It is a lot of grunt work, but to my knowledge no service provides this information. I can tell you that your competition, which is the hedge funds and market makers, have their own proprietary numbers, and they use them to give them an edge.

This might seem like a lot of information to simply buy a call, but it is this information that will allow you to get the edge you need in the marketplace. I believe that this is the way traders should look at buying a call, all of the possibilities that could occur prior to expiration and not just whether they will make money or not at expiration, as that can be very deceiving.

Example: Buying a Put to Open

Buying a put to open is the mirror image of buying a call; everything is exactly the same in the put except the reward is limited to the underlying asset going to zero. I will do a simple exercise to make sure that you understand why buying a put is the same as buying a call.

Your technical analysis tells you it is time to get short AAPL and you decide to buy a put. What put do you buy? You have many choices, from those deep in the money to those that are currently teenies; which one is right?

In options, there is no such thing as buying the absolute right option. That depends on your taste. But there is a wrong way to buy, and that is buying "cheap puts" or "cheap calls," those that are far out of the money and have a small delta. Those puts are not cheap. They are either fairly priced or they are expensive in relation to the ATM and ATM +2/−2 puts.

Here is why.

Although the absolute price is small, the chance that it will ever be worth anything is also very diminutive. Nothing is more frustrating as

	CALLS				Strikes: 12 ▼		PUTS				
Position	Last X	Net Chng	Bid X	Ask X	Exp	Strike	Bid X	Ask X	Position	Last X	Net Chng
(2 14 (1) 100 (Weeklys)											16.03%
	12.70 Q	-.05	12.45 X	12.95 X	MAY2 14	580	.13 Q	.14 I		.14 Q	-.44
	9.65 M	-.35	10.05 X	10.45 I	MAY2 14	582.5	.21 N	.22 Q		.19 C	-.86
	8.00 Z	+.30	7.70 X	8.10 I	MAY2 14	585	.40 N	.42 Z		.41 Q	-1.29
	5.75 A	+.40	5.70 A	5.90 N	MAY2 14	587.5	.77 Z	.81 N		.77 N	-2.00
	3.95 A	+.70	3.95 H	4.05 Q	MAY2 14	590	1.44 N	1.50 Q		1.51 A	-2.36
	2.58 C	+.38	2.51 M	2.58 N	MAY2 14	592.5	2.50 Q	2.54 Q		2.50 Q	-2.82
	1.42 N	+.12	1.41 H	1.46 N	MAY2 14	595	3.85 N	3.95 Q		3.95 A	-3.15
	.74 N	-.12	.73 N	.75 Q	MAY2 14	597.5	5.65 N	5.80 Q		5.70 Z	-3.35
	.34 I	-.21	.36 N	.38 N	MAY2 14	600	7.80 Q	8.00 C		7.85 C	-3.19
	.18 Q	-.17	.18 N	.19 I	MAY2 14	602.5	9.90 C	10.35 C		10.01 X	-3.38
	.08 I	-.16	.09 N	.10 Z	MAY2 14	605	12.30 X	12.75 X		13.20 Z	-2.55
	.06 X	-.11	.05 Z	.06 Q	MAY2 14	607.5	14.75 A	15.25 A		14.85 X	-4.65
Y 14 (8) 100											17.67% (±
	14.50 Q	+1.75	14.20 C	14.45 H	MAY 14	580	1.76 N	1.80 Z		1.76 I	-1.26
	12.30 B	N/A	12.30 C	12.50 M	MAY 14	582.5	2.31 N	2.36 Q		2.29 H	N/A
	10.50 Q	+1.49	10.50 A	10.65 A	MAY 14	585	2.99 Z	3.05 Q		2.94 Z	-1.64
	8.95 A	N/A	8.85 A	9.00 Q	MAY 14	587.5	3.80 N	3.90 C		3.90 C	N/A
	7.35 N	+1.15	7.35 A	7.50 N	MAY 14	590	4.80 Q	4.90 N		4.91 I	-2.09
	6.00 C	N/A	6.00 I	6.15 N	MAY 14	592.5	5.95 N	6.10 X		6.00 N	N/A
	4.90 Q	+.55	4.85 C	4.95 N	MAY 14	595	7.25 N	7.40 A		7.38 I	-2.42
	3.95 A	N/A	3.85 Z	3.95 C	MAY 14	597.5	8.75 N	8.90 C		8.75 X	N/A
	3.05 A	+.40	2.98 C	3.05 Q	MAY 14	600	10.35 Q	10.55 Q		10.40 N	-2.85
	2.34 Q	N/A	2.30 N	2.34 Q	MAY 14	602.5	12.20 N	12.45 C		12.60 A	N/A
	1.78 I	+.08	1.75 A	1.80 Q	MAY 14	605	14.10 N	14.35 N		14.85 M	-3.00

FIGURE 9.3   (AAPL) Apple Inc. One- and Eight-Day Option Chain

an option trader than to nail the price direction on the nose and end up losing money! It is the biggest mistake that rookie traders make.

Using Figure 9.3, suppose you want to buy the May2 14 595 put for 3.85. What needs to transpire in order make money at expiration?

The first thing you need to have happen is that the price must go in the direction that you have predicted. You notice I said "predicted," and the reason is that even if you are reacting to technical analysis it is now a predication; if the price doesn't go lower you will have a losing trade.

How far does price have to decline in order to make a profit?

The math is very simple, and you don't need a computer. The underlying strike is the 595 and you paid a debit of 3.85. In order to figure your breakeven price **at expiration, subtract** the debit from the strike and you have the breakeven price.

$595 - 3.85 = 591.15$, so the stock must close below 591.15 to break even.

What is your risk in this trade?

The standard answer is the \$3.95 that you paid for the put, but this answer is not necessarily correct. If AAPL expires at the current price of around 592.65, your risk is only \$1.60, not \$3.95!

You should be able to see now that buying a put is exactly the same as buying a call except that you are **selling** the underlying asset and not buying it so you must **subtract the premium** from the strike price instead of adding to figure your possible profit or loss. All of the expected-value tables are valid for puts or calls, as you should now know because the process of **conversion and reversal** guarantees that the put and call in the same strike in the same serial will have the same amount of air in them.

The Credit Spread

This is a trade that is referred to in the vocabulary as a **vertical spread**. The trade is initiated by selling an option closest to the at-the-money (ATM) strike price and buying one that is further away. *The idea of the spread is to collect a credit, and if we have predicted the price correctly it will expire worthless.* The credit spread is the bread-and-butter trade for many of my students.

Why trade a credit spread instead of a debit spread?

The late great Hall of Fame Alabama football coach Bear Bryant was once asked why he always wanted a great defense and the offense was a second thought. He said it was very simple—if his opponent couldn't score, the worst he could do was to finish 0-0-10. On the other hand, even if he scored 50 points a game, if his opponent could outscore him he could go 0-10-0!

The credit spread is the same as having a great defense; the opponent (the market) must be correct every time to hurt us. We can win three ways: (1) the market goes in the direction we are predicting it will go; (2) the market does nothing; (3) the market goes against us but not enough to overcome our credit. We only lose if the market goes against us by more than our credit.

If we initiate a **debit spread,** we can only win one way; the market must go in the direction that we want it to go, and it must go far enough to be a winner. It is like buying teenies! We lose if it stays here, and we lose if it goes slightly for or against us.

The credit spread has limited reward and limited risk. The reward is limited to the difference between the strikes initiated minus the premium collected.

Didn't Long-Term Capital get blown out selling air?

Yes, it did, but the difference between this trade and what Long-Term Capital did as a naked seller of premium is that we have limited our risk. It is limited to the difference between strikes and the premium we collect. We can't get a reward as large as Long-Term Capital, but we know that no matter what happens in the market, we will not get blown out of the game on one bad trade. Our risk and reward are defined.

The Call Credit Spread (Bear Vertical)

The call credit spread is initiated when we get a sell signal in our technical analysis. If you feel the market is going lower, you want to sell call verticals, not buy put verticals. The put verticals would be a debit spread, and we don't use debit spreads. You can use any two calls that you want to initiate the spread, but the biggest punch will be if you use the ATM or the ATM +1 as the short leg of your spread and another higher strike (further out of the money) as your long leg.

A credit spread's risk is limited to the difference between the strikes when the spread is initiated minus the credit.

Looking once again at the AAPL option chain in Figure 9.3, you can see that we can trade any call spread that we want to, but it is best if we use the one closest to the ATM for our short leg, as it gives us the greatest punch. If we sell the 592.5 call for 2.58 we know that 2.50 of that is premium and only eight cents is intrinsic value.

How do we know how much is intrinsic and what is air?

We use our conversion and reversal formula to calculate the answer. If the 592.5 put is trading at 2.50 and the call is trading at 2.58, what is the underlying asset price? The answer is approximately 592.58.

After a few tries, this calculation should become second nature to you. I don't need to know the underlying price; I can calculate it in a few seconds using the **conversion and reversal formula.**

Suppose I want to sell the 592.5/595 call credit spread. What is my potential profit and what is my maximum risk?

Sell one 592.5 call @ 2.58. Buy one 595 call @ 1.46, a net credit of 1.02. The difference between the strikes is 2.50 ($-592.5 + 595.0 = +2.50$). My maximum reward is 1.02, the credit I received upon the sale of my call spread, and I receive the maximum reward if the underlying AAPL stock closed at 592.50 or less on expiration. I have my maximum loss if the stock closes above 595.00 on expiration. My maximum loss is 1.48 (the difference between the strike prices minus the credit of 1.02.

The formula listed above will be used for all bear credit spreads to figure profit and loss for any trade.

I want to look at one more bear credit spread before we move on. You decide that you don't want to use the ATM; you would rather use options that are further out of the money. What is the possible profit?

Sell one 595 call @ 1.42. Buy one 600 call @ 0.34, a net credit of 0.98. The difference between the strikes is 5.00 ($-595 + 600 = +5.00$). My maximum reward is 0.98, the credit I received upon the sale of my call spread, and I receive the maximum reward if the underlying AAPL stock closed at 595 or less on expiration. I have my maximum loss if the stock closes above 600 on expiration. My maximum loss is 4.02 (the difference between the strike prices minus the credit of 0.98).

A couple of things should be noted about credit spreads as they move away from the ATM. First, the market must go further against me before my spread would become a loser. Second, if I want the same reward, I must assume more risk. The

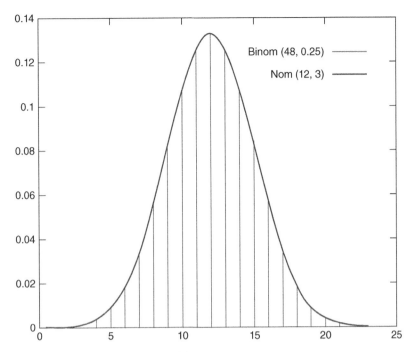

FIGURE 9.4   Binomial Distribution Model

reason is simple: Look at Figure 9.4, which is a binomial distribution model—that is, our friend the distribution curve. As you move further away from uncertainty, the chance that you will be correct is greater, because you have more information. However, that information is not free, it carries more risk for the same reward. If you want to maintain the same risk, you must accept less reward. There is no way possible to change this unless you want to sell naked options, and we have seen the possible negative results. **We don't ever sell naked options!**

How does a credit spread work if we want to do a bull put spread? The answer is exactly the same; it is the opposite trade on the other side of the curve. Here is an example, using the same AAPL option chain.

Looking once again at the AAPL option chain in Figure 9.3 you can see that we can trade any put spread that we want to, but it is best if we use the one closest to the ATM for our short leg, as it gives us the greatest punch. If we sell the 592.5 put for 2.50, we know that 2.50 is all premium.

How do we know it is all air?

We use our conversion and reversal formula to calculate the answer. If the 592.5 call is trading at 2.58 and the put is trading at 2.50 what is the underlying asset price?

The answer is approximately 592.58; the 8c in the call must be intrinsic value; it is the mirror image of selling the bear credit spread.

After a few tries, this calculation should become second nature to you. I don't need to know the underlying price; I can calculate it in a few seconds using the **conversion and reversal formula.**

Suppose I want to sell the 592.5/590 put credit spread: What is my potential profit and what is my maximum risk?

Sell one 592.5 put @ 2.50. Buy one 590 put @ 1.44, a net credit of 1.06. The difference between the strikes is 2.50 (+592.5 − 590 = 2.50). My maximum reward is 1.06, the credit I received upon the sale of my put spread, and I receive the maximum reward if the underlying AAPL stock closed at 592.50 or greater on expiration. I have my maximum loss if the stock closes below 590 on expiration. My maximum loss is 1.44 (the difference between the strike prices minus the credit of 1.06).

The formula listed above will be used for all bull credit spreads to figure profit and loss for any trade.

I want to look at one more bull credit spread before we move on. You decide that you don't want to use the ATM, you would rather use options that are further out of the money. What is the possible profit?

Sell one 590 put @ 1.44. Buy one 585 put @ .40, a net credit of 1.04. The difference between the strikes is 5.00 (−590 + 585 = +5.00). My maximum reward is 1.04, the credit I received upon the sale of my put spread, and I receive the maximum reward if the underlying AAPL stock closed at 590 or greater on expiration. I have my maximum loss if the stock closes above 585 on expiration. My maximum loss is 3.96 (the difference between the strike prices minus the credit of 1.04)

As you can see from Figure 9.4, as predicted, the put spread is the mirror image of the call spread—they are the opposite sides of the bell-shaped curve. These spreads can be used in any market condition. When we marry the option strategy with market conditions later, I will show you how to execute them and manage your risk.

One more credit spread will be discussed, and this spread is more aggressive in nature because it is only used when you want to press your advantage. It is called the 60/40 because the deltas that are used are the 60 delta option and the 40 delta option. Usually, this is going to be the ATM +1/−1 but it could vary slightly. A good rule of thumb is to never use more than the ATM +2/−2, regardless of market conditions.

The Call Credit 60/40 Spread (Bear Vertical)

This spread is initiated by selling the 60 delta call and buying the 40 delta call. It is more aggressive in that you will receive a bigger credit, but if the underlying price stays where the spread is initiated, it will no longer be a winner; it will be a scratch, because we are buying as much premium as we are selling. On the other hand, if you have done a good job in projecting the price action, it is a much bigger winner. This spread can be used in any market condition, and it is one that I prefer.

Employing the option chain in Figure 9.3, you would sell one 590 call @ 3.95 Buy one 595 call @ 1.42, a net credit of 2.53. The difference between the strikes is 5.00 (−590 + 595 = 5.00). My maximum reward is 2.53, the credit I received upon the sale of my call spread. I receive the maximum reward if the underlying AAPL stock closes at 590 or less on expiration. I have my maximum loss if the stock closes above 595 on expiration. My maximum loss is 2.47 (the difference between the strike prices minus the credit of 2.53).

As you can see, we are now selling an option that is in the money so only approximately 1.41 of that is air; the other 2.54 is intrinsic value.

How do we know that?

Using our conversion and reversal formula you should know that the premium (air) at any strike in the same serial is *always equal +/− the bid offer spread*. In this case, the 590 put is trading at 1.44, so the call must have 1.44 of air. We have sold 1.44 of air and we bought 1.41 of premium (air) so, for all practical purposes, we are long as much air as we are short and the net result is that the trade will be a scratch if it is taken off at expiration and the underlying price remains at 592.58 +/− 0.20 cents. I must emphasize that these are all approximate values; the bid–offer spread and any insignificant price change will give you these results. In the real world, you could make a little money on this trade if it closes around 592.28 or you could lose a little, depending on how you take the spread off.

The Put Credit 60/40 Spread (Bull Vertical)

The put spread (bull spread) that can be traded for Figure 9.3 is calculated exactly the same and should be the mirror image of the call spread (bear spread).

Sell one 595 put @ 3.95. Buy one 590 put @ 1.44, a net credit of 2.51. The difference between the strikes is 5.00 (−595 + 590 = 5.00). My maximum reward is 2.51, the credit I received upon the sale of my put spread, and I receive the maximum reward if the underlying AAPL stock closes at 595 or greater at expiration. I have my maximum loss if the stock closes below 590 on expiration. My maximum loss is 2.49 (the difference between the strike prices minus the credit of 2.41).

As you can see, we are now selling an option that is in the money, so only approximately 1.44 of that is air and the other 2.51 is intrinsic value.

How do we know that?

Using our conversion and reversal formula, you should know that the premium (air) at any strike in the same serial *is always equal*. In this case, the 590 put is trading at 1.44, so the call must have 1.44 of air. We have sold 1.44 of air and we bought 1.41 of premium (air), so, for all practical purposes, we are long as much air as we are short and the net result is that the trade will be a scratch if it is taken off at expiration and the underlying price remains at 592.58 $+/- 0.20$ cents. I must emphasize that these are all approximate values; the bid–offer spread and any insignificant price change will give you these results. In the real world, you could make a little money on this trade if it closes around 592.28 or you could lose a little, depending on how you take the spread off.

Since the value of the premium using Figure 9.3 in any strike for the put and call is equal minus the bid–offer spread, you could become even more aggressive and sell a 70/30 or 80/20. I don't use these for my own trading, but I do have students who are very aggressive and use these spreads. They are for large credits, and the trader must assume more risk for this type of trade. I prefer one of the next two types of trades: the **risk reversal** or **backspread.**

The Risk Reversal (Synthetic Long Stock)

Earlier I said that the simplest trade was to buy a call or put outright. The problem with that trade is that you must overcome the air that you have purchased before it can become a winner, and that is why I don't like to use it for my own personal trading. I prefer a synthetic trade known as a risk reversal.

The trade is executed by purchasing a call and selling a put simultaneously at the same strike. This creates a synthetic underlining purchase of 100 shares of stock, or if you are trading contracts (futures or indexes), one contract of the underlying asset. At this point in time, the trade has unlimited reward to the upside and unlimited risk of the underlying asset going to zero. This is the type of trade that we don't make, so is there a way to limit our risk to the downside? Yes, we can buy an out-of-the-money put and then we accomplish our goal. In this case, we have defined our risk to the downside and have given us unlimited upside. In this trade, I want to buy more intrinsic value so that I am not financing a great amount of premium. I will buy the ATM -4 call and sell the ATM -4 put. I will then buy the ATM -5 put for protection.

With Figure 9.3, if you buy the AAPL 585 call @ 8.00, sell the 585 put for .40. When the first step is completed, it will make you long from 592.60.

How do we know that?

Using our conversion and reversal formula, if you pay 8.00 for the 585 call, you know that in order to break even at expiration, the price must be at least 593; however, since we got a 0.40 credit on the put, we subtract that from the breakeven price and we are long from 592.60.

What is our risk/reward at this point?

Our reward is unlimited above 592.60; our risk is also unlimited to a price of zero in the stock. We don't do this type of trade, so we must offset that downside risk. We buy the ATM-5 put, which in this case is the 582.5 strike @ 0.21. The 0.21 is a debit, so it must be added to our synthetic long @ 592.60 and we are long from 592.81.

What is our risk/reward at this point?

Our reward is unlimited above 592.81; our risk has now changed. We have downside of 8.00 in the call plus 2.31 in the short put spread (0.40 − 0.21 = 0.19 − 2.50 = 2.31), for a total of 10.31 in the trade. This is a much larger trade than the credit spreads, and is slightly larger than buying the call outright, but the fact that you must overcome very little premium risk and with a margin of slightly over $1,000 to control over $59,000 of AAPL stock gives you the leverage of over 50 to 1 and places you on even footing with the largest traders in the world!

The mirror image of the risk reversal trade is the put risk reversal, known as a **conversion**. It is called a **conversion** because we are taking the options and "converting the stock to a short position."

The Risk Conversion (Synthetic Short Stock)

The trade illustrated using Figure 9.3 is executed by purchasing a put and selling a call simultaneously at the same strike. This creates a synthetic underlining sale of 100 shares of stock or, if you are trading contracts (futures or indexes), one contract of the underlying asset. At this point in time, the trade has unlimited reward to the asset going to zero and unlimited risk to the upside. This is the type of trade that we don't make, so is there a way to limit our risk to the downside? Yes, we can buy an out-of-the-money call, and then we accomplish our goal. In this case, we have defined our risk to the upside and the trade has given us unlimited reward if the asset goes to zero. I want to buy more intrinsic value so that I am not financing a great amount of premium. I will buy the ATM +4 put and sell the ATM +4 call. I will then buy the ATM +5 call for protection.

Buy the AAPL 600 put @ 7.80 and sell the 600 call for .36. When the first step is completed, it will make you short from 592.56.

How do we know that?

Using our conversion and reversal formula, if you pay 7.80 for the 600 put, you know that in order to break even at expiration, the price must be at least 592.20 (600 − 7.80 = 592.20); however, since we got a 0.36 credit on the call, we **add** that to the breakeven price and we are short from 592.56.

What is our risk/reward at this point?

Our reward is unlimited below 592.56 to a price of zero; our risk is also unlimited to the upside. We don't make this type of trade, so we must offset that upside risk. We do this by **buying** the ATM +5 call, which in this case it is the 582.5 strike @ 0.21. The 0.21 is a debit, so it must be **subtracted** from our synthetic short @ 592.56, and we are short from 592.35.

What is our risk/reward at this point?

Our reward is unlimited to zero below 592.35; our risk has now changed. We have downside of 7.80 in the 600 put plus 2.31 in the short put spread (0.36 − 0.21

= 0.15 − 2.50 = 2.35, for a total of 10.15 in the trade. This is a much larger trade than the credit spreads, and is slightly larger than buying the put outright, but the fact that you must overcome very little premium risk and with a margin of slightly over $1,000 to **short** over $59,000 of AAPL stock gives you leverage of over 50 to 1. **This is how the big traders get around the SEC/FINRA shorting regulations; they use options to create synthetic short stock positions.**

When you read in the *Wall Street Journal* and wonder how the hedge funds and corporate *stockholder advocates* (I love that term) can get in the market without alerting all the market participants, this is how they do it. They stealthily use the options to leverage themselves up. Carl Icahn cut his teeth in the investment arena by trading options, and you can be sure that he is using these strategies now when he is taking large positions in a company. I am not assuming that small investors can take over a company, but I am showing you how professionals look at the market, and it is very different than the average investor. That may be why they are billionaires!

The last straight serial trade I make is aggressive. It is a **backspread,** and I call it the **1 by 2 for even.** It is a powerful way to trade and, as always, offers unlimited reward and limited risk.

The Call Backspread (1 by 2 for Even)

The backspread initiated using Figure 9.3 uses all of the power of the risk reversal/conversion but leverages up the options to do the trade. It has unlimited reward and limited risk, but has many of the benefits of the 60/40 credit spread in that the risk is limited to strike prices. The major difference between the two trades is that it has unlimited reward. Although I call it a 1 by 2 for even (meaning you sell as much premium as you buy), any number of options can be used to leverage it up. The only difference is the risk/reward between the strikes.

Buy two AAPL 600 calls @ 0.36. Sell one 597.5 call for 0.74. The risk/reward on this trade is calculated differently because it is a **ratio spread.** The biggest risk to this trade comes if it expires at exactly at 600. We lose 2 times 0.36 and 1.76 on the 597.5 call (2.50 − 0.74 = 1.76). The total risk on this trade is ((−0.36 × 2 = .72) + (2.50 − 0.74 = −1.76 = 2.48)). We are long from 602.48; the reward is unlimited.

Many novice traders shy away from this type of trade because they fear the risk of getting **pinned** at the 600 strike on expiration. This is a valid concern; however, earlier in the chapter I talked about estimating the premium in the model at any point in time prior to expiration. **Table "Days until Expiration"** shows that the AAPL ATM straddle on the morning of the Friday expiration should be trading at approximately 3.80, and that means if we are trading at the 600 strike that morning, the call should be trading around 1.90. Since we are long two calls, they should have a total value of 3.80. We know our short 597.50 call must have a value of at least 2.50, and it will probably have premium of around 1.20, so it will be trading around 3.80. The fear of doing this trade because of a pin risk is greatly exaggerated; the real risk is the way it is managed on expiration Friday if we are close to either strike. The management of this trade will be dealt with later in the book when we marry the phases of the market to the type of trades that are most suitable for that phase. The put 1 × 2 backspread will be the mirror image of this trade to the downside.

The Put Backspread (1 × 2 for Even)

Buy two AAPL 587.5 puts @ 0.77. Sell one 590 put for 1.44. The risk/reward on this trade is calculated differently because it is a **ratio spread.** The biggest risk to the trade illustrated using Figure 9.3 comes if it expires at exactly at 587.5. We lose 2×0.77 and .106 on the 590 put $(2.50 - 1.44 = 1.06)$. The total risk on this trade is $((-0.77 \times 2 = 1.44) + (2.50 - 144. = -1.06 = 2.50))$, we are short from 585; the reward is unlimited. You will notice that although we used different delta strikes for this trade, the risk is very similar. In most cases, no matter what strikes you use, the risk will be close to the value of the strike spread.

Days until expiration show that the AAPL ATM straddle on the morning of the Friday expiration should be trading at approximately 5.80, and that means if we are trading at the 587.5 strike that morning, the put should be trading around 2.90. Since we are long two puts, they should have a total value of 5.80. We know we are short the 590 put and it has intrinsic value of at least 2.50 and will probably have premium of around 1.20, so it will be trading around 3.80. You should have noticed by now that no matter what strikes we use to do the 1 × 2, as long as they are touching, such as ATM −1−2 or ATM +3 +4, if our short strike is at the money, we should still be at or near a breakeven position on expiration Friday. The key to this trade is managing the risk on Friday. Of course, if it is a big winner; all that is necessary is to take off the spread and sell the ITM money before the close.

▪ Summary

I have now introduced all of the trades that I make using the expiring weekly option serial. They are simple but very effective. It is vital that you can put the option model together with the underlying trades. They are twins, and in order to make consistent profits, you must be able to keep them together.

A tremendous amount of information has been introduced in this chapter. The quiz that follows is 25 questions long with 75 possible points. If you don't get a score of 63, you must reread the material. The market takes no prisoners, and if you are not prepared to fight for every trade, you are not going to succeed.

■ Chapter 9 Quiz

1) The most important psychological aspect of trading is your ability to:
   a) visualize the potential profit in a trade
   b) know where to take profit on a winning trade
   c) know your ability to handle risk
   d) only a and c

2) Selling naked options:
   a) gives the seller obligations but no rights
   b) has unlimited risk and limited reward
   c) has led to the demise of many traders
   d) all of the above

3) Selling naked options:
   a) gives the seller a credit
   b) limits reward but not risk
   c) has limited risk for experienced traders
   d) a and b only

4) Why did Long-Term Capital collapse?
   a) It sold air.
   b) The option model it used was outdated.
   c) The collapse of the Russian currency could not be factored in.
   d) It did not collapse; it was too big to fail.

5) Buying a call to open:
   a) has premium risk in addition to market risk
   b) is a poor trading strategy
   c) has defined risk and reward
   d) both a and c

6) Call buyers have:
   a) assignment risk
   b) exercise rights
   c) rights but no obligations
   d) both b and c

7) A credit spread:
   a) sells air and therefore has unlimited risk
   b) has little upside in relation to its risk
   c) is selling one option and buying another
   d) both a and b

8) A call credit spread is initiated by:
   a) selling a call nearer to the ATM and buying an in-the-money call
   b) buying a call that is out of the money and selling a call in the money
   c) selling any call and buying a call at another strike
   d) selling the ATM call and buying any other call

9) What is true about a put credit spread?
   a) It has different rewards than a call credit spread.
   b) It is the mirror image of a call credit spread.
   c) It is initiated by buying one option and selling another.
   d) Both b and c are true.

10) Calculating the potential profit in a credit spread:
   a) can be done through the formula for conversions and reversals
   b) is the difference between the credit and the strikes involved
   c) is limited to the credit after the trade is completed
   d) all of the above

11) The conversion and reversal formula allows a trader to do what?
   a) tell how much of an ITM put is intrinsic
   b) tell how much of an ITM call is air
   c) compute where the underlying price should be
   d) all of the above

12) The amount of premium in any strike in the same serial:
   a) is constant and will be the same in a put as well as a call
   b) can vary, depending on what option model is being traded
   c) can't be calculated until expiration
   d) both a and c

13) Which of the following is true about conversions and reversals?
   a) Trades that market makers use to take advantage of temporary price dislocation.
   b) They are riskless when executed correctly.
   c) They should not be attempted by retail traders.
   d) All of the above are true.

14) On expiration Friday, the ATM call:
   a) will have the same air as the ATM put
   b) may have no premium at all since the risk is now known
   c) should not be traded because of uncertainty
   d) will have no value after expiration

15) Why is it generally good to buy teenies to initiate a position?
    a) They are worth a cheap shot and pay big dividends when they hit.
    b) They offer a trade with very little time decay.
    c) They will hold their value until the final day of trading.
    d) None of the above; buying teenies to open is a losing trade on average.

16) Buying deep ITM puts:
    a) will initially mimic the underlying stock
    b) will limit the amount of exposure to time decay
    c) will eventually turn into a short stock position
    d) only a and b

17) Debit spreads can:
    a) have a reward greater than any credit spread
    b) be cashed if there is no price movement
    c) have unlimited reward once the debit is paid for by price movement
    d) none of the above

18) When can a bear vertical ATM spread be cashed?
    a) if price goes lower
    b) if price goes higher
    c) if price remains the same
    d) all of the above

19) A 60/40 credit spread has:
    a) theta risk if the price remains constant to expiration
    b) more potential profit than an ATM bear credit spread
    c) more potential loss than an ATM bull credit spread
    d) only b and c

20) What limits the credit spread risk?
    a) It has no limit, as you are selling air.
    b) It is limited to the difference between the strikes used in the spread.
    c) It has no limit on reward.
    d) It is limited to the difference between the strikes used minus the credit.

21) Which of the following is true about pure risk reversal?
    a) It is buying or selling the underlying asset synthetically.
    b) There is both unlimited risk and unlimited reward.
    c) It has no theta risk.
    d) All of the above are true.

22) An ITM risk reversal needs to
    a) buy an additional OTM option to limit the risk
    b) have a small theta risk

c) have unlimited reward
d) all of the above

23) A put and call risk reversal share which of these traits?
   a) Nothing; one is a synthetic put and one is a synthetic call.
   b) They are mirror images.
   c) They have unlimited reward to the short side of the trade.
   d) They have no price risk.

24) A backspread shares which of these traits with a risk reversal?
   a) It has an extra-long option for protection.
   b) It has unlimited reward.
   c) It has limited risk.
   d) All of the above are shared traits.

25) What is true about a 1 × 2 backspread?
   a) It has little theta risk.
   b) It is subject to expiration risk.
   c) It has unlimited reward.
   d) All of the above are true.

Why Trade Weekly Options?

Weekly options will be the subject of this chapter, and you will see the reasons why they are becoming so popular and why I believe they represent absolutely the best possible retail trading opportunity in today's financial universe.

Weekly options have only been in existence since 2011, but in many stocks the front week accounts for more than 30 percent of the total option volume. The growth is still exponential, and with that has come liquidity and great opportunity. I have been an option trader for over 30 years, and during that time more than 95 percent of my income has come as a direct result of trading stock options and futures options. In those 30 years, I have never seen a product with the potential to give the average investor a chance to compete on fairly equal footing with the professional traders. Let's take a look at why I see such an advantage.

In college, my basic statistics course taught me about the challenges of a zero-sum game. Trading options, stock, and futures are all zero-sum games. Simply stated, when I buy or sell something in an auction market, I must find a buyer or seller who is willing to do the opposite side of the trade. In the end, one of us will win what the other loses. If I make this trade to infinity, both of us will have the same P & L, minus commissions. Since our capital is not infinite and commissions are, both of us will eventually end up broke.

That is a very somber note when you are considering making trading your career!

Let's go back to a game of chance again—poker. You enter a game with nine other players. Each of you must invest $100 and you must play the game to the end of each hand. The house "rakes" (commission) $1 per hand. How long does the game last? In this scenario, the game would last approximately 1,000 hands. At that point, the house would have taken all the players' money in the form of commission. This is a zero-sum game plus commissions, very much the same as trading options.

We now play a new poker game with the same 10 players and the same $100 stake to start. It is zero-sum game again; however, this time, the house takes in less, only 10 cents per hand, and the players are free to use any strategy that they want. What has changed? It is still a zero-sum game plus commission, but now it will take 10,000 hands to remove all of the players' money in the form of commission. This time, though, you will see a much different result. At least one of the players will be a winner, and most likely three or four will also win. The rest will bust out, as their lack of skill will show in the long run.

Even though technically it is still a zero-sum game, your superior knowledge will give you the edge and you will have a positive expected value (EV)!

Fortunately, weekly options fall into the second game of poker.

Skill has changed everything around. Instead of following a rote strategy that will guarantee your demise, you are allowed to fold when you are an underdog and continue to play when you are a favorite. In the long run, if the commissions are small enough in relation to the reward, you can overcome them.

Let's get back to trading weekly options and see if we can get a favorable game.

Earlier, I discussed what makes an asset tradable. The first thing that I demand is that it is liquid. I define liquidity as the ability to enter and exit an asset seamlessly in relation to the possible gain. If our possible gain, on average, is $100, but the bid–offer spread is $10, that asset is not liquid. It will cost us $10 to enter and $10 to exit, and if our commission is $10, we are giving up a 30 percent edge in relation to our possible gain. On any individual trade, you may make money, but in the long run, no matter how good you are, you will lose. On the other hand, if our bid–offer spread is only $1 and our commission is $1.00, is it possible to overcome the edge and turn a profit over time?

When you look at Figure 10.1, you will notice that the spreads in AAPL are generally 5 to 6 cents wide. That means that if you were to pay the offer or sell the bid, you would have to give up $5 to $6 to trade an outright option that has the potential to control more than $59,000 of equity. That is liquidity at its finest!

Now look at Figure 10.2; it is an option chain for Bank of America. The spreads are much tighter for most options (one or two pennies), but this market is not liquid—do you know why? There is not enough air in the balloon, and no matter how tight the options are, you are only controlling $1,500 worth of equity, commissions will not be discounted, and you once again have a zero-sum game plus commissions. No amount of skill can overcome the commissions and lack of price movement in this stock.

I have now established what it takes to overcome the zero-sum option market. You need to have a combination of tight bid–offer spreads, low commission, and more skill than your opponent. This is the exact same thing that was described earlier

CALLS						Strikes: 12		PUTS			
Position	Last X	Net Chng	Bid X	Ask X	Exp	Strike	Bid X	Ask X	Position	Last X	Net Chng
2 14 (1) 100 (Weeklys)											16.03%
	12.70 Q	-.05	12.45 X	12.95 X	MAY2 14	580	.13 Q	.14 I		.14 Q	-.44
	9.65 M	-.35	10.05 X	10.45 I	MAY2 14	582.5	.21 N	.22 Q		.19 C	-.86
	8.00 Z	+.30	7.70 X	8.10 I	MAY2 14	585	.40 N	.42 Z		.41 Q	-1.29
	5.75 A	+.40	5.70 A	5.90 N	MAY2 14	587.5	.77 Z	.81 N		.77 N	-2.00
	3.95 A	+.70	3.95 H	4.05 Q	MAY2 14	590	1.44 N	1.50 Q		1.51 A	-2.36
	2.58 C	+.38	2.51 M	2.58 N	MAY2 14	592.5	2.50 Q	2.54 Q		2.50 Q	-2.82
	1.42 N	+.12	1.41 H	1.46 N	MAY2 14	595	3.85 N	3.95 Q		3.95 A	-3.15
	.74 N	-.12	.73 N	.75 Q	MAY2 14	597.5	5.65 N	5.80 Q		5.70 Z	-3.35
	.34 I	-.21	.36 N	.38 N	MAY2 14	600	7.80 Q	8.00 C		7.95 C	-3.19
	.18 Q	-.17	.16 N	.19 I	MAY2 14	602.5	9.90 C	10.35 C		10.01 X	-3.36
	.08 I	-.16	.09 N	.10 Z	MAY2 14	605	12.30 X	12.75 X		13.20 Z	-2.55
	.06 X	-.11	.05 Z	.06 Q	MAY2 14	607.5	14.75 A	15.25 A		14.85 X	-4.65
Y 14 (8) 100											17.57% (+)
	14.50 Q	+1.75	14.20 C	14.45 H	MAY 14	580	1.76 N	1.80 Z		1.76 I	-1.26
	12.30 B	N/A	12.30 C	12.50 M	MAY 14	582.5	2.31 N	2.36 Q		2.29 H	N/A
	10.60 Q	+1.49	10.50 A	10.65 A	MAY 14	585	2.99 Z	3.05 Q		2.94 Z	-1.64
	8.95 A	N/A	8.85 A	9.00 Q	MAY 14	587.5	3.80 N	3.90 C		3.90 C	N/A
	7.35 N	+1.15	7.35 A	7.60 N	MAY 14	590	4.80 Q	4.90 N		4.91 I	-2.09
	6.00 C	N/A	6.00 I	6.15 N	MAY 14	592.5	5.95 N	6.10 X		6.00 N	N/A
	4.90 Q	+.55	4.85 C	4.95 N	MAY 14	595	7.25 N	7.40 A		7.38 I	-2.42
	3.95 A	N/A	3.85 Z	3.95 C	MAY 14	597.5	8.75 N	8.90 C		8.75 X	N/A
	3.05 A	+.40	2.98 C	3.05 Q	MAY 14	600	10.35 Q	10.55 Q		10.40 N	-2.85
	2.34 Q	N/A	2.30 N	2.34 Q	MAY 14	602.5	12.20 N	12.45 C		12.60 A	N/A
	1.78 I	+.08	1.75 A	1.80 Q	MAY 14	605	14.10 N	14.35 N		14.85 M	-3.00

FIGURE 10.1   (AAPL) Apple, Inc. (AAPL) One- and Eight-Day Option Chain

UNDERLYING

Last X	Net Chng	Bid X	Ask X	Size	Volume	Open	High	Lo
15.24 N	+.29	15.20 K	15.21 Q	159 x 15	155,338,090	15.04	15.30	14.9

TRADE GRID

OPTION CHAIN   Spread: Single   Layout: Volume, Open Interest   Exchange: Composite

CALLS					Strikes: 14	PUTS			
Volume	Open Int	Bid X	Ask X	Exp	Strike	Bid X	Ask X	Volume	Open Int
MAY1 14 (3) 100 (Weeklys)									29.50% (+0.5)
5	5	3.15 C	3.25 Q	MAY1 14	12	0 B	.01 H	0	0
0	8	2.66 I	2.76 I	MAY1 14	12.5	0 T	.01 N	0	0
0	0	2.18 I	2.25 I	MAY1 14	13	0 B	.01 M	10	477
0	104	1.67 X	1.74 Q	MAY1 14	13.5	0 B	.01 X	0	5
268	346	1.23 Q	1.24 Q	MAY1 14	14	0 B	.01 M	93	2,542
2,891	4,104	.74 Q	.76 Q	MAY1 14	14.5	.01 Q	.02 M	5,620	6,315
10,708	17,346	.30 H	.31 Q	MAY1 14	15	.07 I	.08 C	9,590	14,633
19,555	15,249	.04 X	.05 Q	MAY1 14	15.5	.31 Q	.32 Q	5,115	6,585
771	12,984	0 B	.01 M	MAY1 14	16	.76 I	.77 Q	2,953	10,651
1,065	18,607	0 B	.01 X	MAY1 14	16.5	1.25 M	1.31 X	632	2,556
41	11,189	0 X	.01 X	MAY1 14	17	1.75 I	1.81 X	143	622
52	5,880	0 Z	.01 M	MAY1 14	17.5	2.25 I	2.31 I	24	282
10	8,683	0 Z	.01 M	MAY1 14	18	2.76 I	2.80 I	0	219
230	2,139	0 M	.01 M	MAY1 14	18.5	3.25 Q	3.35 Q	0	4

FIGURE 10.2   (BAC) Bank of America (BAC) Three-Day Option Chain

on liquidity, but now we have added the variable of skill. You can only beat the market if you have a better strategy than your opponent.

Are weekly options different than longer-term serials?

Weekly options are a miniature version of the longer-term serials, but that is where the similarity ends. Look at Figure 10.3. It is our old friend, Priceline. You should know immediately that the at-the-money call and put both have a .50 delta, which means that they are at the top of the parabolic curve and have the most uncertainty. Now, it is time to look at the ATM put or call credit spread. This type of spread will be one of your bread-and-butter trades. The 1230 strike is the ATM,

UNDERLYING								
Last X	Net Chng	Bid X	Ask X	Size	Volume	Open	High	Low
1230.00 D	+8.96	1229.50 P	1231.50 P	2 x 1	669,764	1222.01	1237.15	1220.15

TRADE GRID

OPTION CHAIN — Spread: Single — Layout: Last X, Net Change — Exchange: Composite

CALLS				Exp	Strike	PUTS			
Last X	Net Chng	Bid X	Ask X			Bid X	Ask X	Last X	Net Chng
APR4 14 (3) 100 (Weekly)								25.17% (±24.635)	
22.00 Q	+5.00	20.40 X	21.70 X	APR4 14	1215	5.60 X	6.40 W	6.10 Z	-6.10
20.00 C	+4.30	18.70 W	20.40 X	APR4 14	1217.5	6.30 X	7.20 X	6.61 C	-9.29
17.01 I	+2.91	17.10 W	18.30 X	APR4 14	1220	7.10 X	8.10 X	8.10 Z	-6.30
15.50 C	+3.15	15.60 I	16.80 X	APR4 14	1222.5	8.10 X	9.20 X	8.39 W	-9.81
15.00 Z	+3.70	14.10 X	15.00 I	APR4 14	1225	9.20 H	10.10 X	9.80 Z	-8.00
13.00 C	+2.80	12.80 X	13.80 X	APR4 14	1227.5	10.30 X	11.10 H	10.61 W	-8.79
12.00 Z	+2.70	11.50 X	12.50 W	APR4 14	1230	11.40 X	12.30 X	12.00 A	-10.20
11.00 X	+3.19	10.40 W	11.30 X	APR4 14	1232.5	12.80 X	13.60 X	13.40 A	-10.17
9.30 X	+1.50	9.30 W	10.10 X	APR4 14	1235	14.10 X	15.00 X	14.80 N	-7.80
8.50 Q	+1.75	8.30 X	9.10 X	APR4 14	1237.5	15.60 X	16.40 X	16.30 X	-13.90
7.30 Q	+1.30	7.30 X	8.00 Z	APR4 14	1240	17.10 X	18.00 X	17.70 N	-12.40
8.52 C	+3.52	6.50 X	7.20 X	APR4 14	1242.5	18.80 X	19.60 X	20.50 N	-10.60
6.20 Q	+1.10	5.70 X	6.20 Q	APR4 14	1245	20.50 X	21.30 X	21.50 Z	-16.30

FIGURE 10.3 PCLN Three-Day Option Chain

so if we want to do a credit spread, the first choice would be to use this strike as our short, and the ATM +1, +2/−1, −2 as our long strike. If we use the ATM −2, it would be the 1225 strike and we can sell the bull put spread for approximately $2.20. As per our formula, for the risk/reward in a credit spread, this trade would risk $2.80 to make $2.20; it has better than a **2/3 risk/reward ratio** and will be a key number to initiate trades.

Figure 10.4 is another PCLN option chain, but this one is for 178 days, or approximately six months, instead of Figure 10.3, a serial that will expire in three days. If we want to sell the ATM −1 spread here, it would be the 1230/1225 bull put spread and we could do it for a slightly better price of $2.60. This is logical, as there is more time to expiration and therefore more uncertainty; thus, we should get a bigger reward.

UNDERLYING								
Last X	Net Chng	Bid X	Ask X	Size	Volume	Open	High	
1230.00 D	+8.96	1229.50 P	1231.50 P	2 x 1	669,764	1222.01	1237.15	122

OPTION CHAIN — Spread: Single — Layout: Last X, Net Change — Exchange: Composite

CALLS				Exp	Strike	PUTS			
Last X	Net Chng	Bid X	Ask X			Bid X	Ask X	Last X	Net Chng
126.00 Q	+8.78	119.50 C	123.40 X	OCT 14	1200	88.50 X	91.40 X	96.40 Z	0
114.30 X	0	116.90 C	120.80 X	OCT 14	1205	90.60 C	93.60 X	132.80 C	0
120.50 Q	+20.00	114.30 T	118.10 C	OCT 14	1210	93.20 I	96.00 X	101.40 Q	0
120.83 C	0	111.60 T	115.60 X	OCT 14	1215	95.40 X	98.40 X	99.30 Z	-11.10
108.70 Q	+4.00	109.30 C	113.00 X	OCT 14	1220	97.80 X	101.00 X	125.64 C	0
121.48 C	0	106.80 C	110.60 X	OCT 14	1225	100.40 X	103.40 X	159.20 C	0
89.50 N	0	104.20 T	108.00 X	OCT 14	1230	103.00 X	106.00 X	148.50 C	0
106.00 Q	0	102.50 C	105.70 X	OCT 14	1235	105.30 X	108.60 X	138.20 M	0
114.00 Q	0	99.80 C	103.10 X	OCT 14	1240	108.10 C	111.00 C	121.00 C	0
103.00 Q	0	97.40 C	100.70 X	OCT 14	1245	110.70 C	113.80 C	159.30 C	0
99.60 N	+4.20	95.20 C	98.40 X	OCT 14	1250	113.50 C	116.50 X	151.30 C	0
90.75 C	0	92.90 C	96.20 X	OCT 14	1255	116.20 C	119.20 C	165.75 C	0
91.00 Q	+1.00	90.70 C	93.90 X	OCT 14	1260	119.00 X	122.00 X	166.70 T	0
N/A	N/A	88.50 C	91.70 X	OCT 14	1265	121.80 X	124.80 X	167.20 X	0

FIGURE 10.4   (PCLN) PCLN 178-Day Option Chain

Let's compare the merits of these two trades.

Trade one sells the 1230/1225 bull put spread for three days for a credit of approximately $2.20. We risk $2.80 to make 2.20 for a period of three days.

Trade two sells the 1230/1225 bull put spread of 178 days for a credit of approximately $2.60. We risk 2.40 to make 2.60 for a period of 178 days.

The advantage of trading weekly option credit spreads should now be apparent!

Why would you make a trade for 178 days that could only make 40 cents more than a trade that will mature in 3 days? You wouldn't, if you know anything about trading options. You could sell the weekly three-day serial credit spread 25 times for a total credit of $55.00 in the same time that would make 40 cents in the 178-day serial!

If the credit spread strategy has such an advantage over longer dated serials, will this hold when I go to my more aggressive trades?

I will now examine if we can get the edge using the more aggressive strategies that I suggested earlier in the book. I want to go from a large dollar stock to one that is smaller but still very liquid. In this example, I will use Facebook (FB). Facebook was not a pubic company until 2013, so you can see how quickly a stock can go from an IPO to one of the most actively traded stocks in the world.

Figure 10.5 is a combination of two serials in FB. One is expiring in 2 days; the other in 212 days.

	CALLS				Strikes: 12		PUTS				
Position	Last X	Net Chng	Bid X	Ask X	Exp	Strike	Bid X	Ask X	Position	Last X	Net Chng
MAY4 14 @ 100 (Weeklys)											36.57% (E
	2.76 Q	+.47	2.70 I	2.73 Q	MAY4 14	56.5	.07 A	.08 Z		.09 C	-.11
	2.32 N	+.47	2.25 H	2.28 N	MAY4 14	57	.11 A	.12 Q		.13 C	-.17
	1.88 Z	+.40	1.82 H	1.85 N	MAY4 14	57.5	.19 Z	.20 A		.18 C	-.23
	1.43 X	+.30	1.43 H	1.45 N	MAY4 14	58	.29 N	.30 Z		.29 Z	-.27
	1.11 C	+.26	1.08 N	1.10 N	MAY4 14	58.5	.44 N	.45 N		.44 M	-.34
	.81 Z	+.20	.78 N	.80 Z	MAY4 14	59	.64 A	.66 N		.64 C	-.42
	.56 Z	+.15	.54 I	.56 N	MAY4 14	59.5	.90 N	.92 N		.91 N	-.48
	.37 C	+.08	.36 I	.38 A	MAY4 14	60	1.22 Q	1.24 N		1.20 Q	-.54
	.23 M	+.05	.23 A	.24 Z	MAY4 14	60.5	1.59 N	1.61 H		1.54 N	-.57
	.15 C	+.03	.15 H	.16 Z	MAY4 14	61	2.00 H	2.02 Z		2.00 H	-.59
	.11 Q	+.03	.10 Z	.11 A	MAY4 14	61.5	2.45 Q	2.47 N		2.40 H	-.80
	.08 X	+.01	.07 Z	.08 A	MAY4 14	62	2.91 N	2.94 Z		2.89 H	-.66

Position	Last X	Net Chng	Bid X	Ask X	Exp	Strike	Bid X	Ask X	Position	Last X	Net Chng
	20.16 C	-.81	20.10 X	20.50 X	DEC 14	40	1.01 A	1.06 I		1.02 Q	-.03
	16.50 M	+.10	16.00 X	16.40 X	DEC 14	45	1.89 A	1.98 A		1.91 M	-.18
	12.81 C	+.81	12.45 X	12.65 C	DEC 14	50	3.25 C	3.40 C		3.29 I	-.26
	10.40 Q	0	10.85 X	11.05 C	DEC 14	52.5	4.15 C	4.30 C		4.14 I	-.26
	9.60 M	-.05	9.40 X	9.60 C	DEC 14	55	5.20 C	5.35 C		5.65 I	0
	8.12 A	0	8.10 C	8.25 C	DEC 14	57.5	6.35 A	6.55 C		6.50 M	-.25
	7.22 C	+.42	6.90 C	7.10 C	DEC 14	60	7.70 C	7.85 A		7.65 Q	-.35
	6.00 A	-.21	5.90 C	6.05 C	DEC 14	62.5	9.15 C	9.30 A		9.25 N	0
	5.00 N	+.15	5.00 A	5.10 M	DEC 14	65	10.75 A	10.90 C		10.80 M	-.50
	4.30 N	-.15	4.20 C	4.35 C	DEC 14	67.5	12.45 A	12.60 A		12.25 Q	0
	3.60 M	+.20	3.50 C	3.65 A	DEC 14	70	14.25 A	14.40 X		14.15 C	0
	2.40 Q	+.01	2.45 A	2.56 C	DEC 14	75	16.15 C	18.30 A		17.45 Q	0

FIGURE 10.5 (FB) Facebook 2- and 212-Day Option Chain

■ Buying a Call or a Put Outright

Earlier I said that buying a call or put outright was the basic trade and that we should generally use the ATM −1/−2 to buy calls and the ATM +1/+2 to buy puts. Let's make a comparison of using the expiring weekly option versus the 212 day. Because strikes are different as you go out in time, I will use the approximate −1/−2 strike in the December serial.

Buy one MAY4 58 call for 1.45. Using our conversation and reversal formula, we know that we have purchased approximately 29 cents of air and that in order for this trade to break even the price must advance to 59.74 before the serial expires in two days. The expected value in two days is +/−1.50, so there is a good chance that we will get there if the market is rallying.

Buy one DEC14 55 call for 9.60. Using our conversation and reversal formula, we know that we have purchased approximately 5.50 of air and that the trade must advance to 64.60 by December in order to break even. The expected value is +/−15.9. Personally, I would never make this trade in December. I would much rather use the weekly option and roll back; if I still have a buy signal, I could roll back more than 17 times and not have the huge premium risk.

The Risk Reversal (Synthetic Long or Short Stock)

In order to overcome the problems of premium without giving up a big edge by buying parity options, the synthetic long or short gives us the same opportunity for profit as an outright call or put, but limits our risk for premium loss. I will use the −4 call and −4 put to initiate a long position. I will then buy a −5 put to remove the unlimited risk to the downside. I will initiate a short position, and I will use the +4 put and the +4 call, and buy a +5 call to eliminate the risk to the upside.

Buy one MAY4 14 57.5 call @ 1.85. Sell one MAY4 57.5 put @ .20. Buy one MAY 57 put @ .11.

As you compress time and price, the absolute premium that you pay to buy an option will decrease tremendously. The premium risk will be in the same ratio as the higher-priced stock, but the absolute risk will be greatly reduced.

As an example, trading Facebook using the ATM −4 strike, you only have $11 of premium risk in the expiring option. However, if you are trading Priceline in the same time period, the risk in the ATM −4 would be over $700! The amount of **dollar risk** you can assume in making a trade is as important as if not more important than the trade itself; **as the absolute dollar risk goes down, it is better to buy the options outright. As the dollar risk raises, the synthetic**

long or short is more beneficial. In either case, the weekly option is far superior to using any other serial.

The Backspread (1 × 2 for Even)

The final trade that I use is the backspread. I call it a 1 × 2 for even because I am trying to reduce the premium risk as much as possible. In some cases, you will be able to put the trade on for a small credit; in others, it might be a slight debit. The trade is similar to buying either an outright or a synthetic, as it has unlimited reward and limited risk. This example will look at the difference between a medium-priced stock and a large one, and how the trade works best. Figure 10.6 is Priceline, with three days until expiration.

You can see that the problem with trading such a high-priced stock is the spread that must be employed, because the premium in each strike is so large that you can't use touching strikes. In fact, you have to use strikes that are more than $20 apart. **The 1 × 2 is not conducive to this type of environment**. Although theoretically it is exactly the same as trading smaller stocks, the big dollar risk doesn't make this trade practical unless you have a large amount of risk capital. **The bigger the strike risk, the less you want to use this strategy**.

Figure 10.7 is AAPL with one (1) and eight (8) days until expiration. Once again, you can see the problem as time increases. In order to do the 1 × 2 with eight days remaining, you probably need to go out 8 to 10 strikes. However, as time decreases, it is much easier to do the trade. Remember, when you do a 1 × 2, the tighter the strikes the less risk you have as expiration comes into play. The ATM +1 call spread could be initiated very close to even, and all higher spreads could be used.

UNDERLYING								
Last X	Net Chng	Bid X	Ask X	Size	Volume	Open	High	Low
1230.00 D	+8.96	1229.50 P	1231.50 P	2 x 1	669,764	1222.01	1237.15	1220.15

TRADE GRID

OPTION CHAIN Spread: Single Layout: Last X, Net Change Exchange: Composite

Strikes: 14

	CALLS							PUTS		
Last X	Net Chng	Bid X	Ask X	Exp	Strike	Bid X	Ask X	Last X	Net Chng
APR4 14 (3) 101 (Weekly)									25.17% (±24.635)
22.00 Q	+5.00	20.40 X	21.70 X	APR4 14	1215	5.60 X	6.40 W	6.10 Z	-6.10
20.00 C	+4.30	18.70 W	20.40 X	APR4 14	1217.5	6.30 X	7.20 X	6.61 C	-9.29
17.01 I	+2.91	17.10 W	18.30 X	APR4 14	1220	7.10 X	8.10 X	8.10 Z	-6.30
15.50 C	+3.15	15.60 I	16.80 X	APR4 14	1222.5	8.10 X	9.20 X	8.39 W	-9.81
15.00 Z	+3.70	14.10 X	15.00 I	APR4 14	1225	9.20 H	10.10 X	9.80 Z	-8.00
13.00 C	+2.80	12.80 X	13.80 X	APR4 14	1227.5	10.30 X	11.10 H	10.61 W	-8.79
12.00 Z	+2.70	11.50 X	12.50 W	APR4 14	1230	11.40 X	12.30 X	12.00 A	-10.20
11.00 X	+3.19	10.40 W	11.30 X	APR4 14	1232.5	12.80 X	13.60 X	13.40 A	-10.17
9.30 X	+1.50	9.30 W	10.10 X	APR4 14	1235	14.10 X	15.00 X	14.80 N	-7.60
8.50 Q	+1.75	8.30 X	9.10 X	APR4 14	1237.5	15.60 X	16.40 X	16.30 X	-13.90
7.30 Q	+1.30	7.30 X	8.00 Z	APR4 14	1240	17.10 X	18.00 X	17.70 N	-12.40
8.52 C	+3.52	6.50 X	7.20 X	APR4 14	1242.5	18.80 X	19.60 X	20.50 N	-10.60
6.20 Q	+1.10	5.70 X	6.20 X	APR4 14	1245	20.50 X	21.30 X	21.50 Z	-16.30

FIGURE 10.6 (PCLN) Priceline Three-Day Option Chain

Position	Last X	Net Chng	Bid X	Ask X	Exp	Strike	Bid X	Ask X	Position	Last X	Net Chng
CALLS						Strikes: 12 ▼		PUTS			
2 14 (1) 100 (Weeklys)											16.03% (a
	12.70 Q	-.05	12.45 X	12.95 X	MAY2 14	580	.13 Q	.14 I		.14 Q	-.44
	9.65 M	-.35	10.05 X	10.45 I	MAY2 14	582.5	.21 N	.22 Q		.19 C	-.86
	8.00 Z	+.30	7.70 X	8.10 I	MAY2 14	585	.40 N	.42 Z		.41 Q	-1.29
	5.75 A	+.40	5.70 A	5.90 N	MAY2 14	587.5	.77 Z	.81 N		.77 N	-2.00
	3.95 A	+.70	3.95 H	4.05 Q	MAY2 14	590	1.44 N	1.50 Q		1.51 A	-2.36
	2.58 C	+.38	2.51 M	2.58 N	MAY2 14	592.5	2.50 Q	2.54 Q		2.50 Q	-2.82
	1.42 N	+.12	1.41 N	1.46 N	MAY2 14	595	3.85 N	3.95 Q		3.95 A	-3.15
	.74 N	-.12	.73 N	.75 Q	MAY2 14	597.5	5.65 N	5.80 Q		5.70 Z	-3.35
	.34 I	-.21	.36 N	.38 N	MAY2 14	600	7.80 Q	8.00 C		7.85 C	-3.19
	.18 Q	-.17	.18 N	.19 I	MAY2 14	602.5	9.90 C	10.35 C		10.01 X	-3.38
	.08 I	-.16	.09 N	.10 Z	MAY2 14	605	12.30 X	12.75 X		13.20 Z	-2.56
	.06 X	-.11	.05 Z	.06 Q	MAY2 14	607.5	14.75 A	15.25 A		14.85 X	-4.65
14 (8) 100											17.67% (±
	14.50 Q	+1.75	14.20 C	14.45 H	MAY 14	580	1.76 N	1.80 Z		1.76 I	-1.26
	12.30 B	N/A	12.30 C	12.50 M	MAY 14	582.5	2.31 N	2.36 Q		2.29 H	N/A
	10.50 Q	+1.49	10.50 A	10.65 A	MAY 14	585	2.99 Z	3.05 Q		2.94 Z	-1.64
	8.95 A	N/A	8.85 A	9.00 Q	MAY 14	587.5	3.80 N	3.90 C		3.90 C	N/A
	7.35 N	+1.15	7.35 A	7.50 N	MAY 14	590	4.80 Q	4.90 N		4.91 I	-2.09
	6.00 C	N/A	6.00 I	6.15 N	MAY 14	592.5	5.95 N	6.10 X		6.00 N	N/A
	4.90 Q	+.55	4.85 C	4.95 N	MAY 14	595	7.25 N	7.40 A		7.38 I	-2.42
	3.95 A	N/A	3.85 Z	3.95 C	MAY 14	597.5	8.75 N	8.90 C		8.75 X	N/A
	3.05 A	+.40	2.98 C	3.05 Q	MAY 14	600	10.35 Q	10.55 Q		10.40 N	-2.85
	2.34 Q	N/A	2.30 N	2.34 Q	MAY 14	602.5	12.20 N	12.45 C		12.60 A	N/A
	1.78 I	+.08	1.75 A	1.80 Q	MAY 14	605	14.10 N	14.35 N		14.85 M	-3.00

FIGURE 10.7   (AAPL) Apple Inc. (AAPL) One- and Eight-Day Option Chain

The biggest risk for this trade is if the market places your short strike at the money on expiration day.

Summary

It is important to look at each individual stock before you decide which type of trade is suitable. Some trades are better than others in an individual stock, depending on the way the premium is priced. Learning which trade to use, when, is a very important consideration.

Weekly credit spread, 60/40 credit spread

The weekly credit spreads will fit with any stock as long as you can maintain a 2/3 risk/reward ratio. Some of my students like to move further away from the ATM, and that is their choice. You have less price risk but you have greater premium risk. I personally like to use the ATM +1/−1 or the 60/40. It is a Vega-neutral spread, and it employs the 60 delta and 40 delta options.

Outright buy of a call or put

This depends solely on the price of the stock. As you move further up the price ladder, the amount of air you must overcome makes this type of trade very difficult. The premium in stocks over $100 usually precludes this trade.

Risk reversal synthetic long or short

Once you move to the higher-priced stocks, you must go to the synthetic in order to overcome the premium. Although the option model works the same for higher-priced and lower-priced stocks, the dollar risk comes into play, and since our goal is to minimize the dollar risk and maximize our leverage, you must use the risk reversal on high-priced stocks.

The backspread (1 × 2 for even)

This spread works very well in modestly priced stocks where you can use touching strikes. As you move further away from the ATM, the chances are less that you have to cash this trade. In higher-priced stocks, the strike risk becomes too large, and I suggest that you abandon this type of trade.

■ Chapter 10 Quiz

1) Weekly options:
   a) are a new trading vehicle and therefore not liquid
   b) are the fastest-growing segment of the derivatives market
   c) account for more than 30 percent of all stock option volume
   d) both b and c

2) Weekly options:
   a) are a zero-sum game
   b) have smaller commissions than long dated options
   c) have a different parabolic curve than longer dated serials
   d) all of the above

3) In order to defeat a zero-sum game, you must:
   a) have a large amount of risk capital
   b) have low commissions and tight bid offer spreads
   c) have more skill than your opponent
   d) b and c only

4) Weekly option credit spreads offer:
   a) liquidity
   b) opportunity to cash a trade each week as opposed to once a month
   c) limited risk limited reward trades with a high percentage of win
   d) all of the above

5) Priceline (PCLN) priced over $1,000 a share is a good candidate for:
   a) backspreads 1 × 2 for even
   b) outright purchase of a call or put

c) synthetic long or short through a risk reversal
d) all of the above

6) Facebook (FB) priced under $60 a share is a good candidate for:
   a) outright purchase of a call or put
   b) backspreads 1 × 2 for even
   c) synthetic long or short through a risk reversal
   d) all of the above

7) Apple Inc. (AAPL) priced at $600 a share is a good candidate for:
   a) outright purchase of a call or put
   b) backspread 1 × 2 for even
   c) 60/40 credit spread
   d) only b and c

8) Bank of America (BAC) priced at $14 a share is a good candidate for:
   a) nothing; there is not enough air in the balloon
   b) backspreads 1 × 2 for even
   c) synthetic long or short through a risk reversal
   d) 60/40 credit spreads

9) A long or short risk reversal:
   a) should be used when there is a lot of air in the balloon
   b) should be used on all stocks priced above $100
   c) should never be used on stocks below $100
   d) none of the above

10) Weekly options offer excellent opportunity for:
    a) outright buys of calls and puts
    b) credit spreads
    c) backspreads 1 × 2 for even
    d) all of the above

CHAPTER 11

Midterm Review

This chapter will be a review of the material that has been presented so far. A 50-question test will be given at the end of the chapter. It will have 150 possible points, and you will need to get a score of at least 135 before you go to the second half of the book. Some of the terms introduced are unique to this book and may be different from what you have learned in the past. It is imperative that you have a working knowledge of these terms before you continue on to the second half of the book.

Earlier, I talked about how Jack Nicklaus always used the same swing to play golf; he just changed clubs based on the distance. In the past two chapters, I showed you what clubs I use to trade options. The clubs ranged from the very conservative credit spreads to the aggressive risk reversals and all trades in between. There are hundreds of strategies possible to trade options, but I believe the four simple trades that I showed you will accomplish just about anything if they are used properly.

I deliberately did not introduce any of the typical graphs that show how the profit or loss will play out on expiration; I don't think that is the way to trade. You need to be able to price the model using the formula for conversions and reversals. That is the way that your opponent is going to play the game, and using analyzers is very difficult because they are only accurate after the market closes on expiration Friday.

Even with as little as an hour remaining, the model will have premium. That is why I use the table "Days until Expiration." **It is dynamic and will help you to estimate the premium that most likely will be left in the ATM straddle at any point in the last 14 days of trading.** You can construct your own table for other stocks by observing the ATM straddle each day for the last 14 trading days and recording the price each day. The ATM price will not always be exactly the same in each serial cycle, but it will be close enough for you to estimate how much air will be left in the balloon in a stock at any point in the last 14 days of trading.

I want to review the groundwork that was laid out in the first half of the book to emphasize what I consider to be the keys to trading.

Psychology

I believe that it is important to have the right mind-set as a trader. When things are going great, you must be on the alert for problems. When things are going bad, you have to keep plugging away and maintain your discipline. Think of taking a loss as the beginning of the next winner. If you control your losses, the winners take care of themselves. Losing trades are inevitable; the way you handle them will be the key to your success or failure. When the markets reach bubble tops or bottoms, it will not be the economic fundamentals that drive them; it will be the emotional view that the market can never go down again or some fundamental change will prevent the market from going up. Remember to trade the market you have, not the one you want. **The market is never wrong; it is never tired or sick. It is always right. Don't try to fight it, and you will be successful!**

Liquidity

If you are around the markets long enough, you will see what I mean by trading only in a liquid market. A retail trader has no hope of success if you try to beat the pros in illiquid markets. Unless you trade in markets that have tight bid–offer spreads and good volume, you will not be able to make money. The combination of commissions and a wide bid–offer spread will take away any edge you have, skillwise. It is like playing in the poker game where you must pay a commission and have no choice of strategy. Eventually, the house gets all of your money; in this case, it is the broker clearing your trades.

Market Pricing

All auction markets are driven when the buyer and seller decide to exchange value, and that **price discovery** leaves a print that ensures that the market was in equilibrium even if it is only for a few seconds. There must be a buyer for every seller and vice versa. The market can only go higher if the buyers are willing to pay more and it can only go lower if the sellers are willing to take less. There must be a buyer for every seller. If there is no buyer or seller at the next price level, the market will **gap** until the buyers and sellers are again in equilibrium.

Phases of the Market

The markets continually repeat the same patterns, and there is a mathematical reason to justify the patterns forming. **Congestion** is the dominant pattern, and it is where the **strong hands and weak hands** constantly change position. When one dominates the other, there is a **breakout to the trend,** which may be joined by **new money.** Eventually, the markets will get overdone in one direction, in which case greed or fear will cause a **blowoff** to occur, forcing the weak hands to cover at any price, and the market will then begin the cycle once again.

Relationship of Time and Price

The relationship of time and price is constant in any liquid market. Without time and price axis labels, it is impossible to tell what time frame or market you are observing—they all look identical. The sum of all shorter time frames will equal the longest time frame. This is pretty simple; if the market has been rallying for the past six months in the daily time frame, all of the shorter time frames will be positive. It is not to say all will be positive at the same time, but the sum of the shorter time frames will be positive.

Option Vocabulary

Options have their own vocabulary, and without a working knowledge of the lexicon it is impossible to trade options.

Option Model

Options are a probability model and mimic the underlying asset. As uncertainty changes, the air in the balloon expands and contracts to reflect that opinion. At expiration, the model has no air left and each individual strike is either worthless or has all intrinsic value. The option model has the greatest uncertainty at the current market price (at the money) and therefore it is all air and no intrinsic value. All other strikes have less air until the probability reaches either 100 percent (parity) or zero; in either case, there is no air left in those strikes. **The ATM will always have** air even with a few seconds left to trade in the expiring serial, because there will still be uncertainty.

Option Chain

The option chain is the vehicle used to execute option trades, and it reflects the option model's probability curve. The put and call of the same strike in each serial have the same amount of premium. The ATM will always have the most premium (air) because it is the greatest point of uncertainty. It is important to understand which stock options can be traded and which stock options are not liquid. If the option bid–offer spread is too wide or there is not enough air in the balloon, the option is no longer liquid. It is important to constantly monitor a large number of stocks to make sure that your portfolio doesn't get outdated.

Option Trading Strategies

Your ability to handle risk is the most import component of trading options. **Selling unlimited risk (naked options) is always wrong.** Buyers of **outright options** always have limited risk and unlimited reward. Sellers of **credit spreads** have limited risk and limited reward. However, they win three ways if the price stays where the spread is sold, if the price goes in their predicted direction, or if the price moves against them by less than the credit received. All **risk reversals have limited risk and unlimited reward.** The **synthetic long or short** reacts roughly the same as an outright buy or sale of the underlying stock; the major difference is that unlike the underlying stock, it has limited risk to go along with unlimited reward. The **backspread has unlimited reward and limited risk.** Buying two options and selling one for very close to even in premium gives an outstanding chance for reward with minimum premium risk.

Weekly Options

Weekly options are a miniature version of longer dated options with many similar characteristics. The major factor separating them is that the **premium can be sold each week, which allows for a much greater chance to earn regular income.** If you are correct in the price direction of your trade, you get a much bigger bang for your buck using weekly options.

◼ Summary

Anytime that you are confused about a trading topic, you can quickly go to this chapter and find the topic that you are looking for. You can then go back to the other chapters and review in detail. In part two of the book, we will marry the different option strategies with the phases of the market and learn how to initiate and take off the various options trades. The test that follows should give you a very good idea of how well you have digested the materials presented to this point.

■ Test for Chapters 1–10

1) An option chain resembles:
    a) a standard bell-shaped curve
    b) a triangle breakout pattern
    c) a trending pattern
    d) none of the above

2) Which of the following is true about in-the-money options?
    a) They all expire in the money.
    b) They will have no premium at expiration.
    c) They always have intrinsic value at expiration.
    d) It cannot be determined from this information.

3) Fundamental traders generally:
    a) only look at supply and demand for a stock
    b) are predictive in nature
    c) are reactive in nature
    d) never consider technical factors

4) Which of the following is true about stock indexes rallying after a bad unemployment number?
    a) It is highly unusual and is generally a selling opportunity.
    b) It is caused by high-frequency traders.
    c) It is called market expectation.
    d) All of the above are true.

5) Technical traders never take _____ into consideration.
    a) P/E ratios of stocks they are looking to buy
    b) overbought or oversold conditions
    c) market retracement levels
    d) media buying or selling advice

6) Technical traders usually buy:
    a) double bottoms
    b) breakouts from congestion
    c) blowoff bottoms
    d) all of the above

7) Double tops occur when:
   a) the weak hands turn strong
   b) the strong hands take profit
   c) new money enters the market
   d) all of the above

8) What happens once a market breaks out from congestion?
   a) A trending market has begun.
   b) It can go back into congestion.
   c) A double top must have been violated.
   d) High-frequency traders will be scrambling for cover.

9) What controls all bear trending markets?
   a) the weak hands
   b) the strong hands
   c) new money
   d) none of the above

10) When the angle of the bull market approaches 60 degrees, what will happen?
    a) The last of the weak hands will be getting forced out.
    b) Longs will be the strong hands.
    c) New money will come in on the long side of the market.
    d) None of the above will occur.

11) The South Sea Company was set up to:
    a) take advantage of new trade routes to the South Seas
    b) be the world's first franchise
    c) fund the Crown's debt from the Spanish War of Succession
    d) all of the above

12) Why did Sir Isaac Newton lose his fortune in the South Sea bubble?
    a) The South Sea stock was allowed to trade freely.
    b) The Crown lost a great deal of money developing the trade routes to the South Seas.
    c) Land companies drove up the price of the trade routes.
    d) He was greedy.

13) What caused the railroad panic of 1893?
    a) Congress allowed too many free acres for railroad construction.
    b) There was competition among railroads.
    c) Wall Street was greedy in financing unneeded infrastructure.
    d) Travel from coast to coast declined.

14) Price discovery is:
   a) where value changes hands
   b) where price is in equilibrium
   c) not recognized by fundamental traders
   d) a and b

15) Liquidity is characterized by:
   a) high volume
   b) a large float or open interest
   c) tight bid–offer spreads
   d) all of the above

16) A rally in the market is caused by:
   a) a lack of sellers
   b) no strong hands to fight the buyers
   c) more buyers than sellers
   d) aggressive buyers

17) What condition creates an upside price gap?
   a) Buyers are active in the market.
   b) Sellers are active in the market.
   c) There are no sellers to meet buyer demand.
   d) Overnight geopolitical news is very positive.

18) Futures markets are characterized by:
   a) different-sized contracts for each product
   b) an expiration date for trading
   c) good-faith margin deposits
   d) all of the above

19) Stock index futures:
   a) are a safe investment
   b) mirror the underlying cash index
   c) are settled in stock from the index
   d) have no specific expiration date

20) The Forex market:
   a) is guaranteed by the Forex currency exchange
   b) is dominated by large banks
   c) has fixed expiration dates
   d) is liquid for small traders

21) Congestion markets can extend for how long?
   a) Never more than six months; then they are known as a trend.
   b) They can extend until they breakout to a trend.
   c) Indefinitely; there is no time limit.
   d) All of the above are true.

22) When is a trending market confirmed?
   a) The double top or double bottom is violated.
   b) The market makes a new higher high and a higher low.
   c) The market has a 45-degree downtrend confirmed.
   d) New money enters the market.

23) What is true about assignment?
   a) It is the right of an option buyer to exercise.
   b) It rarely happens to option buyers.
   c) An option seller has an obligation to deliver the underlying asset.
   d) None of the above is true.

24) What is a serial?
   a) another word for a near-term put
   b) the grouping of options that have the same expiration
   c) the order in which options are priced
   d) all of the above

25) The strike price is:
   a) the value of a call at expiration
   b) the price at which a call must be delivered by the buyer
   c) the price at which the seller must buy or sell the underlying asset
   d) the at-the-money strike

26) Even in a bull market of 45 degrees:
   a) weak hands will push the market down
   b) there can be a congestion phase
   c) the strong hands can become the weak hands
   d) all of the above will occur

27) The at-the-money option always:
   a) has the most amount of premium
   b) has the least amount of premium
   c) is closest to the underlying asset's current price
   d) a and c

28) What is delta?
   a) the rate of change of the option to the underlying price of an asset
   b) a positive number for calls

c) a negative number for puts

d) all of the above

29) What is gamma?

    a) the change in premium as volatility increases

    b) a negative for calls

    c) the speed at which the delta changes for a one-point change in the underlying asset

    d) all of the above

30) The Black–Scholes option model:

    a) was the first option model

    b) has changed because of high-frequency traders

    c) is not reliable in volatile markets

    d) none of the above

31) When does the option model have the most uncertainty?

    a) at the current price of the underlying asset

    b) when an option reaches parity

    c) when an option becomes a teenie

    d) none of the above

32) How is poker similar to options?

    a) Some information concerning the market is revealed.

    b) Both rely on probability models to succeed.

    c) Luck can be overcome in the long run.

    d) All of the above are true.

33) How is blackjack similar to options?

    a) Your opponent has unlimited capital.

    b) Both rely on probability models and skill to succeed.

    c) Luck can overcome your opponent in the short run.

    d) All of the above are true.

34) In terms of options, what is a tick?

    a) a small insect

    b) the smallest price change allowed in an option or underlying asset

    c) amount varies from stock to stock

    d) none of the above

35) Which of the following is true about theta?

    a) It is the loss of premium as options move closer to expiration.

    b) It is the increase of premium when there is more uncertainty in the market.

    c) It is the decrease of premium as uncertainty diminishes.

    d) Theta is not a term associated with options.

36) An option that reaches parity is synonymous with:
   a) an option that currently has no premium
   b) an option that can be exercised
   c) an option that can be assigned
   d) all of the above

37) The standard contract size for all US exchange-traded stocks:
   a) is 100 shares
   b) is regulated by the OCC and SEC
   c) expires on Friday after the close
   d) all of the above

38) If the at-the-money option has premium expanding, what is most likely true?
   a) The out-of-the-money options will have more air.
   b) The in-the-money options will have more air.
   c) Volatility of the underlying asset is probably increasing.
   d) All of the above are true.

39) At expiration, which option will have the most premium?
   a) the at the money
   b) the 40 delta put
   c) the 40 delta call
   d) none of the above

40) Once an option reaches parity, what happens if the volatility doesn't change?
   a) It will remain at parity.
   b) It will mimic the underlying stock 100 percent.
   c) It can never end up as a teenie.
   d) It is always at risk for market direction.

41) The amount of premium in the at-the-money option is determined by:
   a) the Black–Scholes model
   b) the rate at which the underlying stock is moving
   c) the supply and demand for the option in the specific expiration serial
   d) all of the above

42) The longest time frame is:
   a) not related to shorter time frames
   b) not valid if the market is blowing off
   c) the sum of all shorter time frames
   d) generally in congestion

43) Another name for the longest time frame is:
   a) the major trend that we are observing
   b) the strong hands running over the weak hands

c) new money entering a bear market

d) none of the above

44) In a bull market, the shorter time frames:

    a) are always bullish

    b) are not relevant

    c) can be bearish

    d) none of the above

45) The deferred serial will have:

    a) more air in the balloon as it has more uncertainty

    b) more air in the out-of-the-money options

    c) parity options and teenies

    d) all of the above

46) If volatility doubles in the expiring month, what will happen?

    a) The at-the-money options will double in price.

    b) The differed serial expirations will double.

    c) There will no longer be parity options.

    d) Volatility cannot double in the front month.

47) What is true about out of-the-money options?

    a) They always expire out of the money.

    b) They will have no premium at expiration.

    c) They always have intrinsic value at expiration.

    d) It cannot be determined from this information.

48) What is intrinsic value?

    a) the amount of premium in an option

    b) the opposite of extrinsic value

    c) the same as a credit

    d) none of the above

49) Buying long options can create which of the following positions?

    a) The trader owns a call.

    b) The trader owns a put.

    c) The trader owns both a put and a call.

    d) All of the above are true.

50) Selling or writing options has which of the following characteristics?

    a) It gives the seller the right to exercise on or before expiration.

    b) It gives the seller the obligation to deliver the underlying asset at expiration.

    c) It gives the seller the right to assign options at expiration.

    d) None of the above is true.

Standard Deviation—The Mathematics of the Price Cycle

This chapter will deal with the pricing model and how it relates to the binomial distribution that makes up the option curve. It will explain mathematically why the market goes through different phases.

I am keeping the math to a minimum in this book, but once you start to combine the option model with the trading model, you will need to know a little about how I came up with each phase of the market and why standard deviations are relevant to trading.

Figure 12.1 is the binomial distribution that was shown earlier in the book. This version has included the Greek symbol sigma, σ, which indicates a standard deviation. I will not go into the equations necessary to get the graph of Figure 12.1, but it is calculated by taking the square root of the average of the squared differences of values from their mean value. **A standard deviation is a measure of volatility; as data points move further from the mean, the population of the sample grows more unstable**.

What that means in layman's terms is that you want to make sure that if you are getting a certain return on an investment, that it is done with low volatility.

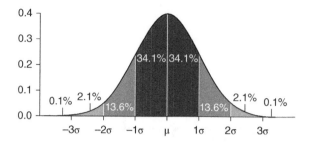

FIGURE 12.1 Binomial Curve with Sigma (σ)

In financial circles, the standard deviation is used to measure the risk associated with an asset and the amount that the risk varies from the mean over time. If a certain asset has yielded 10 percent per annum over the past 50 years, it is important to be aware of the amount of variance that has occurred during that period. If the asset lost money in 48 of the 50 periods, then no matter what the annual rate of return is, it can't be used for a normal investment—the volatility is too high. Most likely, it had one or two great periods and the rest of the time it lost money. On the other hand, if it made money in 48 of 50 periods, it is very stable, can be relied on with a "95 percent level of confidence," and is a very good asset to own. The logic also carries over into the phases of the market.

You will notice that since the price data **in a liquid asset** are evenly distributed above and below the mean, we should have a very good idea of how stable the asset is. If it is liquid, the price should be rotating around the mean. For our trading purposes, we know that the **mean is always the at-the-money option strike** where the most uncertainty is associated. As we get more information and the market moves further from the mean, the options either move closer to parity or they lose all value. This is a mathematical certainty. There is another mathematical certainty; the price of the liquid asset will rotate around the mean price roughly +/−65 percent of the time, or approximately one standard deviation on either side of the mean, and I call this congestion.

Examine Figure 12.2; it is a market in the congestion phase, which was discussed earlier in the book. What you are really looking at is the bell-shaped distribution from Figure 12.1. The mean is the middle of the congestion phase and the double tops and bottoms are +/−1σ on the left and right of the mean. The reason that the markets remain in congestion is that the uncertainty about the direction of the current price causes the strong hands and weak hands to constantly change dominance until one of them overwhelms the other and the market breaks out. The amount of volume associated with the congestion phase is also consistent with the price pattern.

Figure 12.3 is represented by +/−2σ, although the time that the market is in congestion is much longer. The distribution of price occurs after we "break out to the trend," and this is also consistent with what happens when the strong hands are

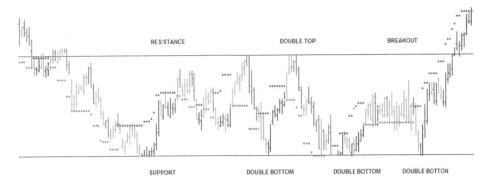

FIGURE 12.2   Congestion Phase

FIGURE 12.3   Triangle Breakout to a Trend

able to force the weak hands out of the market. They gain strength, and this attracts new money. The weak hands are forced out, and they may join forces with their old adversaries to form a new alliance. If the new strong hands begin to run over their opponents, the market will go $+/-3\sigma$ and the blowoff will occur.

Figure 12.4 is the classic V blowoff. This represents the smallest percentage of time of the three phases but offers one of the best trading opportunities. Although the amount of time spent in this phase is very small in relation to the rest of the market, in some instances the price movement that is generated is almost as much as the other two phases combined. I know that some traders do nothing but wait for the blowoff phase and that they do extremely well with it—in fact, it is my favorite trade because the price pattern is so clearly defined. The strong hands have overwhelmed the weak hands and at the very bottom/top, the weak hands "puke out," a colorful term in the business that is very descriptive of how you feel when you finally get out—it is as though you have just gone through the stomach flu!

As the weak hands become price insensitive, it attracts "new money" that has been waiting on the sidelines. New money signifies participants that are not currently in the market. They could have been the strong hands that took profit on the way

CLASSIC V BLOWOFF PATTERN

FIGURE 12.4   Classic V Blowoff Pattern

up/down or they could be the pukers that now join the new money. In any case, the remnants of the strong hands are now feeling great pressure to take profit, and their greed is now replaced with fear. They bid up/sell off the rest of their position, and the race back to the other side of the distribution curve creates the distinctive V.

After the cycle is complete, it will start over again. The market will constantly rotate around the current price level, which is the at-the-money straddle. The angle at which the market is declining or advancing is the key to understanding the current phase. It can go from one congestion pattern to another without a trend. It can go from one blowoff to another without going into congestion or a trend. Or it can go through the normal cycle, which is congestion, breakout to the trend, and then the final blowoff.

When I am trading and the market is moving around, I am constantly thinking about the distribution curve. As we roll from one strike to another and the premium levels change, I think of the "Days until Expiration" table in the back of the book to anticipate what will occur if the market goes into congestion at any time. Congestion is always the toughest phase to trade. I am a reactionary trader, but once I take a trade, I become a predictive trader, and, as such, I need the market to respond in the direction that I have chosen.

This section is very important to your mind-set. The markets are going to continually try to fool you, and when things are going bad you need to have a security blanket. When the fear sets in, knowing how the market is distributing price should help you to control your emotions—and believe me, even after more than 30 years, it is still a tough fight. Going back to your distribution model should give you some comfort; if the market is in congestion, you can see where the next opportunity should appear. If it is trending, it will help you to continue with the trend. Finally, when you are in a blowoff situation and the greed is overwhelming you, it will give you the confidence to take the winner off and look to reverse at a time when many of your opponents are making the classic mistake of selling a blowoff bottom or buying a blowoff top.

Summary

This is the last section on the mathematics of trading options. I have tried to present the same material in a number of different ways so that you can have various views of the same problem. In the next section, we will start to combine the trading model with the option model and begin to trade.

Chapter 12 Quiz

1) The binomial distribution model:
   a) is only valid if the asset is liquid
   b) can help you to learn how to trade in illiquid products
   c) limits how far price can go in any direction
   d) only a and c

2) An asset that has most of it data points spread out from the mean:
   a) is most likely to be very volatile
   b) needs a very high rate of return to be considered for an investment
   c) will rarely be suitable for most investors
   d) all of the above

3) A congestion market is characterized by:
   a) a rotation of price about the mean
   b) a rotation of price about the at-the-money straddle
   c) invisible barriers at $+/-1\ \sigma$
   d) all of the above

4) What is true about the at-the-money straddle?
   a) It is always less than 1σ from the current underlying price.
   b) It is always in strong hands.
   c) It is always in equilibrium.
   d) All of the above are true.

5) What is true about the mean?
   a) It is always the at-the-money option strike.
   b) It will have the highest delta.

c) It varies from asset to asset.

d) Both a and c are true.

6) Standard deviation:

    a) is only valid in the at the money strike

    b) is a measure of volatility

    c) works best in volatile markets

    d) creates a limit to how far price can fluctuate

7) What is true about a blowoff market?

    a) The market will be at $+/-3\sigma$.

    b) It cannot be traded by a retail trader.

    c) High-frequency traders create the market.

    d) None of the above is true.

8) A trending market will usually occur:

    a) $+/-2\sigma$

    b) when the shorts are squeezed out

    c) when the longs are squeezed out

    d) all of the above

9) A congestion market usually occurs:

    a) within $+/-1\sigma$ of the mean

    b) when the strong and weak hands change position

    c) when new money joins the strong hands

    d) a and b only

10) Double tops and bottoms usually occur when:

    a) the strong hands and weak hands change position

    b) the market cannot move more than $+1/-1\sigma$ from the current at-the-money straddle

    c) the market is recovering from a blowoff

    d) a and b only

Trading in a Congestion Phase of the Market

This chapter will focus on initiating and managing trades when the market is in congestion. It will use a two-time-frame trade and then suggest how the trade should be managed.

As we have seen earlier, the most common price pattern is congestion. The current price will have a tendency to rotate above and below the mean price until the strong hands finally overpower the weak hands and the market breaks out. Generally, the first trade I make in a congestion pattern is a loser. I am not able to see the support and resistance levels that are forming until a double top or bottom is hit and the strong and weak hands change ownership. Once I see the pattern change, I can then initiate a trade.

For simplicity's sake, we will always execute off of the AAPL option chain that we have used so far in the book. Since all of the trading theories use the ATM +/− 1 or 2 strikes, I will use the price of AAPL with the two-time-frame chart. I will assume that there is no position in place when I make the trade. Once the first trade is made, I will adjust accordingly.

Figure 13.1 is a market in extreme congestion. It appears that it entered the current state from the end of a downtrend, but that is not important. What is important is that it cannot break out $+/-1\sigma$ from its mean. After the initial rally, the strong hands change to sellers and the market heads back to the first bottom.

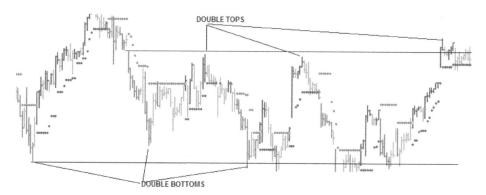

FIGURE 13.1 Congestion Market

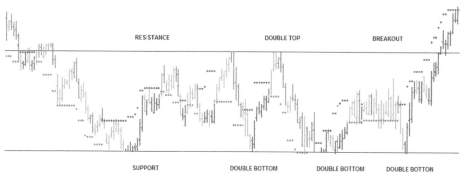

FIGURE 13.2 Congestion Double Tops and Double Bottoms

It doesn't quite reach the bottom; many times it will not make a perfect bottom or top, as it did in Figure 13.2, and that is why I use more than one time frame. If I see that I am within 5 percent of the original bottom, I look for a spot to enter to the long side. **I then go to the shortest time frame that I am observing. As soon as my technical analysis gives me a buy, I initiate the trade**.

Figures 13.3a and 13.3b are examples of looking at a market in two time frames. If you are only observing the longest time frame, Figure 13.3a appears to be a 45-degree bull market that is very smooth and trading in a low-volatility environment. However, when you look at Figure 13.3b, it is the same market observed in a shorter time frame. As you can see, the shorter time frame has more volatility and offers more chances to trade. In this case, you can pick up the double bottom and use it to enter when you get a buy signal, which is why using two time frames helps you to get an extra hedge. Trades can be set up off of the guiding time frame, and your execution is initiated on the shorter one.

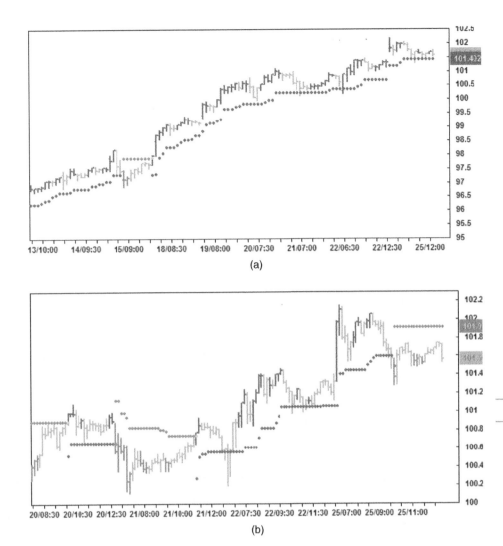

FIGURE 13.3   Observing a Market in Two Time Frames

We will assume for the purposes of this book that the charts are of AAPL and the buy point on the shortest time frame is the ATM strike. Figure 13.4 is our option chain for execution. **Using this method, you can extrapolate the theory and turn it into practice. If you can master the theory, all of your trades will be interchangeable no matter what asset you use.**

The price of our sample trade must be around 592.5; you should be able do the conversion and reversal formula to figure that out. You can now decide which type of trade that you want to make, from the most conservative outright buy of an

	CALLS				Strikes: 12 ▼		PUTS				
Position	Last X	Net Chng	Bid X	Ask X	Exp	Strike	Bid X	Ask X	Position	Last X	Net Chng
2 14 (1) 100 (Weekly)											16.03%
	12.70 Q	-.05	12.45 X	12.95 X	MAY2 14	580	.13 Q	.14 I		.14 Q	-.44
	9.65 M	-.35	10.05 X	10.45 I	MAY2 14	582.5	.21 N	.22 Q		.19 C	-.66
	8.00 Z	+.30	7.70 X	8.10 I	MAY2 14	585	.40 N	.42 Z		.41 Q	-1.29
	5.75 A	+.40	5.70 A	5.90 N	MAY2 14	587.5	.77 Z	.81 N		.77 N	-2.00
	3.95 A	+.70	3.95 H	4.05 Q	MAY2 14	590	1.44 N	1.50 Q		1.51 A	-2.36
	2.58 C	+.38	2.51 M	2.58 N	MAY2 14	592.5	2.50 Q	2.54 Q		2.50 Q	-2.82
	1.42 N	+.12	1.41 H	1.46 N	MAY2 14	595	3.85 N	3.95 Q		3.95 A	-3.15
	.74 N	-.12	.73 N	.75 Q	MAY2 14	597.5	5.65 N	5.80 Q		5.70 Z	-3.35
	.34 I	-.21	.36 N	.38 N	MAY2 14	600	7.80 Q	8.00 C		7.85 C	-3.19
	.18 Q	-.17	.18 N	.19 I	MAY2 14	602.5	9.90 C	10.35 C		10.01 X	-3.38
	.08 I	-.16	.09 N	.10 Z	MAY2 14	605	12.30 X	12.75 X		13.20 Z	-2.56
	.06 X	-.11	.05 Z	.06 Q	MAY2 14	607.5	14.75 A	15.25 A		14.85 X	-4.65
Y 14 (8) 100											17.67%
	14.60 Q	+1.75	14.20 C	14.45 H	MAY 14	580	1.76 N	1.80 Z		1.76 I	-1.26
	12.30 B	N/A	12.30 C	12.50 M	MAY 14	582.5	2.31 N	2.36 Q		2.29 H	N/A
	10.50 Q	+1.49	10.50 A	10.65 A	MAY 14	585	2.99 Z	3.05 Q		2.94 Z	-1.64
	8.95 A	N/A	8.85 A	9.00 Q	MAY 14	587.5	3.80 N	3.90 C		3.90 C	N/A
	7.35 N	+1.15	7.35 A	7.50 N	MAY 14	590	4.80 Q	4.90 N		4.91 I	-2.09
	6.00 C	N/A	6.00 I	6.15 N	MAY 14	592.5	5.95 N	6.10 X		6.00 N	N/A
	4.90 Q	+.55	4.85 C	4.95 N	MAY 14	595	7.25 N	7.40 A		7.38 I	-2.42
	3.95 A	N/A	3.85 Z	3.95 C	MAY 14	597.5	8.75 N	8.90 C		8.75 X	N/A
	3.05 A	+.40	2.98 C	3.05 Q	MAY 14	600	10.35 Q	10.55 Q		10.40 N	-2.85
	2.34 Q	N/A	2.30 N	2.34 N	MAY 14	602.5	12.20 N	12.45 C		12.60 A	N/A
	1.78 I	+.08	1.75 A	1.80 Q	MAY 14	605	14.10 N	14.35 N		14.85 M	-3.00

FIGURE 13.4 (AAPL) Apple Inc. One- and Eight-Day Option Chain

option to the most aggressive risk reversal. Let's go through the possible scenarios and decide what we want to do.

■ Trade One: Buying an Outright Option

Buying a Call

The basic option trade is to buy an option outright. You have limited risk and unlimited reward. The problem with buying outright options is that you are always fighting the time decay, and in the weekly option serial, that is a load. I do buy outrights, but only when the volatility is high. I know that might sound crazy—why would I pay more for the air? I do it because the price movement is usually so high that you can overcome the time decay. Many times, even if you are slightly wrong with the price direction, you can still make money because nervous sellers keep bidding up the price of the option market. If I am buying an option outright, I want to buy one that is either at the money or is the ATM −2 to −4. The liquidity of the in-the-money option will determine whether or not I will use it or go closer to the money. Observing Figure 13.4, you can see that as the calls get deeper in the money the spread between the bid and the offer keeps getting larger. The reason for that is the market makers don't want to own/sell those big deltas; it counters their strategy for trading options. The only time they are going to sell them to you is if they can do the conversion or reversal on the other side of the trade. I touched on this earlier, but until you trade, you might not appreciate the significance of the big bid–offer spread in the deep in-the-money options.

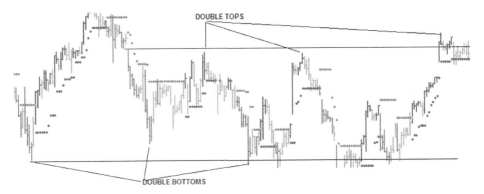

FIGURE 13.5 Congestion Double Tops

For call buys, I prefer the **ATM to ATM −1, −2**. Look at Figure 13.5. The ATM −1 has a bid–offer spread of about 10c, but by the time you reach the ATM −6, that spread has gone out to 50c. I can tell from the ATM straddle that the expected move until expiration is a little over $5. How can I pay a spread of 10 percent for the call and hope to make money? The answer is that it is impossible; don't even try! **Even in a contract like AAPL, one of the most liquid in the world, the deeper in-the-money options become illiquid and cannot be used for trading, the bid–offer spread plus commissions will make it much tougher to turn a profit in the long run**. Another reason not to use the parity options is because your risk will mimic the underlying. Even though you still have limited risk, if you buy an option near parity and get a big move against you, it will lose almost as many deltas as the underlying stock, giving you a nasty black eye.

Buying an outright call at a double bottom gives you a nice shot at a winner. First, you have support that is close by, and if necessary you might even add to this trade at support. Second, there is some volatility, and with the price angle accelerating it has a good chance to advance to the mean $+1\sigma$ very quickly. **When the shortest technical time frame you are observing gives a buy signal, initiate the trade**.

Rolling Up

Once you are in the trade, you must manage the risk. The reward almost always takes care of itself, so I constantly worry about the risk, not the potential reward. As long as the trade goes in your favor, let the trade run. Your only adjustment would be to **"roll up or roll back." I never roll up until the new ATM is at least four strikes above my current long call**. I like to roll up to limit my intratrade risk. I am willing to pay the premium to make sure that in case of a sudden move against me, I don't mimic the underlying asset tick for tick on the way down. **I roll up by doing a vertical spread, selling the long call, and buying a new call at the current ATM −1 −2.**

Rolling Back

I roll back when the market is still in my favor on Friday. I buy the horizontal spread, selling the expiring weekly call that I am long, and buying the next weekly ATM −1−2 call.

Managing Risk in an Outright Call Buy

I know that my risk is limited, and that I have positioned myself with a pretty nice risk/reward trade. I can get out; if the bottom below is violated by a certain small percentage or my shortest indicator tells me to take my loss, I am out of the trade. I know that there will probably be some price action around the low of the current move. I anticipate that, and so I always allow a few ticks below that low to stop me out. Sometimes it works; other times I end up selling the low of the move. The important thing is that you make the same trade each time; nothing works all of the time. I will stay in the trade until I reach the other side of congestion, and I will look to reverse and get short if the double top holds and my shortest technical signal gives me a reversal signal. If the market takes out the double top, I will stay with the trade, as it could turn into a monster winner if the new trend is to the upside.

Buying an Outright Put Option

Buying an outright put is the exact mirror image of the outright call. **The only difference is that it is initiated at the double top.**

Figure 13.5 is the same as Figure 13.1. However, in this example time has moved forward and the market has rallied back to a double top. The strong hands, which have been the longs, cannot push it past $+1\sigma$ and the short hands, which have been on the defensive, take control. **When the shortest technical time frame you are observing gives a sell signal, initiate the trade buying a put.**

When I am buying a put, I use the exact same strikes that I use when buying a call, but because we want the market to sell off, we must use **strikes above the current ATM**. If you are new to options, this can be a little tricky because you must reverse your thinking, and the deeper in-the-money options will be above the current price. I prefer the **ATM to ATM +1/+2**. If you go to the deeper in-the-money puts, you have the same liquidity problem as you did buying the deep in-the-money calls. The big bid–offer spread is going to make it very difficult for you to overcome the slippage in the long run.

Rolling Down

Managing a put buy is very similar to managing a call; you must still deal with your risk. As long as the trade goes in your favor, let the trade run. Your only adjustment would be to **"roll down" or "roll back." I never roll down until the new ATM is at least four strikes lower than my current long put**. I roll down to limit my intratrade risk. I am willing to pay the premium to make sure that in case of a sudden move to the upside I don't get stuck tick for tick. **I roll down by doing a vertical spread, selling the long put, and buying a new put at the current ATM +1+2**.

Rolling Back

I roll back when the market is still in my favor on Friday. I buy a horizontal spread, selling the expiring weekly put that I am long, and buying the next weekly ATM to ATM +1+2 put.

Managing Risk in an Outright Put Buy

It is just the opposite of managing the risk in the call. I know that my risk is limited, and that I can get out, if the top above is violated by a certain small percentage or my shortest indicator tells me that the market is reversing. I will stay in the trade until I reach the other side of congestion, and I will look to reverse and get long if the double bottom holds and my shortest technical signal gives me a buy. If the market takes out the double bottom, I will stay with the trade, as it could turn into a large winner if the new trend is to the downside.

■ Trade Two: Credit Spreads

Sell a Bullish Credit Spread

A double bottom is a great spot to sell a bullish credit spread. You have support right below, at the nominal double bottom, and you have plenty of price room to the previous high; the market has some velocity to the upside. Check to see if you can get the 2/3 ratio that we want when we sell a credit spread. If we sell the ATM −1 **vertical put spread** we get the correct price for the trade. Sell the 592.5 put for approximately 2.50 and buy the 590 put for approximately 1.44, giving us a credit of 1.06. Our maximum risk is approximately 1.44 and our reward is 1.06, which is better than our required 2/3 ratio. In dollar terms, we would be willing to sell the credit spread at 1.00 so anything above that is good. **If you had trouble following this example, don't go any further until you can appreciate this trade. Please go back to the chapter on credit spreads.**

The risk/reward is very good. If you are more aggressive, you could consider the 60/40 spread and see if you can do it "Vega neutral." That means that you are collecting a credit equal to or greater than the debit **in terms of air, not nominal price**. If the spread expires here, it will be a scratch or near it. Unlike the ATM −1 put spread, we do not make money if the price doesn't change; the best we can do is scratch the trade. The 60/40 gives us more upside if we are correct; it is more aggressive, because we can only make money if we have correctly predicted the direction of price.

Looking at the option chain, if I sell the ATM +1 put and buy the ATM −1, I am doing the 60/40 delta trade. I can sell the 595 put for approximately 3.85 and buy the 590 put for approximately 1.44. Does this match our criteria for doing a 60/40 trade?

If you have been practicing your conversion and reversal formula, it is a layup. They both have approximately 1.44 of air, so the trade is right in line. If the market expires exactly at this price, I will lose 1.44 of air in my long put and the short put will also lose the same amount of premium, so I scratch the trade. The amount of premium doesn't have to match to the penny; it needs to be close. If it is 10c or so off against you still do the trade if your technical analysis is bullish. Our risk in this trade is bigger, but so is our reward. If we are correct in the prediction of the price movement, we rate to make as much as 2.40 in this trade, more than double the straight credit spread.

Rolling Up a Bullish Credit Spread

If the market rallies after you initiate the bullish credit spread you must still manage your winner. You can do nothing and allow the spread to expire worthless, or if you are more aggressive you can roll it up. Similar to the outright buy of a call, I never do anything until the price advances **to at least ATM +4 from my short leg of the credit spread. Sell the ATM +4 +3**. If you are aggressive, you can let the old spread stay on the books, as you are now a very big favorite to cash the trade. If you are conservative and are concerned about a sudden reversal of fortunes, you can buy back the short leg of the original spread. I prefer to leave the long leg on, as it is probably near to being a teenie and could turn into a lottery ticket. **Never sell the long leg and hold the short leg, as you will create an unlimited risk situation**. As long as the market goes in your favor, continue to roll the spreads up for maximum possible gain.

Rolling Back a Bullish Credit Spread

On Friday, I roll back the bullish credit spread by first selling the new ATM/ATM −1 in the next weekly or the 60/40. I only buy back my existing spread if it is in danger of going out as a loser. If it is beyond the expected range, I will leave it in place. Even if the market starts to move against me that late in the week, I can always take the expiring spread off. Many times it will be so far out of the money that even adverse price movement will not affect the trade.

Managing the Risk in a Bullish Credit Spread

Personally, when I am doing credit spreads, I have found historically that trying to trade credit spreads and constantly taking small losses actually adds up to bigger losses because of the bid–offer spread and commissions that I must overcome. All trades that I teach have limited risk involved, so the worst case is you will have a loser and you go on to the next trade. Just by luck, you should cash 50 percent of these trades because that is the delta. With any skill, using your technical analysis, that number should go well into the 50s or low 60s. Cashing the 60/40 requires that you are right the same amount, 50 percent; however, it is much tougher to scratch this type of trade because if it sits here until expiration, it could be a small loser, whereas the ATM −1 pure credit spread is always a winner if the price rotates around the mean.

I said I don't try to scalp around trades, but I do take a defensive posture by selling another credit spread on the other side of the market. That will turn the original position into an **iron condor**. I don't use iron condors to initiate a spread, because you must pay double commissions and double the bid–offer spread, but I will use them to try and scratch a losing trade.

I do the following to initiate the iron condor:

If I get a reversal signal, I don't buy back the credit spread. I am short. I sell another credit spread on the other side of the market. So if I am short an ATM +1 call spread, I then try to "iron condor" it off by selling an ATM −1 put credit spread. One of the two spreads will go out worthless, and if you are lucky, both of them will. I only buy back my original spread if it is a scratch or a winner. I don't want to open myself up to a constant whipsawing by trying to buy them back and reselling them again.

How I manage winners is pretty simple: As long as the trade is going my way, I let it run. If it goes a great deal in my favor, I will "roll it up" or "roll it back." I roll it up when the new ATM is at least four strikes above my current short position leg. I don't buy back the short spread because my expected value (EV) is very positive at this time. I am probably at least a 20-to-1 favorite to cash this trade, and I am laying 2/3. However, if I can buy my short position back for .05 or less, I will buy it back and leave my long leg in place. **I never sell my long leg and keep the short leg on; this gives you very limited reward and unlimited risk**.

Sell a Bearish Credit Spread

The bearish credit spread is the mirror image of the bullish spread. Instead of using an ATM −1 put spread, **the ATM +1 vertical call spread** is used. The calculations will be exactly the same for the premium levels. In this case, you will be looking to initiate this spread near a double top. If you had a bullish spread on, you can leave it in place if it is outside of the expected value, or you can cash it out and take profit; that is a personal risk tolerance issue. The option chain will look exactly the same as the bullish spread; the only difference is that you are using the call side of the market to execute the trade. **When the shortest technical time frame you are observing gives a sell signal, initiate the trade by selling a vertical call spread**.

The calculations used in this spread are the same as the ones for the bullish credit spread. If it is an ATM +1 spread, you need your 2/3 risk ratio. If it is a 60/40, the premium levels in both of the calls should be the same or at worst a slight debit.

Rolling Down a Bearish Credit Spread

If the market goes in your direction after you sell the bearish credit spread, you must still manage your winner. You can do nothing and allow the spread to expire worthless, or, if you are more aggressive, you can roll it down. Similar to the outright buy of a put, I never do anything until the price declines **to at least ATM −4 from my short leg of the credit spread. Sell the ATM +4 +3 call spread**. If you are aggressive, you can let the old spread stay on the books, as you are now a very big favorite to cash the trade. If you are conservative and are concerned about a sudden reversal of fortunes, you can buy back the original spread. **Never sell the long leg and hold the short leg, as you will create an unlimited risk situation**. As long as the market goes in your favor, continue to roll the spreads up for maximum possible gain.

Rolling Back a Bearish Credit Spread

On Friday, I roll back the bearish credit spread by first selling the new ATM/ATM + call spread in the next weekly or the 60/40. I only buy back my existing spread if it is in danger of going out as a loser. If it is beyond the expected range, I will leave it in place. Even if the market starts to move against me that late in the week, I can always take the expiring spread off. Many times, it will be so far out of the money that even adverse price movement will not affect the trade.

Managing the Risk in a Bearish Credit Spread

I manage the risk in the bearish credit spread in the same manner as the bullish vertical. I don't try to constantly scalp the losers, as I find that unproductive. Instead, I will turn the spread into an **iron condor** by selling a bullish credit spread.

If I get a reversal signal, I don't buy back the credit spread I am short; I sell another credit spread on the other side of the market. So if I am short an ATM

+1 call spread, I then try to "iron condor" it off by selling an ATM −1 put credit spread. One of the two spreads must go out worthless, and if you are lucky, both of them will. I only buy back my original spread if it is a scratch or a winner. I don't want to open myself up to a constant whipsawing by trying to buy them back and reselling them again.

How I manage winners is pretty simple: As long as the market continues to break I let it run until the trade runs into support. If the support doesn't hold I will roll the spread down and continue to do that until I have a losing trade.

Which type of credit spread you take is entirely up to you. It is a function of how much risk you can handle emotionally if things go wrong. There is no right or wrong trade; it is the degree of risk you can handle. I am an aggressive trader, so I like the 60/40, even though it has more risk; I believe that the higher reward is worth it.

◼ Trade Three: Risk Reversals

Risk Reversal (Synthetic Long)

The risk reversal is the first aggressive spread trade that you can make. Your risk in this trade will be the same as an outright buy from a price perspective; however, by using the premium in the put you will diminish the premium risk. The trade will be initiated when the shortest technical time frame that you are observing turns positive. I like to use the ATM−1 for this trade because it has less air to be offset by the put. Margin is always a consideration, and to offset the margin problem I buy the outright call first and then I sell the put spread. Some of my students do all three legs at once. The third way to do the trade is to sell the put spread first and then buy the call.

Looking at Figure 13.5, we know the current stock price of AAPL is around 592.50 using the ATM −1. We can pay approximately 4.05 for the call and sell the ATM −1 −4 put spread for 1.23. This makes us long from approximately 592.72. We give up a small edge to buying the outright stock, but the best we could have done was to either buy the parity call or the ATM −2 −3 call is to be long from at least .20c higher. The risk reversal combines all of the power of the naked option, but with less overall premium risk. The trade is aggressive, and if the underlying stock begins to break, initially we will lose money tick for tick. However, your risk is limited to the price of the call plus the loss in the put spread.

The biggest edge using risk reversals becomes obvious when you consider margin. If you were to buy 100 shares of AAPL outright and had a Reg T margin requirement of 50 percent, you would need at least $29,000 in your account to buy the stock. Using the risk reversal, the cost goes down to about $1,500 and gives you the same reward if the trade goes the way that you have predicted. On the other hand, if AAPL were to suddenly have a disaster and the stock opened $200 lower/higher, your total risk is about $1,500 versus $20,000 owning the stock. If it gaps $200 higher, you make the same amount as owning the stock outright! It is this leverage that makes the weekly options such a great trading vehicle.

Rolling Up a Synthetic Long

I will roll up if the ATM moves more than two strikes to the upside. I **sell a vertical call spread, replacing my old ATM −2 with a new ATM −2**. I don't need to replace the put spread because it is a winner, and I use it as a means to finance my new call premium. If you want to reduce the premium risk to zero, you can sell the new ATM −2 −4 put spread, but you don't have to. If you don't mind having a little more intratrade risk you don't have to roll up. I roll up to reduce my intratrade risk, as my protection from the put spread is now closer to my long risk reversal. I roll up to guard against a wild opening to the downside. I want my protection closer to my long. When I roll up, I already have booked a $5 winner and I am now long with a premium risk of about $4. I believe that not rolling up when the ATM goes two strikes in your favor is a mistake; however, many very successful traders might argue the point, as you are probably going to give up some liquidity by paying the extra commissions and breakage. If the trade continues to go in your favor, you give up a little bit of premium, but if the market gaps against you, it will still be the winner.

Rolling Back a Synthetic Long

On Friday, I roll back the risk reversal by first **selling** the horizontal call spread. In this trade, you must sell your long call and buy the next weekly serial ATM −2 call. After the roll is in place, I sell the ATM −2 −4 put spread. Unless the trade is going badly and my expiring ATM −2 −4 put spread is in danger of going in the money, I let it expire worthless. If it is close, you will have to monitor it. My rule is, when in doubt, cover and go on to the next trade.

Managing Risk in a Synthetic Long

As with all limited-risk trades, I can get out if the bottom below is violated by a certain small percentage or my shortest indicator tells me to take my loss. I am out of the trade. This trade is managed similar to owning a call outright. There will probably be some price action around the low of the current move; I always allow a few ticks below that low to stop me out. Exactly what measure you use is up to you, as long as you limit your risk. The important thing is that you make the same trade each time. I will hold the trade until I reach the other side of congestion, and I will look to reverse and get short if the double top holds. If it doesn't hold, I will allow my long to run, as we may be having a breakout to the trend on the upside and I have a great head start.

Risk Reversal (Synthetic Short)

The synthetic short is actually called a risk conversion because you convert the long stock into a short stock position. **I will use the term risk reversal for both the long and short positions, as the mechanics of execution are exactly the same.** The synthetic short is a mirror image of the long trade. The difference is that since you are initiating a short position, you must think in reverse. You will now buy the ATM +2 put and sell the ATM +2 +4 call spread. The rest of the trade is managed exactly the same as the synthetic long.

The biggest edge using the short risk reversal is that it allows you to short the stock, with no FINRA restrictions. When you hear about large hedge funds shorting stock, it is almost always through the options. If they are wrong, their risk is limited, and if they are correct, they get the stock through exercise. Additionally, they are not subject to the short-selling margin. Unlike a synthetic long, they have reward limited to the stock going to zero, so technically it is not an unlimited reward/limited risk trade.

Rolling Down a Synthetic Short

I will roll down my synthetic short if the ATM moves more than two strikes to the downside. I **sell a vertical put spread replacing my old ATM +2 with a new ATM +2**. I don't need to replace the call spread, because it is a winner and my premium risk is greatly reduced. You can sell the ATM +2 +4 call spread to remove all premium risk if you wish. Rolling down to the lower strike helps to prevent a problem if the stock were to suddenly open on a gap higher. I already have booked a $5 winner and I am now short with a premium risk of about $4. You don't have to roll down if you are willing to take the intratrade risk. Personally, I am always looking to reduce market risk.

Rolling Back a Synthetic Short

Rolling back a synthetic short is the same operation as rolling back a synthetic long. Friday, I roll back the risk reversal by first **selling** the horizontal put spread. In this trade, you must sell your long put and buy the next weekly serial ATM +2 put. After the roll is in place, I sell the ATM −2 −4 put spread. Unless the trade is going badly and my expiring ATM −2 −4 put spread is in danger of going in the money, I let it expire worthless. If it is close, you will have to monitor it. If you are unable to monitor it during the day, it is best to cover and go to the next trade.

Managing Risk in a Synthetic Short

As with all limited-risk trades, I can get out if the top above is violated by a certain small percentage or my shortest indicator tells me to take my loss. This trade is managed similar to owning an outright put. There will probably be some price action around the high of the current move; I always allow a few ticks above that high to stop me out. Exactly what measure you use is up to you, as long as you limit your risk. The important thing is that you make the same trade each time. I will hold the trade until I reach the other side of congestion, and I will look to reverse and get long if the double bottom holds. If it doesn't hold, I will allow my short to run, hoping that the bottom will fail to hold and we have a good start on a potential big winner.

■ Trade Four: Backspread (1 × 2 for Even)

The Bullish Backspread (1 × 2 for Even)

The final trade that I do is the backspread. When the shortest time frame that I am observing gives me a buy signal, I initiate the trade. This spread can be tricky and needs to have the right amount of air in the balloon or my strikes may be too wide to use it properly. **During periods of very high volatility, I don't use this trade**; I use the risk reversal or an outright buy. To implement this trade effectively you must "**split the strikes,**" which means that they will no longer touch when you have a lot of air in the balloon. If you sell the ATM, you must buy the ATM +2/−2 in order to execute this trade for even or a small debit, because the premium is very evenly distributed (more uncertainty, more premium). If the trade goes against you, meaning that it rallies slowly, it must advance past two strikes in order to break even. This can create some major heartburn, so I suggest that you don't initiate a split strike trade in the expiring weekly.

Figure 13.6 is the original Figure 13.5, and you can see what I mean about split strikes. The one-day option has an expected range of +/− $5.08; the eight-day has an expected range of +/− $12.15. There is more uncertainty in the eight-day option, so there should be more air in the balloon. If you are bullish, the one-day trade can be initiated by buying the 1 × 2 call spread using the ATM +1, ATM +2 (2); that spread can be put on for even or a small debit.

If the market is trading near the ATM +2 strike near expiration, the ATM +1 will have very little air left, so that option will be trading around parity, which would be 2.50 in a 2.50-point strike spread. Your long options will go out worthless if we settle directly on the ATM +2 strike; consequently, the spread would go out at $2.50, your maximum loss. The risk is somewhat mitigated by the fact that even with as little as 1 hour left until expiration, the ATM +2 call should still have at least $1.00 of premium left in it, and the real risk is more like 0.50 to 0.75. You will have time to take corrective action. **The main danger of this spread is that the market goes in the direction you predicted but it will move too slowly and will threaten to stall near your long strike**. If the market remains beneath the ATM +1 strike, all of the options would go out worthless and you have

CALLS					Strikes: 12 ▼		PUTS				
Position	Last X	Net Chng	Bid X	Ask X	Exp	Strike	Bid X	Ask X	Position	Last X	Net Chng
2 14 (1) 100 (Weeklys)											16.03%
	12.70 Q	-.05	12.45 X	12.95 X	MAY2 14	580	.13 Q	.14 I		.14 Q	-.44
	9.65 M	-.35	10.05 X	10.45 I	MAY2 14	582.5	.21 N	.22 Q		.19 C	-.86
	8.00 Z	+.30	7.70 X	8.10 I	MAY2 14	585	.40 N	.42 Z		.41 Q	-1.29
	5.75 A	+.40	5.70 A	5.90 N	MAY2 14	587.5	.77 Z	.81 N		.77 N	-2.00
	3.95 A	+.70	3.95 H	4.05 Q	MAY2 14	590	1.44 N	1.50 Q		1.51 A	-2.36
	2.58 C	+.38	2.51 M	2.58 N	MAY2 14	592.5	2.50 Q	2.54 Q		2.50 Q	-2.82
	1.42 N	+.12	1.41 H	1.46 N	MAY2 14	595	3.85 N	3.95 Q		3.95 A	-3.15
	.74 N	-.12	.73 N	.75 Q	MAY2 14	597.5	5.65 N	5.80 Q		5.70 Z	-3.35
	.34 I	-.21	.36 N	.38 N	MAY2 14	600	7.90 Q	8.00 C		7.85 C	-3.19
	.18 Q	-.17	.18 N	.19 I	MAY2 14	602.5	9.90 C	10.35 C		10.01 X	-3.36
	.08 I	-.16	.09 N	.10 Z	MAY2 14	605	12.30 X	12.75 X		13.20 Z	-2.55
	.06 X	-.11	.05 Z	.06 Q	MAY2 14	607.5	14.75 A	15.25 A		14.85 X	-4.65
Y 14 (8) 100											17.67%
	14.50 Q	+1.75	14.20 C	14.45 H	MAY 14	580	1.76 N	1.80 Z		1.76 I	-1.26
	12.30 B	N/A	12.30 C	12.60 M	MAY 14	582.5	2.31 N	2.36 Q		2.29 H	N/A
	10.50 Q	+1.49	10.50 A	10.65 A	MAY 14	585	2.99 Z	3.05 Q		2.94 Z	-1.64
	8.95 A	N/A	8.65 A	9.00 Q	MAY 14	587.5	3.80 N	3.90 C		3.90 C	N/A
	7.35 N	+1.15	7.35 A	7.50 N	MAY 14	590	4.80 Q	4.90 N		4.91 I	-2.09
	6.00 C	N/A	6.00 I	6.15 N	MAY 14	592.5	5.95 N	6.10 X		6.00 N	N/A
	4.90 Q	+.55	4.85 C	4.95 N	MAY 14	595	7.25 N	7.40 A		7.38 I	-2.42
	3.95 A	N/A	3.85 Z	3.95 C	MAY 14	597.5	8.75 N	8.90 C		8.75 X	N/A
	3.05 A	+.40	2.98 C	3.05 Q	MAY 14	600	10.35 Q	10.55 Q		10.40 N	-2.85
	2.34 Q	N/A	2.30 N	2.34 Q	MAY 14	602.5	12.20 N	12.45 C		12.60 A	N/A
	1.78 I	+.08	1.75 A	1.80 Q	MAY 14	605	14.10 N	14.35 N		14.85 M	-3.00

FIGURE 13.6 (AAPL) Apple Inc. One- and Eight-Day Option Chain

very little risk. **When the shortest time frame you are observing gives a buy signal, initiate the trade buy, selling the ATM or ATM +1 strike and buying two of the next higher strike, ATM +1 (2) or ATM +2 (2).**

Rolling Up the Bullish Backspread (1 × 2 for Even)

If the spread goes in your favor you want to roll it up when your short strike is more than two strikes in the money. The first step to rolling up a 1 × 2 is to sell your extra-long call. **This turns the original spread into a long put spread with no risk.** If you remember, earlier I talked about this phenomenon where a short call spread becomes a long put spread when price rolls through the short strike. In the 1 x 2 you want to lock in your winner, and this will do. The next step is to **sell the new ATM or ATM +1 strike and buy two of the next higher strike ATM +1 (2) or ATM +2 (2).**

Rolling Back the Bullish Backspread (1 × 2 for Even)

Rolling back the 1 × 2 on Friday will depend on where the trade is in relation to where you initiated it. If the trade is in your favor (the market is above your long strike), I roll back the 1 × 2 by first **selling** the extra call, creating a credit spread in the original trade. If it is at a loss (the market is below your long strike but above the short strike), I cover the initial trade.

In this trade, you must sell your long call and buy the next weekly serial ATM −2 call. After the roll is in place, I sell the ATM −2 −4 put spread. Unless the trade is going badly and my expiring ATM −2 −4 put spread is in danger of going in the money, I let it expire worthless. If it is close, you will have to monitor it. My rule is, when in doubt, cover and go on to the next trade.

Managing Risk in a Bullish Backspread (1 × 2 for Even)

Managing the risk in the bullish 1 × 2 is slightly different than the other trades that we have discussed. It has virtually no downside if we are wrong in predicting the correct price movement. This is why many traders like to use this spread; it has one-directional risk. Since there is no free lunch, it must have risk somewhere, and in this case it is that if we are correct in the direction of the price movement, but we are wrong about the rate at which it changes, we can end up with a losing trade.

I don't adjust this trade until either of these occurs:

a) The long side of our trade (2) becomes at least the ATM +1 strike.
b) The market arrives at the long strike on expiration Friday.

In the first scenario, (a), the trade is a winner, and now we want to take advantage of that. In order to get the full benefit, I will roll it up when the (2) long legs become the ATM +1. At that point in time, I will be short a call spread and long one extra call. The short call spread will now act as a long put spread if the market breaks back toward the original ATM. **You may be wondering how a short call spread turns into a long put spread. It is because the spread reverses as you go through the strike price of the long option**.

This is an important concept that many novices and quite a few experienced traders don't fully understand. Look at Figure 13.6 again. If you had sold the 605 607.5 put spread earlier in the expiration as a credit spread, it has rolled over to a debit spread. You have already maxed out your risk, so if the market continues to break, the spread won't lose any more money. However, if the market would suddenly reverse, it would act as a call spread, and if it rallied back above 607.5 the credit spread would go to zero. **When I roll up, I sell one of the long calls and let the other one act as the long leg of the short spread**.

If the market arrives at the long strike (2) on Friday, the short leg will be near or at parity, and if the market expires on the long strike, the spread will lose the maximum amount on the trade. Earlier, I said that you can go to the "Days until Expiration" table in Appendix II to have a very good idea how much air will be left in the model on expiration Friday. **As a general rule, if you don't split strikes you will find that the trade will be near breakeven or a small loser because of the air left in the long strike (2)**. If you have split strikes, you have a much bigger problem because the short leg will be at parity and will now have at least two strikes' worth of intrinsic value. That is why I don't do split strikes 1 × 2; it can be very dangerous if you don't get the move that you need.

The Bearish Backspread (1 × 2 for Even)

The bearish backspread is the opposite trade of the bullish backspread. Theoretically, it doesn't have unlimited reward because the asset can only go to zero, but for all practical purposes, it is the exact same trade but uses puts instead of calls. **I initiate the trade when the shortest time frame that I am observing gives me a sell signal**. Because volatility is generally higher during breaking markets, I don't get a chance to use this trade as much as the bullish 1 × 2. In a break from the top of congestion, the volatility hasn't generally reached a level that would preclude this trade; however, in bear markets it will be very tough to execute this trade and I almost exclusively use the risk reversal or credit spreads.

Buying options outright and the 1 × 2 can be very hard to execute because of the huge amount of air in the balloon. Again, when you have a lot of air in the balloon to implement this trade effectively you must "**split the strikes,**" which means that they will no longer touch. If you sell the ATM you must buy the ATM −2 in order to execute this trade for even or a small debit, because the premium is very evenly distributed (more uncertainty, more premium). If the trade goes against you, meaning that it breaks slowly, it must break past two strikes in order to break even.

The main danger of the bearish 1 × 2 spread is that the market breaks, but it will move too slowly and will threaten to stall near your long strike. If the market remains above the ATM −1 strike all of the options would go out worthless and you have very little risk. To initiate this trade, sell the ATM or ATM −1 strike and buy two of the next lower strike ATM −1 (2) or ATM −2 (2).

Rolling Down the Bearish Backspread (1 × 2 for Even)

Rolling this spread down is the mirror image of rolling the bullish backspread up. You want to roll it down when your short strike is more than two strikes in the money. The first step to rolling down a 1 × 2 is to sell your extra long put. **This turns the original spread into a long call spread with no risk**. The next step is to **sell the new ATM or ATM −1 strike and buy two of the next lower strike ATM −1 (2) or ATM −2 (2)**.

Rolling Back the Bearish Backspread (1 × 2 for Even)

Rolling back the 1 × 2 on Friday will depend on where the trade is in relation to the initial position. If the trade is in my favor (the market is below my longest strike), I roll back the 1 × 2 by first **selling** the extra put, creating a credit spread in the original trade. If it is at a loss (the market is below my short strike but above the long strike), I cover the initial trade. I then sell the ATM −1 put spread and buy the ATM −1, −2 (2) put in the next expiring serial. Unless the trade is going badly and my expiring ATM −1 −2 put spread is in danger of going in the money, I let it expire worthless. If it is close, you will have to monitor it. My rule is, when in doubt, cover and go on to the next trade.

Managing Risk in a Bearish Backspread (1 × 2 for Even)

Managing the risk in the bearish 1 × 2 is the same as it is in the bullish 1 × 2. It has virtually no downside if the market rallies above our short strike. The biggest risk is that we are correct in predicting the break, but the rate at which the market is breaking will place us at our long strike at expiration.

On the winning side, I adjust when:

The short side of my trade (2) becomes at least the ATM −1 strike. I will roll down by selling the extra-long put and turning the original spread into a long call spread. This is the exact same trade that I did when I rolled the bullish backspread up. I then buy the 1 × 2 backspread. If the profit hits on Friday, I close out my original trade and roll back to the next weekly serial. I will continue to do this roll until my shortest technical indicator turns bullish.

If the trade is a loser, meaning the market is breaking but it is nearing our long strike, I know that if I haven't split strikes there should still be enough premium in my long strike to mitigate much of my risk. The biggest risk will always be on Friday if the market arrives at the long strike (2). You will have to make a decision—either take the loss and roll back to the next serial or manage the trade during the day. I stay with the trade until about midday; if it is still a problem, then I cover and take my loss or perhaps a scratch. I will then roll it back to the next weekly serial, and it will be managed as a new trade; I will let it run until I get a bullish signal.

◼ Summary

This chapter married the market theory with trading in congestion. Most of your trades will be done in the congestion phase of the market, as it represents the biggest portion of price distribution ($+1/-1\sigma$). In addition to recognizing the correct phase of the market, you must be able to decide the proper trade to use.

As a rule, you can always use credit spreads, as they represent the greatest chance to turn a profit. You can win even if the price goes slightly against you. They have limited risk, and also limited reward. Personally, when I am trading credit spreads I like the 60/40 trade, as I am willing to scratch if price doesn't go my way, but I like the bigger punch that they offer.

The outright buy needs to have air coming into the balloon to be effective, but if too much premium has already been pumped in, it can be a problem, and so I believe that the risk reversal is always a better choice.

The risk reversal has greater risk than the outright buy, but the fact that the premium risk is greatly offset makes this my number one directional trade. It allows unlimited reward with limited risk and can be initiated no matter how much air is in the balloon.

The 1 × 2 also has unlimited reward, but if the premium levels don't allow you to do touching strikes, the risk of the market slowing down near expiration increases, and it can cause problems. I like this trade in low-volatility environments, but many of my students like this trade in any environment. I suggest if you can't get this trade in touching strikes that you use one of the three alternatives.

This chapter is very important, and you must understand the principles before you go further. The quiz for this chapter is longer; if you have trouble getting at least 90 percent of the points correct, you must go back and review it before you can go on to the next phase of the market.

■ Chapter 13 Quiz

All the questions refer to trades made in the congestion phase of the market, whether stated or not.

1) In the congestion phase of the market, buying a call can be initiated at:
   a) a double bottom
   b) when the shortest time frame you are observing turns positive
   c) when your technical indicators turn positive
   d) all of the above

2) In the congestion phase of the market, buying a put can be initiated at:
   a) a double top
   b) when the shortest time frame you are observing turns negative
   c) when your technical indicators turn negative
   d) all of the above

3) In the congestion phase of the market, what is true about volatility?
   a) It is low, as price is not moving more than $+1/-1\sigma$.
   b) It is high, as there will be maximum uncertainty as to future price direction.
   c) It is impossible to tell what volatility will be at any point in the market cycle.
   d) Volatility is not important in the congestion phase of the market.

4) In the congestion phase of the market, what is true about buying options outright?
   a) It is always dependent on the uncertainty in the market (volatility).
   b) It is always a safe play, as the risk is limited and the reward is unlimited.

c) It should only be done in a low-volatility environment.

d) It should only be done in a high-volatility environment.

5) Buying calls in a rising volatility environment generally:

a) is not a good trade; if the market is rallying volatility will be dropping

b) can make money even if the price goes down slightly

c) is no longer a safe trade

d) none of the above

6) When should a bull credit spread (vertical) be initiated?

a) the market reaches a double bottom

b) your shortest technical indicator turns positive

c) volatility is dropping

d) both a and b

7) A bull ATM credit spread (vertical) can make money even if:

a) the market remains at the same price

b) the market rallies

c) the market breaks slightly

d) all of the above

8) A bear ATM credit spread (vertical) can make money even if:

a) the market remains at the same price

b) the market rallies slightly

c) the market breaks

d) all of the above

9) What is true about a 60/40 bull credit spread?

a) It has the same reward as a 60/40 bear spread.

b) It has a greater reward than an ATM credit spread.

c) It can only make money if you are correct in predicting price.

d) All of the above are true.

10) A credit spread should never be used when:

a) volatility is rising

b) you can buy an outright option for the same risk

c) a credit spread can always be used in congestion

d) none of the above

11) When should profit be taken on a credit spread?

a) when price goes through the long strike

b) when price goes through the short strike

c) on any Friday

d) when it expires

12) How can an ATM credit spread be defended?
    a) Stop yourself out and reversing to the opposite credit spread.
    b) Turn it into an iron condor.
    c) You have limited risk, so don't defend it.
    d) None of the above is true.

13) If you turn an ATM credit spread into an iron condor, which of the following is true?
    a) You can never lose more than the net credit no matter what price does.
    b) You will cash one side of the trade if you don't readjust.
    c) You can cash both sides of the trade if price expires between your short strikes.
    d) Both b and c are true.

14) A bullish risk reversal should be initiated in congestion when:
    a) the market is within 5 percent of a double bottom
    b) the shortest time frame you are observing turns positive
    c) your technical indicators turn positive
    d) all of the above

15) A bearish risk reversal should be initiated when:
    a) the market is within 5 percent of a double top
    b) the shortest time frame you are observing turns bearish
    c) your technical indicators turn negative
    d) all of the above

16) How does a bullish risk reversal resemble a call?
    a) Both have unlimited reward and limited risk.
    b) Both should be initiated in a low-volatility environment.
    c) Both can make money even if the price goes slightly lower.
    d) Both b and c.

17) How does a bullish risk reversal in congestion resemble a put?
    a) Both have unlimited reward and limited risk.
    b) Both should be initiated in a high-volatility environment.
    c) Both can make money even if the price goes slightly lower.
    d) Both b and c.

18) What is true about rolling up a bullish risk reversal?
    a) It should be rolled up if the underlying asset begins to break.
    b) It should be rolled up if the long strike goes at least to an ATM +2.
    c) You should never let the winner run.
    d) You don't need to roll up if you want to accept the intratrade risk.

19) What is true about rolling down a bearish risk reversal?
    a) It should be rolled down if the underlying asset begins to break.
    b) It should be rolled down if the long strike goes at least to an ATM −2.
    c) It should be rolled down if the volatility suddenly rises.
    d) You don't need to roll down if you want to accept the intratrade risk.

20) When should you roll back a winning bullish risk reversal?
    a) anytime the long strike goes to ATM +2
    b) when you reach a double top
    c) on Friday, before the close of expiration
    d) never

21) When should you roll back a winning bearish risk reversal?
    a) anytime, as long as the market is not rallying
    b) when you reach a double bottom
    c) on Friday, before the close of expiration
    d) only a and b

22) A 1 × 2 bullish backspread works best:
    a) at double bottoms
    b) at double tops
    c) in a low-volatility environment
    d) in a high-volatility environment

23) A 1 × 2 bearish backspread works best:
    a) at double tops
    b) when the market is rallying
    c) in a low-volatility environment
    d) in a high-volatility environment

24) Splitting strikes in a 1 × 2 backspread:
    a) increases risk
    b) decreases risk
    c) has greater profit potential than touching strikes
    d) works best in a low-volatility environment

25) A credit spread:
    a) sells air and therefore has unlimited risk
    b) has little upside in relation to its risk
    c) is selling one option and buying another
    d) both a and b

Trading in a Trending Phase of the Market

The last chapter focused on trading when the market was in congestion. Eventually, no matter how long congestion lasts, the double top or double bottom will fail to hold $+/-1\sigma$ and the trending phase of the market will begin. Trending markets are different, and when they begin, the style that is used to trade will also change. The trades themselves will not change, but when and how to use them will change.

Usually, the first trade in the trend will be a very nice winner. This is because you should be either long or short from the other side of the market's double top or bottom. The weak hands will be covering their loss, and they may decide to join the strong hands and go with the breakout. Money that has been on the sidelines will be waiting for this opportunity to join the trend. The trend will be confirmed by the market making a higher low or lower high.

This chapter will focus on initiating and managing trades when the market is trending. A trending market can be used in either one or two time frames. I prefer always to use two, as it takes profit sooner and cuts down on intratrade risk.

We will again execute off of the AAPL option chain that we have used so far in the book. Since all of the trading theories use the ATM $+/-1$ or 2 strikes, I will use the price of AAPL with the two-time-frame chart.

Figure 14.1 is a market that is trending. This pattern is typical of a long-term bullish trend. The market exited its congestion phase quite a few time periods ago, when it broke above $+1\sigma$, and is now trading in the $+1+3\sigma$ phase of the market.

FIGURE 14.1 Trending Market

	CALLS				Strikes: 12 ▼		PUTS				
Position	Last X	Net Chng	Bid X	Ask X	Exp	Strike	Bid X	Ask X	Position	Last X	Net Chng
Y2 14 (1) 100 (Weeklys)										16.03%	
	12.70 Q	-.05	12.45 X	12.95 X	MAY2 14	580	.13 Q	.14 I		.14 Q	-.44
	9.65 M	-.35	10.05 X	10.45 I	MAY2 14	582.5	.21 N	.22 Q		.19 C	-.86
	8.00 Z	+.30	7.70 X	8.10 I	MAY2 14	585	.40 N	.42 Z		.41 Q	-1.29
	5.75 A	+.40	5.70 A	5.90 N	MAY2 14	587.5	.77 Z	.81 N		.77 N	-2.00
	3.95 A	+.70	3.95 H	4.05 Q	MAY2 14	590	1.44 N	1.50 Q		1.51 A	-2.36
	2.58 C	+.38	2.51 M	2.58 N	MAY2 14	592.5	2.50 Q	2.54 Q		2.50 Q	-2.82
	1.42 N	+.12	1.41 H	1.46 N	MAY2 14	595	3.85 N	3.95 Q		3.95 A	-3.15
	.74 N	-.12	.73 N	.75 Q	MAY2 14	597.5	5.65 N	5.80 Q		5.70 Z	-3.35
	.34 I	-.21	.36 N	.38 N	MAY2 14	600	7.80 Q	8.00 C		7.85 C	-3.19
	.16 Q	-.17	.18 N	.19 I	MAY2 14	602.5	9.90 C	10.35 C		10.01 X	-3.38
	.08 I	-.16	.09 N	.10 Z	MAY2 14	605	12.30 X	12.75 X		13.20 Z	-2.55
	.06 X	-.11	.05 Z	.06 Q	MAY2 14	607.5	14.75 A	15.25 A		14.85 X	-4.65
Y 14 (8) 100										17.67%	
	14.50 Q	+1.75	14.20 C	14.45 H	MAY 14	580	1.76 N	1.80 Z		1.76 I	-1.26
	12.30 B	N/A	12.30 C	12.50 M	MAY 14	582.5	2.31 N	2.36 Q		2.29 H	N/A
	10.50 Q	+1.49	10.50 A	10.65 A	MAY 14	585	2.99 Z	3.05 Q		2.94 Z	-1.64
	8.95 A	N/A	8.65 A	9.00 Q	MAY 14	587.5	3.80 N	3.90 C		3.90 C	N/A
	7.35 N	+1.15	7.35 A	7.50 N	MAY 14	590	4.80 Q	4.90 N		4.91 I	-2.09
	6.00 C	N/A	6.00 I	6.15 N	MAY 14	592.5	5.95 N	6.10 X		6.00 N	N/A
	4.90 A	+.55	4.85 C	4.95 N	MAY 14	595	7.25 N	7.40 A		7.38 I	-2.42
	3.95 A	N/A	3.85 Z	3.96 C	MAY 14	597.5	8.75 N	8.90 C		8.75 X	N/A
	3.05 A	+.40	2.98 C	3.05 Q	MAY 14	600	10.35 Q	10.55 Q		10.40 N	-2.85
	2.34 Q	N/A	2.30 N	2.34 Q	MAY 14	602.5	12.20 N	12.45 C		12.60 A	N/A
	1.78 I	+.08	1.75 A	1.80 Q	MAY 14	605	14.10 N	14.35 N		14.85 M	-3.00

FIGURE 14.2 AAPL One-Day and Eight-Day Option Chain

Notice that even though the overall trend is very positive, it is still rotating around its mean. In this case, unlike congestion, the mean is positive and therefore the market rally is fairly constant.

Figure 14.2 is the AAPL one-day and eight-day option chain that we have looked at before.

■ Trade One: Buying an Outright Option

Buying a Call

In the last chapter I talked about buying options outright and why I like volatility to be rising, as opposed to declining. The bullish market that is represented in

Figure 14.1 appears to be a very slow moving bull similar to the one that has been trading from 2012 to 2014. Buying a call outright in this type of market is tough, as the VIX is almost always declining in a low-volatility bullish market. I don't suggest buying outright calls with this type of price action. If you like to buy them then you can, but it is not the preferred method, as you are fighting the anchor of time decay.

If you are buying a call option outright, I suggest that you use the same strategy as in the congestion phase either at the money or the ATM −2 to −4. The liquidity of the in-the-money option will determine whether I will use it or go closer to the money.

For call buys, I prefer the ATM to ATM −1 −2. When the shortest technical time frame you are observing gives a buy signal, initiate the trade.

Rolling Up; Taking Short-Term Profit

Once you are in the trade you must manage it; that doesn't change no matter what phase of the market you are trading. As long as the trade goes in your favor, let the trade run. By that, I mean if your shortest technical time frame that you are observing continues to give you a positive signal, stay with the trade. If your shortest time frame gives you a sell signal, I suggest that you exit the trade and take profit. If you are trading multiple shares or contracts, you should lock in profit by selling part of your inventory. **As a rule of thumb, when I am long multiple positions I recommend selling 50 percent when my shortest time frame turns negative.**

Many traders don't like to take profit in a bullish market because if the market is pausing before it is going higher, they must buy back into it at a higher price. This can create some emotional issues and is a personal preference call; there is not an absolute right or wrong way to take profit. **If you find that it is a problem to trade in a trending market using two time frames, don't do it; stay in the trade until your longest time frame gives the sell signal.**

You should still roll this trade up whether or not you are using one of two time frames. That is the great advantage of trading options; you can always roll up to limit your intratrade risk without giving back a lot of profit potential. **I never roll up until the new ATM is at least four strikes above my current long call.** I like to roll up to limit my intratrade risk. I am willing to pay the premium to make sure that in case of a sudden move against me I don't mimic the underlying asset tick for tick on the way down. **I roll up by doing a vertical spread, selling the long call, and buying a new call at the current ATM −1,−2.**

Rolling Back

I roll back when the market is still in my favor on Friday. I buy the horizontal spread, selling the expiring weekly call that I am long, and buying the next weekly ATM −1 −2 call.

Managing Risk in an Outright Call Buy

I know that my risk is limited, and I can get out and take my loss if the shortest-term indicator I am observing tells me the market is changing. I may end up selling the bottom tick using my short-term indicator, and that is always a risk, but as long as you do the same thing each time, it will work for you in the long run. Nothing in trading works all of the time, and you must get used to that problem. Always allow trending trades to run as long as your technical indicators stay positive, as there is no way to tell how long the asset will continue to appreciate.

Buying an Outright Put Option

Figure 14.3 is a bear market. Generally, bear markets will be characterized by fear, and that translates into higher volatility. Buying an outright put is similar to buying a call but has one major difference: **The VIX should be rising and not falling.** Buying puts in a rising volatility market is much different than buying calls in a falling volatility market. In many rapidly declining markets, you can make money even if you are slightly wrong because the amount of air going in to the balloon can

FIGURE 14.3 Bear Market

make the put inflate even if the price of the underlying asset rallies slightly. **When the shortest technical time frame you are observing gives a sell signal, initiate the trade buying a put.**

Buying a put in a bear market is similar to buying a call in a bull market. I use the exact same strikes that I use when buying a call, but because we want the market to break, we must use **strikes above the current ATM.** I prefer the **ATM to ATM +1/+2.** If you go to the deeper in-the-money puts, you have the same liquidity problem as you did buying the deep in-the-money calls. The big bid–offer spread is going to make it very difficult for you to overcome the slippage and commission in the long run.

Rolling Down; Taking Short-Term Profit

Put trades have a theoretical limit as to how low price can go zero. But for our purposes, they will continue to have limited risk and unlimited reward. As long as the market continues to break, let the trade run. If your shortest time frame gives you a buy signal, I suggest that you exit the trade and take profit. If you are trading multiple shares or contracts, you should lock in profit by purchasing a percentage of your short inventory back. **As a rule of thumb when I am short multiple positions, I recommend buying 50 percent of my shorts back when my shortest time frame turns positive.** This can create the same problem as selling your longs in a bull market: If you want to reenter, there is a chance you might have to sell at a lower price when you initiate the trade. **If you find that it is a problem to trade in a bear market using two time frames, don't do it; stay in the trade until your longest time frame gives the sell signal.**

You should still roll this trade down, whether you are using one of two time frames and single or multiple positions. You can always roll your puts down to limit your intratrade risk without giving back a lot of profit potential. I never roll down until the new ATM is at least four strikes below my current long put. **I roll down by doing a vertical spread, selling the long put, and buying a new put at the current ATM +1,+2.**

Rolling Back

I roll back when the market is still in my favor on Friday. I buy a horizontal spread, selling the expiring weekly put that I am long, and buying the next weekly ATM to ATM +1+2 put.

Managing Risk in an Outright Put Buy

Put risk is always limited. I buy back my shorts when my short-term indicator turns positive and I am in a losing position. I may end up buying the top tick using my short-term indicator, and that is always a risk; cutting your loss short is never wrong. It might not work on an individual trade, but it always works in the long run. Make sure that trending trades run as long as your technical indicators stay negative; bear markets can last a long time—just ask people who have tried to fight them.

■ Trade Two: Credit Spreads

Sell a Bullish Credit Spread

Selling credit spreads in a trending market is slightly different from selling in congestion. You won't have a double bottom or top to set up your trade. The market will be in a rotation about its mean but now the mean will have a positive slope. You still need to get the proper risk/reward ratio, which for an ATM vertical is 2/3. We are willing to risk $3 for every possible $2 we can make. Reviewing the AAPL trade from the last chapter, the ATM −1 **vertical put spread,** we get the correct price for the trade. Sell the 592.5 put for approximately 2.50; buy the 590 put for approximately 1.44, giving us a credit of 1.06. Our maximum risk is approximately 1.44 and our reward is 1.06, which is better than our required 2/3 ratio. In dollar terms, we would be willing to sell the credit spread at 1.00, so anything above that is good. The risk reward is very good.

If you are more aggressive you could consider the 60/40 spread and see if you can do it "Vega neutral." That means that you are collecting a credit equal to or greater than the debit **in terms of air, not nominal price**. If the spread expires here, it will be a scratch trade or very close one way or the other. Unlike the ATM −1 put spread, we do not make money if the price doesn't change; the best we can do is scratch the trade. The 60/40 gives us more upside if we are correct; it is more aggressive, because we can only make money if we have correctly predicted the direction of price. The option chain shows that if I sell the ATM +1 put and buy the ATM −1 put, I am doing the 60/40 delta trade. I can sell the 595 put for approximately 3.85 and buy the 590 put for approximately 1.44.

Both puts have approximately 1.44 of air and so the trade is right in line. If the market expires exactly at this price, I will lose 1.44 of air in my long put and the short put will gain the amount of premium that I lost, so I scratch the trade. The amount of premium doesn't have to match to the penny; it needs to be close. If it is 10c or so off against you, still do the trade if your technical analysis is bullish. Our risk in this trade is slightly bigger, but so is our reward. If we are correct in the prediction of the price movement, we rate to make as much as 2.40 in this trade, more than double the straight credit spread.

Rolling Up a Bullish Credit Spread; Taking Short-Term Profit

If the market rallies after you initiate the bullish credit spread you must still manage your winner. You can do nothing and allow the spread to expire worthless, or if you are more aggressive, you can roll it up. Similar to the outright buy of a call, I never do anything until the price advances **to at least ATM +4 from my short leg of the credit spread. Sell the ATM +4 +3 put spread.** If you are aggressive, you can let the old spread stay on the books, as you are now a very big favorite to cash the trade. If you are conservative and are concerned about a sudden reversal of fortunes, you can buy back the original spread. **Never sell the long leg and hold the short leg, as you will create an unlimited risk situation. As long as the market continues to rally, roll the spreads up for the maximum possible gain.**

Rolling Back a Bullish Credit Spread

On Friday, I roll back the bullish credit spread by first selling the new ATM/ATM −1 put spread in the next weekly or the 60/40. I only buy back my existing spread if it is in danger of going out as a loser. If it is beyond the expected range, I will leave it in place. Even if the market starts to move against me that late in the week, I can always take the expiring spread off. Many times, it will be so far out of the money that even adverse price movement will not affect the trade.

Managing the Risk in a Bullish Credit Spread

You should expect to cash a higher percentage of your bullish credit spreads than you do in congestion. Therefore, I don't use the iron condor as an initial defense. In this case, if the bullish credit spread goes against me by more than one strike and my longest-term indicator is still bullish, I will sell another put spread at the lower strike. **Initiate the trade if the underlying asset price moves to ATM −2. Sell the ATM −2 −3 put spread. This will double the size of the strike risk but will also double the size of the profit potential. If you are trading 60/40 spreads, make the same rolldown.**

If the underlying market continues to break, you can add spreads as long as your longest time frame remains in a bullish mode. The original put spreads you sold will become debit call spreads. I have covered this several times before, and you should understand this principle by now. If you are confused, please go back to the section on pricing the markets. If the market continues to break and your technical indicators give you a sell signal, you can take a defensive posture by turning your credit spreads into an iron condor. **Initiate the corrective trade by selling the**

ATM +1 call spread X − 1 times. The first bullish put spread should be trading near parity and has very little risk left in it, so there is no reason to use call spreads to cover that risk. That is the reason that you sell the call spread one time less than the bullish put spreads that you used to initiate the trade.

Sell a Bearish Credit Spread

The bearish credit spread is the mirror image of the bullish spread. Instead of using an ATM −1 put spread, **the ATM +1 vertical call spread** is used. The calculations will be exactly the same for the premium levels. If you had a bullish spread on, you can leave it in place if it is outside of the expected value or you can cash it out and take profit; that is a personal risk tolerance issue. The option chain will look exactly the same as the bullish spread; the only difference is that you are using the call side of the market to execute the trade. **When the shortest technical time frame you are observing gives a sell signal, initiate the trade by selling a vertical call spread.**

The calculations used in this spread are same as the ones for the bullish credit spread. If it is an ATM +1 spread, you need your 2/3 risk ratio. If it is a 60/40, the premium levels in both of the calls should be the same or, at worst, a slight debit.

Rolling Down a Bearish Credit Spread; Taking Short-Term Profit

If the market goes in your direction after you sell the bearish credit spread you must still manage your winner. You can do nothing and allow the spread to expire worthless, or if you are more aggressive you can roll it down. Similar to the outright buy of a put I never do anything until the price declines **to at least ATM −4 from my short leg of the credit spread. Sell the ATM +4 +3 call spread.** If you are aggressive, you can let the old spread stay on the books, as you are now a very big favorite to cash the trade. If you are conservative and are concerned about a sudden reversal of fortunes, you can buy back the original spread. **Never sell the long leg and hold the short leg, as you will create an unlimited risk situation.** As long as the market goes in your favor, continue to roll the spread down until you get a reversal signal.

Rolling Back a Bearish Credit Spread

On Friday, I roll back the bearish credit spread by first selling the new ATM/ATM +1 call spread in the next weekly or the 60/40. I only buy back my existing spread if it is in danger of going out as a loser. If it is beyond the expected range, I will leave it in place. Even if the market starts to move against me that late in the week, I can always take the expiring spread off. Many times, it will be so far out of the money that even adverse price movement will not affect the trade.

Managing the Risk in a Bearish Credit Spread

I manage the risk in the bearish credit spread in the same manner as the bullish vertical. I don't try to constantly scalp the losers, as I find that unproductive. Instead I will turn the spread into an **iron condor** by selling a bullish credit spread.

If I get a reversal signal, I don't buy back the bearish credit spread I am short. I sell another credit spread on the other side of the market. So if I am short an ATM +1 call spread, I then try to "iron condor" it off by selling an ATM −1 put credit spread. One of the two spreads must go out worthless. If you are lucky, both of them will. I only buy back my original spread if it is a scratch or a winner. I don't want to open myself up to a constant whipsawing by trying to buy them back and reselling them again.

Which type of bearish credit spread you take is entirely up to you. It is a function of how much risk you can handle emotionally if things go wrong. There is no right or wrong trade; it is the degree of risk you can handle. I am an aggressive trader, so I like the 60/40, even though it has more risk. I believe that the higher reward is worth it.

■ Trade Three: Risk Reversals

Risk Reversal (Synthetic Long)

The risk reversal in a trending market is ideal. You don't have to worry about whether volatility is advancing or declining because you are selling almost as much premium as you are buying. Your risk in this trade will be slightly greater from a price perspective than an outright call buy, **but the virtual elimination of the premium risk makes me lean toward this trade for aggressive directional trades. The trade will be initiated when the shortest technical time frame that you are observing turns positive.** In a trending market, I like to use the ATM −1. You will have no liquidity problems for this trade, as the ATM −1 option is usually the second most liquid. Since this trade requires three legs, you can do all three at once, as most platforms will allow you to use a three-legged spread. I don't do that, as I believe that you are giving up a big edge to the market makers. I suggest two ways to initiate this spread. First, buy the call outright and then sell the put spread. Second, sell the put spread first and then buy the outright call. Looking at Figure 14.3, we know the current stock price of AAPL is around 592.50; using the ATM −1, we can pay approximately 4.05 for the call and sell the ATM−1 −4 put spread for 1.23. This makes us long from approximately 592.72. We give up a small edge to buying the outright stock, but the best we could have done was to either buy the parity call or the ATM −2 −3 call is to be long from at least 20c higher.

Rolling Up a Synthetic Long; Locking in Profits

I will roll up if the ATM moves more than two strikes to the upside. **I sell a vertical call spread, replacing my old ATM −2 with a new ATM −2.** I don't have to replace the put spread because it will offer some protection against a catastrophic gap opening, but rolling up locks is more profit. I believe that not rolling up when the ATM goes two strikes in your favor is a mistake; however, many very successful traders might argue the point that you are giving up the edge by paying the extra commissions and breakage. They have a very good point, but I believe that anytime I can decrease my market risk, I am going to take that trade. I will continue to roll up as long as my technical indicators remain bullish.

Rolling Back a Synthetic Long

On Friday, I roll back the risk reversal by first **selling** the horizontal call spread. In this trade, you must sell your long call and buy the next weekly serial ATM −2 call. After the roll is in place, I sell the ATM −2 −4 put spread. Unless the trade is going badly and my expiring ATM −2 −4 put spread is in danger of going in the money, I let it expire worthless.

Managing Risk in a Synthetic Long

Personally, I use my shortest time frame to exit the trade. Most likely, the major trend will be bullish so I will be neutral the market. **I exit by selling my long call;** I let the put spread in place, as it can help me in two ways. First, if the rally continues and I took profit near the bottom of the short-term break, it will provide me with extra profit. Second, if the exit was good and the market breaks before I get my next buy signal, I don't need to do the three legs again. I simply rebuy the call. If my major trend turns bearish, I cover the put spread and either reduce my profit in the overall trade or increase it slightly if the break is very minor.

Risk Reversal (Synthetic Short)

As I said in the previous chapter, the synthetic short in a trending market is actually called a risk conversion, because you convert the long stock into a short stock position. **I will use the term risk reversal for both the long and short positions, as the mechanics of execution are exactly the same.** The synthetic short is a mirror image of the long trade. The difference is that since you are initiating a short position, you must think in reverse. You will now buy the ATM +2 put and sell the ATM +2 +4 call spread. The rest of the trade is managed exactly the same as the synthetic long.

It doesn't matter at what phase of the market you initiate a synthetic short, the biggest edge using the short risk reversal is that it allows you to short the stock with no FINRA restrictions. I am going to emphasis this in each chapter. The longer you trade, the more you will understand what edge this gives you.

Rolling Down a Synthetic Short; Taking Short-Term Profits

As long as all of my technical indicators remain bearish, I will roll down my synthetic short if the ATM moves more than two strikes to the downside. I **sell a vertical put spread, replacing my old ATM +2 with a new ATM +2.** You can sell the ATM +2 +4 call spread to remove all premium risk, or you can let the old spread remain intact. You don't have to roll down if you are willing to take the intratrade risk, and I know many successful traders who never roll down.

Rolling Back a Synthetic Short

Rolling back a synthetic short is the same operation as rolling back a synthetic long. Friday, I roll back the risk reversal by first **selling** the horizontal put spread. In this trade, you must sell your long put and buy the next weekly serial ATM +2 put. After the roll is in place, I sell the next week ATM −2 −4 put spread. Unless the trade is going badly and my expiring ATM −2 −4 put spread is in danger of going in the money, I let it expire worthless. If it is close, you will have to monitor it. If you are unable to monitor it during the day, it is best to cover and go to the next trade.

Managing Risk in a Synthetic Short

When I get a buy signal in my shortest time frame, **I exit by selling my long put.** This trade is the mirror of the long risk reversal. I let the call spread in place to help me. If I have taken profit near a short-term top or the market remains close to my buy, it can be used to finance my reentry with a new put if I get a new short-term sell signal.

The biggest edge using risk reversals becomes obvious when you consider margin. Instead of paying a Reg T amount of 50 percent, you end up buying the stock for about 3 to 5 percent of the face value, with all of the profit potential and none of the major risk of owning shares.

▪ Trade Four: Backspread (1 × 2 for Even)

The Bullish Backspread (1 × 2 for Even)

This trade works very well in a trending market. I prefer to use it in a downtrend, as the price action is generally better. Generally in a breaking market volatility is rising, and since you are long two options for every one that you are short, you benefit greatly if air is coming into the balloon. On the other hand, if the market suddenly reverses and goes higher, your risk is limited to the debit you paid. **If volatility is already very high—say in the upper 20 percent of historical volatility—I don't recommend using this trade.** You will have to split strikes, and that can take away much of the edge that you get by using the backspread. **When the shortest time frame you are observing gives a buy signal, initiate the trade by selling the ATM or ATM +1 strike and buy two of the next higher strike ATM +1 (2) or ATM +2 (2).**

Rolling Up the Bullish Backspread (1 × 2 for Even); Taking Profit

If the spread goes in your favor, you want to roll it up when your short strike is more than two strikes in the money. The first step to rolling up a 1 × 2 is to sell your extra long call. **This turns the original spread into a long put spread with no risk.** The next step is to **sell the new ATM or ATM +1 strike and buy two of the next higher strike ATM +1 (2) or ATM +2 (2).** You don't have to roll up if you don't want to, but it is recommended to manage your intraday risk.

Rolling Back the Bullish Backspread (1 × 2 for Even)

Rolling back the 1 × 2 on Friday will depend where the trade is in relation to where you initiated it. If the trade is in your favor (the market is above your long strike), I roll back the 1 × 2 by first **selling** the extra call, creating a credit spread in the original trade. If you don't have the ability to monitor the residual call spread, close the entire trade. If it is at a loss (the market is below your long strike but above the short strike), I cover the initial trade. Next you must go to the next week ATM +1 +2 call and initiate the new trade.

Managing Risk in a Bullish Backspread (1 × 2 for Even)

Managing the risk in the bullish 1 × 2 is different in a trending market. It has the same downside in that, if the market reverses, its risk is limited to the initial debit or credit. However, if the trade is going your way and you get a short-term sell signal, it is important that you take the entire spread off. What you will find is the unpleasant side effect of the trade "racing" to the downside. **If you didn't roll up, you will be naked a near parity call and also short a near parity put spread. Your long call spread will have rolled over into a short put spread.** Some inexperienced traders learn this lesson the hard way, and it is an eye-opener. Backspreads are fantastic when the market is in a big trend, but if it suddenly turns choppy, you will need to cover quickly.

The Bearish Backspread (1 × 2 for Even)

The bearish backspread in a selloff is usually very favorable because volatility is inevitably on the rise. Theoretically, the trade doesn't have unlimited reward because the asset can only go to zero, but for all practical purposes, it is the exact same trade. **Initiate the trade when the shortest time frame that you are observing gives a sell signal. If the volatility is in the upper 20 percent of the historical average, don't use this trade.** Because volatility is generally higher during breaking markets, I don't get a chance to use this trade as much as the bullish 1 × 2. To implement this trade effectively, you must "**split the strikes,**" which means that they will no longer touch when you have a lot of air in the balloon. If you sell the ATM, you must buy the ATM −2 in order to execute this trade for even or a small debit, because the premium is very evenly distributed (more uncertainty, more premium). If the trade goes against you, meaning that its price retreats slowly, it must break past two strikes in order to break even.

The main danger of the bearish 1 × 2 spread is that the market breaks but it will move too slowly and will threaten to stall near your long strike. If the market remains above the ATM −1 strike, all of the options would go out worthless and you have very little risk. To initiate this trade, sell the ATM or ATM −1 strike and buy two of the next lower strike ATM −1 (2) or ATM −2 (2).

Rolling Down the Bearish Backspread (1 × 2 for Even); Taking Profit

Rolling this spread down is the mirror image of rolling the bullish backspread up. You want to roll it down when your short strike is more than two strikes in the money. The first step to rolling down a 1 × 2 is to sell your extra long put. **This turns the original spread into a long call spread with no risk.** The next step is to **sell the new ATM or ATM −1 strike and buy two of the next lower strike ATM −1 (2) or ATM −2 (2).**

Managing Risk in a Bearish Backspread (1 × 2 for Even)

Managing the risk in the bearish 1 × 2 is different in a trending market. It has the same downside in that, if the market reverses, its risk is limited to the initial debit or credit. However, exactly like the call spread, if the trade is going your way and you get a short-term buy signal, you should close the entire spread. It is better to take this trade off too early than to let it "blow back" in your face. Sometimes you will take the trade off at the top tick, and that is part of trading, but in the long run, a big reversal in this trade is very disheartening. If the major trend continues lower, when your short-term signal gets short again, initiate the spread again.

▮ Summary

This chapter dealt with the four basic trades when the market breaks out of congestion at +/−1σ and moves to the trending phase +/−2 −3σ. This phase comprises a smaller portion of the distribution curve but generally comprises most of the price movement and represents a very good profit opportunity. The risk in the trending phase is much different than in congestion. Generally speaking, the bullish trend is characterized by low volatility and a smooth process. Markets can have volatile rallies, and many times the first break above a double top can be quick and very wild, but as a rule, when the long-term trend is positive, it will become docile.

A breaking market usually is driven by fear, and that means as the trend grows, the dip buyers are nowhere to be found; they turn and become "rally sellers." Since it has been more than five years since the 2009 bull started to form, it is sometimes hard to remember the panic of 2008, but you can be sure that something will happen to cause it to start again, and these four trades will put you in a good position to take advantage of it.

■ Chapter 14 Quiz

All the questions refer to trades made in the trending phase of the market, whether stated or not.

1) In the trending phase of the market, when can buying a call be initiated?
    a) Buy anytime the technical signals are bullish.
    b) Buy when the shortest time frame you are observing turns positive.
    c) Buy when the market breaks out above congestion.
    d) All of the above are correct.

2) In the trending phase of the market, when can buying a put be initiated?
    a) Buy anytime technical signals are bearish.
    b) Buy when the shortest time frame you are observing turns negative.
    c) Buy when your technical indicators turn negative.
    d) All of the above are correct.

3) In the trending phase of the market, what will volatility be?
    a) It will be low, as price is not moving between $+/-2, 3\sigma$.
    b) It will be high if the market is rallying.
    c) It is impossible to predict what volatility will be at any point in the market cycle.
    d) None of the above is correct.

4) In the trending phase of the market, what is true about buying options outright?
    a) It is the first choice of most traders.
    b) It is usually a safe bet, as the risk is limited and the reward is unlimited.
    c) It should only be done in a low-volatility environment.
    d) It is best in a rising volatility environment.

5) Buying calls in a rising volatility environment generally:
   a) is not a good trade; if the market is rallying volatility will be dropping
   b) can make money even if the price goes down slightly
   c) is no longer a safe trade
   d) none of the above

6) When should a bull credit spread (vertical) be initiated?
   a) The market breaks out above double tops.
   b) Your shortest technical indicator turns positive.
   c) Volatility is dropping.
   d) Both a and b are correct.

7) In a trending market a bull ATM credit spread (vertical) can make money even if:
   a) the market remains at the same price
   b) the market rallies
   c) the market breaks slightly
   d) all of the above

8) In a trending market a bear ATM credit spread (vertical) can make money even if:
   a) the market remains at the same price
   b) the market rallies slightly
   c) the market breaks
   d) all of the above

9) In a trending market, a 60/40 bull credit spread:
   a) has more reward than a 60/40 bear spread
   b) has a greater reward than an ATM credit spread
   c) can only make money if you are correct in predicting price
   d) only b and c

10) In a trending market, when should you not use a bullish credit spread:
   a) when volatility is rising
   b) when you can buy an outright option for the same risk
   c) a credit spread can always be used in any market condition
   d) all of the above

11) In a trending market, when can price profit be taken on a credit spread?
   a) when price goes through the long strike
   b) when your shortest-term signal gives you a reversal
   c) on any Friday
   d) when it expires

12) In a trending market, how can an ATM credit spread be defended?
    a) Stop yourself out and reverse to the opposite credit spread.
    b) Turn it into an iron condor.
    c) You have limited risk; don't defend it.
    d) None of the above is correct.

13) In a trending market, if you turn an ATM credit spread into an iron condor, you can:
    a) never lose more than the net credit no matter what price does
    b) cash one side of the trade if you don't readjust
    c) cash both sides of the trade if price expires between your short strikes
    d) both b and c

14) During a trending market, a risk reversal should be initiated:
    a) when the shortest time frame you are observing turns bearish
    b) when the shortest time frame you are observing turns positive
    c) when your technical indicators turn positive
    d) all of the above

15) A bullish risk reversal resembles a call in that:
    a) both have unlimited reward and limited risk
    b) both should be initiated in a low-volatility environment
    c) both can make money even if the price goes slightly lower
    d) both b and c

16) A bearish risk reversal in a trending market resembles a put in that:
    a) both have unlimited reward and limited risk
    b) both should be initiated in a high-volatility environment
    c) both can make money even if the price goes slightly lower
    d) both b and c

17) In a trending market, when should a bullish risk reversal be rolled up?
    a) The underlying asset begins to break.
    b) The long strike goes at least to an ATM +2.
    c) Never let the winner run.
    d) You don't need to roll up if you want to accept the intratrade risk.

18) When should a bearish risk reversal be rolled down?
    a) The underlying asset begins to break.
    b) The long strike goes at least to an ATM −2.
    c) The volatility suddenly rises.
    d) You don't need to roll down if you want to accept the intratrade risk.

19) In a trending market, when should you roll back a winning bullish risk reversal?
   a) anytime the long strike goes to ATM +2
   b) when you reach a double top
   c) on Friday before the close of expiration
   d) never

20) When should you roll back a winning bearish risk reversal?
   a) anytime, as long as the market is not rallying
   b) when you reach a double bottom
   c) on Friday, before the close of expiration
   d) only a and b

21) In a trending market, when does a 1 × 2 bullish backspread work best?
   a) if the trend continues in the direction in which you initiated the trade
   b) if both a and c conditions are met
   c) if it is initiated in a low-volatility environment
   d) if it is initiated in a high-volatility environment

22) During a trending market, 1 × 2 bearish backspread works best:
   a) at double tops
   b) when the market is rallying
   c) in a low-volatility environment
   d) in a high-volatility environment

23) Splitting strikes in a 1 × 2 backspread:
   a) increases risk
   b) decreases risk
   c) has greater profit potential than touching strikes
   d) works best in a low-volatility environment

24) In a trending market, rolling up a bullish 1 × 2 backspread:
   a) decreases intratrade risk
   b) is not necessary if you are not concerned about intratrade risk
   c) should only be done in a low-volatility environment
   d) only a and b

25) In a bearish trending market, rolling back a 1 × 2 bearish backspread:
   a) is not necessary if you want to take profit
   b) should be done on Friday
   c) decreases intratrade risk
   d) can be done at anytime

Trading in the Blowoff Phase of the Market

This chapter will feature the final stage of the market, the blowoff, and it is my favorite. When this trade is initiated, almost all the information about the current market is in place. Initially we broke out above or below the congestion at $+/- 1\sigma$ and moved through the trend at $+/- 2,3\sigma$; the market has arrived at $+/- 3\sigma$ and only a small amount of data is not contained under the distribution curve. One of the reasons that I like volatile stocks is that they have blowoffs more frequently.

At this point, the greed of the strong hands will nearly be satisfied and the fear of the weak hands will have reached a point that they are no longer price sensitive; the only thing that they care about is getting back their short options. They will be buying back their short options in order to survive and live another day. They are most likely running out of capital, and the clearinghouse is getting very nervous. They get the tap on the shoulder: Either cover or the brokerage firm will cover for you. Not a good place to be trading from.

Volatility will be through the roof if the market is bottoming. On a rally it should be high, but not as high as if it were breaking.

Here is a good example of what I mean:

During the housing collapse in 2008, volatility set record highs. It reached its zenith on October 24, 2008, with the VIX trading at 89.16 and the price of the OEX market trading at 414.93.

	CALLS					Strikes: 12 ▼			PUTS				
Position	Last X	Net Chng	Bid X	Ask X	Exp		Strike	Bid X	Ask X	Position	Last X	Net Chng
2 14 (1) 100 (Weeklys)												16.03% (
	12.70 Q	-.05	12.45 X	12.95 X	MAY2 14		580	.13 Q	.14 I		.14 Q	-.44
	9.65 M	-.35	10.05 X	10.45 I	MAY2 14		582.5	.21 N	.22 Q		.19 C	-.86
	8.00 Z	+.30	7.70 X	8.10 I	MAY2 14		585	.40 N	.42 Z		.41 Q	-1.29
	5.75 A	+.40	5.70 A	5.90 N	MAY2 14		587.5	.77 Z	.81 N		.77 N	-2.00
	3.95 A	+.70	3.95 H	4.05 Q	MAY2 14		590	1.44 N	1.50 Q		1.51 A	-2.36
	2.58 C	+.38	2.51 H	2.68 N	MAY2 14		592.5	2.50 Q	2.54 Q		2.50 Q	-2.82
	1.42 N	+.12	1.41 H	1.46 N	MAY2 14		595	3.85 N	3.95 Q		3.95 A	-3.15
	.74 N	-.12	.73 N	75 Q	MAY2 14		597.5	5.65 N	5.80 Q		5.70 Z	-3.35
	.34 I	-.21	36 N	38 N	MAY2 14		600	7.80 Q	8.00 C		7.85 C	-3.19
	.18 Q	-.17	.18 N	.19 I	MAY2 14		602.5	9.90 C	10.35 C		10.01 X	-3.38
	.08 I	-.16	.09 N	.10 Z	MAY2 14		605	12.30 X	12.75 X		13.20 Z	-2.55
	.06 X	-.11	.05 Z	.06 Q	MAY2 14		607.5	14.75 A	15.25 A		14.85 X	-4.65
Y 14 (8) 100												17.67% (±
	14.50 Q	+1.75	14.20 C	14.45 H	MAY 14		580	1.76 N	1.80 Z		1.76 I	-1.26
	12.30 B	N/A	12.30 C	12.50 M	MAY 14		582.5	2.31 N	2.36 Q		2.29 H	N/A
	10.50 Q	+1.49	10.50 A	10.65 A	MAY 14		585	2.99 Z	3.05 Q		2.94 Z	-1.64
	8.95 A	N/A	8.85 A	9.00 Q	MAY 14		587.5	3.80 N	3.90 C		3.90 C	N/A
	7.35 N	+1.15	7.35 A	7.50 N	MAY 14		590	4.80 Q	4.90 N		4.91 I	-2.09
	6.00 C	N/A	6.00 I	6.15 N	MAY 14		592.5	5.95 N	6.10 X		6.00 N	N/A
	4.90 Q	+.55	4.85 C	4.95 N	MAY 14		595	7.25 N	7.40 A		7.38 I	-2.42
	3.95 A	N/A	3.85 Z	3.95 C	MAY 14		597.5	8.75 N	8.90 C		8.75 X	N/A
	3.05 A	+.40	2.98 C	3.05 Q	MAY 14		600	10.35 Q	10.55 Q		10.40 N	-2.85
	2.34 Q	N/A	2.30 N	2.34 Q	MAY 14		602.5	12.20 N	12.45 C		12.60 A	N/A
	1.78 I	+.08	1.75 A	1.80 Q	MAY 14		605	14.10 N	14.35 N		14.85 M	-3.00

FIGURE 15.1   (AAPL) Apple Inc. AAPL One- and Eight-Day Option Chain

To make a comparison of what this would mean to an individual stock, go back to the daily AAPL option chain and look at the prices. Figure 15.1 is the AAPL option chain with the stock trading at a volatility of nearly 16 percent. The at-the-money straddle with one day remaining was roughly $5. That meant the option sellers had factored into the market a price movement of +/− 3σ of $10. Earlier, you learned how to price options if the volatility changed, and it is a factor of the air coming into the balloon (Vega). To figure out the price of the ATM if AAPL went from 16 percent to 89 percent, you divide 89 by 16 and multiply it by $5 (the current straddle); the answer is that the ATM in AAPL would go to +/− $27, a 500 percent increase, and that was with one day to go.

The second example is a very volatile stock that we looked at earlier, Priceline. Figure 15.2 is the option chain for PCLN with 178 days to go. It is trading at a volatility of around 31.5 percent and the ATM is trading at roughly $220. To figure what would happen to that ATM, divide 89 by 31.5 and multiply it by $220. The answer is that the new straddle would be trading at roughly $621 and has an expected range of over $1,240; in other words, the entire cap of the company!

Think this can't happen again?

Well if you think it can't, then you don't have a good handle on the markets. **This is why we are never naked options—not only can it happen, it will happen; the only question is when!** Some of the biggest traders of all time have learned that lesson the hard way, and they have taken out many banks and hedge funds with other people's money in them.

If the markets can explode like this, what happens if the volatility changes but the price doesn't?

UNDERLYING

	Last X	Net Chng	Bid X	Ask X	Size	Volume	Open	High	
▷	1230.00 D	+8.96	1229.50 P	1231.50 P	2 x 1	669,764	1222.01	1237.15	1220

OPTION CHAIN Spread: Singe Layout: Last X, Net Change Exchange: Composite

Strikes: 14

CALLS						PUTS			
Last X	Net Chng	Bid X	Ask X	Exp	Strike	Bid X	Ask X	Last X	Net Chng
▷ MAY 14 (24) 100									38.96% (±99
▷ MAY4 14 (31) 100 (Weeklys)									37.44% (±103
▷ MAY5 14 (38) 100 (Weeklys)									33.49% (±107
▷ JUN 14 (59) 100									32.68% (±129
▷ JUL 14 (87) 100									31.68% (±153
▽ OCT 14 (178) 100									31.56% (±220
126.00 Q	+8.78	119.50 C	123.40 X	OCT 14	1200	88.50 X	91.40 X	96.40 Z	0
114.30 X	0	116.90 C	120.80 X	OCT 14	1205	90.60 C	93.60 X	132.80 C	0
120.50 Q	+20.00	114.30 T	118.10 C	OCT 14	1210	93.20 I	96.00 X	101.40 Q	0
120.83 C	0	111.60 T	115.60 X	OCT 14	1215	95.40 X	98.40 X	99.30 Z	-11.10
108.70 Q	+4.00	109.30 C	113.00 X	OCT 14	1220	97.60 X	101.00 X	125.64 C	0
121.48 C	0	106.80 C	110.60 X	OCT 14	1225	100.40 X	103.40 X	159.20 C	0
89.50 N	0	104.20 T	108.00 X	OCT 14	1230	103.00 X	106.00 X	148.50 C	0
106.00 Q	0	102.50 C	105.70 X	OCT 14	1235	105.30 X	108.60 X	138.20 M	0

FIGURE 15.2 (PCLN) Priceline Inc. 178-Day Option Chain

On May 4, 2009, the price of the OEX reached 414.93 again, but this time it was on a rally instead of a break. Traders had anticipated that the worst was over and began to sell puts again. The volatility was still historically high but the VIX had come down to 36.16.

What happened to the people who bought their PCLN straddles at $621?

Unfortunately, they also blew out, but this time it was because they were **long premium in a collapsing volatility market.** Even if there was no time decay in the six months between the zenith and the current volatility, the price of the PCLN straddle would be back to $252 (89.93/−36.16 = −2.46) ($621/2.46) = $252 and the underlying stock price would be exactly where it was six months earlier. The straddle price was still higher than it was six months before, but it is the equivalent of owning a $621 stock that ended up being worth $252.

When the market is at extremes, many traders heed the old expression that it is impossible to catch a falling knife. You will learn that not only is it possible—it is one of the best trades that you can make! Some professional traders do nothing but scan the markets to find this type of trade. The key is to know how to initiate it and how to manage it.

Trade One: Buying an Outright Option

Figure 15.3 is the classic downside blowoff pattern. You have probably seen this pattern many times in the past and were interested in it but were advised to stay away because you can't catch a falling knife. This chapter will teach you what trades you

FIGURE 15.3 Classic V Blowoff pattern

can use and what trades will result in a disaster. **In order to trade the blowoff, you must use two time frames. Before, that was an option; now it is not an option at all. It is impossible to catch the falling knife, but is not impossible to catch it on the first bounce!**

Buying a Call

Buying a call outright in a blowoff is extremely difficult. The premium levels are simply too high. Remember from earlier in the book you learned that the premium levels in each strike are the same. The market makers put them in line through conversions and reversals. It is a riskless trade for them and it keeps the premium equally distributed among the strikes in the option chain. So if a market is blowing off to the bottom, you can be confident that the shorts will be covering at any price. As they buy back their short puts, it inflates the balloon in proportion to the price they are paying to cover, and consequently that premium will overflow into the calls. Even with a few days to go in a blowoff, the premium levels will be dangerously high, and it will be very tough to make money. For this reason, buying a call is not the correct play. **Never buy calls in a blowoff; there are many other trades that are superior.**

Buying an Outright Put Option

It is the exact same problem as you had buying a call. In most cases, the premium will be too great to overcome. Even if you get a big move to the downside, you will lose money. In the fall of 2008, put buyers thought they had the deal of the century.

Many media experts begged them to cover their risk by using puts. Quite a few unethical investment advisers preyed on the panicked longs and sold "secrets" that not only were horrible but compounded the problem. Fortunately, most of the most egregious advisers were later brought to justice and many of them are currently in jail. **Never buy puts in a blowoff; there is a huge downside to this trade and very little upside.**

Trade Two: Credit Spreads

Sell a Bullish 60/40 Credit Spread

Selling credit spreads in a blowoff is different than trading in congestion or trending markets. The reason is that the premium levels rate is extremely high, the air in the balloon is going to make the ATM and ATM +/−1 nearly the same. This is logical as well as mathematically correct. The market will still gyrate around its mean, but with so much uncertainty, the strikes near the ATM will all have similar amounts of premium. Consequently, it will be hard to get the correct 2/3 risk ratio that we looked for in our other trades. If you want to make the ATM your short strike, you will probably need to go to the ATM −2 or −3 for your long strike. This creates more risk and not much extra reward because the market will be flying around at the blowoff bottom. **For that reason, you shouldn't initiate this trade. In this environment, the 60/40 bullish credit spread is a much better choice.** The strikes will most likely be the ATM +2 /−2, but this increased spread gives you real punch for your money. The blowoff is the most directional trade that you will make, and you want a trade that will give you the best chance to catch a big winner. **The 60/40 trade is initiated when the shortest time frame you are observing gives a bullish technical indicator.**

The key to all blowoff trades is to allow the market to tell you that it is ready to stop breaking or rallying. The way that is done is to let your shortest time frame roll over and then make the trade. You are not trying to catch the knife; you are trying to get onboard for what figures to be a nice rally or break.

Rolling Up a Bullish 60/40 Credit Spread; Taking Short-Term Profit

If the market rallies after you initiate the bullish credit spread, you must still manage your winner. The price action in this environment should be very quick. Many times it will cover as much ground up and down in a day as the congestion phase of the market did in a week. Rolling up is much more important in a blowoff market. Unlike before, where it was a suggestion, here it is a rule. You don't want to give up big profits if the market suddenly reverses and heads back to the bottom or top.

When the market advances to at least ATM +4 from my short leg of the credit spread, sell the new ATM 60/40 put spread. If the longest time frame that you are trading is now giving a reversal signal, you can let the old spread stay on the books, as you are now a very big favorite to cash that trade also. If you are conservative and are concerned about a sudden reversal of fortunes, you can buy back the original spread.

Rolling Back a 60/40 Bullish Credit Spread

On Friday, I roll back the bullish credit spread by first selling the new 60/40 spread in the next weekly. I only buy back my existing spread if it is in danger of going out as a loser. If it is beyond the expected range, I will leave it in place. Even if the market starts to move against me that late in the week, I can always take the expiring spread off. Many times, it will be so far out of the money that even adverse price movement will not affect the trade.

Managing the Risk in a Bullish 60/40 Credit Spread

Managing the risk in a 60/40 spread in a blowoff depends on how aggressive you are. It will be harder to turn this spread into an iron condor because the strikes are spread wider due to the increased premium levels. If the spread is a loser when the shortest time frame turns negative, you can't average down if the longest time frame hasn't turned to bullish. If the longest time frame is still bearish, I will take my loser and look for a new entry position if the shortest time frame again goes bullish. If I get a reversal in my shortest time frame and my longest time frame has turned positive, I will average down by selling another 60/40 spread at the better price. **Initiate the trade if the underlying asset price moves to ATM −2. Sell the ATM +2/−2 60/40 put spread. This will double the size of the strike risk but will also double the size of the profit potential.** If the underlying market continues to break, you can add spreads as long as your longest time frame remains in a bullish mode. The original 60/40 put spreads you sold will become debit call spreads. If the longest-term technical indicator reverses and gives you a bearish signal, cover the spreads and take a loss, looking for a new entry point if the shortest signal turns bullish.

Sell a Bearish Credit 60/40 Spread

The bearish credit spread will take place if the market is in a blowoff to the upside. The conditions will be slightly different than a downside blowoff. In this case, the strong hands are the bulls and the shorts are throwing in the towel. You should expect high volatilities but, generally speaking, they will not be as high as a breaking market.

Most likely, it will still be very difficult to get the proper 2/3 risk/reward ratio, so go directly to your 60/40 spread. In this case, we are not trying to catch the falling knife; we are watching a rocket ship reach its zenith and waiting for gravity to take over. **The 60/40 bearish credit trade is initiated when the shortest time frame you are observing gives a short technical indicator. Sell the ATM −2/+2 call spread.**

Rolling Down a Bearish 60/40 Credit Spread; Taking Short-Term Profit

The price action in the upside blowoff phase should be very quick. Rolling down in this spread is a rule. You don't want to give up big profits if the market suddenly reverses and heads back up to new highs. **When the market breaks to at least ATM −4 from my long leg of the credit spread, sell the new ATM 60/40 call spread.** If the longest time frame that you are trading is now giving a bearish signal, you can let the old spread stay on the books, as you are now a very big favorite to cash that trade also. If you are conservative and are concerned about a sudden reversal of fortunes, you can buy back the original spread.

Rolling Back a 60/40 Bearish Credit Spread

On Friday, I roll back the bearish 60/40 spread in the next weekly. I only buy back my existing spread if it is in danger of going out as a loser. If it is beyond the expected range, I will leave it in place. Even if the market starts to move against me that late in the week, I can always take the expiring spread off. Many times, it will be so far out of the money that even adverse price movement will not affect the trade.

Managing the Risk in a Bearish 60/40 Credit Spread

Managing the risk in a bearish 60/40 spread in a blowoff is the mirror image of managing the bullish 60/40. You will probably have the same problem with split strikes because of the higher levels of volatility. If the spread is a loser when the shortest time frame turns positive, you can't average up as you would in a trending market, because the longest time frame will not have turned negative. In this case, I will take my loser and look for a new entry position if the shortest time frame again goes bearish. If I get a reversal in my shortest time frame and my longest time frame has turned positive, I will average up by selling another 60/40 spread at the better price. **Initiate the trade if the underlying asset price moves to ATM +2. Sell the ATM −2 /+2 60/40 call spread. This will double the size of the strike risk but will also double the size of the profit potential.** If the underlying market continues to rally, you can add spreads as long as your longest time frame remains in a bearish frame. The original 60/40 call spreads you sold will become debit put spreads. If the longest-term technical indicator reverses and gives you a bullish signal, cover the spreads and take your loss, looking for a new entry point if my shortest signal turns negative.

In a blowoff market environment, don't trade the traditional ATM +/−1. Look directly to the 60/40 spread.

■ Trade Three: Risk Reversals

Risk Reversal (Synthetic Long)

The risk reversal in a blowoff market is a bread-and-butter trade. It is almost impossible to make a directional trade buying outright options when the volatility levels get to extremes, so using a risk reversal is the ideal trade. You have very little premium risk in the trade and you get the full punch from the price movement if you are correct. If you are wrong and the market gaps against your position, the risk is still limited to the strike risk in the corresponding call/put spread. **The trade will be initiated when the shortest technical time frame that you are observing turns positive.** The only variation in this trade will be that you must increase the strike risk in the short put spread to accommodate the extremes of premium. If you are using the ATM−1,−2 call/put, you probably will need to buy the ATM −5, −6 put to complete the trade. This does increase your downside risk but it is worth it to keep any premium to a minimum in case the market suddenly stalls and the short sellers take the air out of the balloon.

Rolling Up a Synthetic Long; Locking in Profits

I will roll up if the ATM moves more than two strikes to the upside. I **sell a vertical call spread, replacing my old ATM −1,−2 with a new ATM −1,−2.** I don't have to replace the put spread because it will offer some protection against a catastrophic gap opening, but rolling up locks in more profit. I believe that not rolling up when the ATM goes two strikes in your favor is a mistake. I don't make it a rule, as it is in the 60/40 credit spread, but I believe in cutting intratrade risk as much as possible.

Rolling Back a Synthetic Long

On Friday, I roll back the risk reversal by first **selling** the horizontal call spread. In this trade you must sell your long call and buy the next weekly serial ATM −1−2 call. After the roll is in place I sell the ATM−5 −6 put spread. Unless the trade is going badly and my expiring ATM−5 −6 put spread is in danger of going in the money, I let it expire worthless.

Managing Risk in a Synthetic Long

This trade is managed similar to the trending market trade. If I get a sell signal in my shortest time frame that I am trading and the longest trend is still negative, I exit the trade by selling the call and buying back my put spread. If the long-term trend has changed, I exit my call and leave the put spread in place. Most likely I am locking in profit. If the short-term signal becomes bullish again, I replace the original call with the ATM −1,−2 and recycle the trade. If the major trend turns bearish before I get a signal to reenter, I buy back my put spread and look for a new entry point.

Risk Reversal (Synthetic Short)

The risk reversal at the blowoff top will be treated very similar to the blowoff bottom. Since we are initiating it from the short side of the market, the OTM calls should not be blown up as much as the puts in the blowoff low. The premium risk will be somewhat mitigated, and you can probably sell the ATM +2, 4, or 5 call spread. **The trade will be initiated when the shortest technical time frame that you are observing turns negative.** If you are using the ATM +1,+ 2 put/call, you probably will need to buy the ATM +2,+4 call to complete the trade. The upside risk is cut down considerably if are able to buy a call closer to your short.

Rolling Down a Synthetic Short; Locking in Profits

I will roll down if the ATM moves more than two strikes to the downside. I **sell a vertical put spread, replacing my old ATM +1,+2 with a new ATM +1,+2.** I don't have to replace the call spread because it will offer some protection against a catastrophic gap opening, but rolling down locks in more profit. I believe that not rolling down when the ATM goes two strikes in your favor is a mistake. I don't make it a rule, as it is in the 60/40 credit spread, but I believe in cutting intratrade risk as much as possible.

Rolling Back a Synthetic Short

On Friday, I roll back the risk reversal by first **selling** the horizontal put spread. In this trade, you must sell your long put and then buy the next weekly serial ATM +1+2 put. After the roll is in place, I sell the ATM +1,+2 +4 −5 call spread. Unless the trade is going badly and my expiring ATM +1, +2 +4 −5 call spread is in danger of going in the money, I let it expire worthless.

Managing Risk in a Synthetic Short

This trade is managed similar to a bearish trade in a trending market. If I get a buy signal in the shortest time frame that I am trading and the longest trend is still bullish

I exit the trade by selling the put and buying back my call spread. If the long-term trend has changed I exit my put and leave the call spread in place. If the short term signal becomes bearish again I replace the original put with the ATM +1,+2 and recycle the trade. If the major trend turns bullish before I get a signal to reenter, I buy back my call spread and look for a new entry point.

Risk reversals are the only way to go when you want to get short a runaway market and want an unlimited reward, limited risk trade. No FINRA problems, no Reg T problems, and you will get the full benefit if you are correct as to the next move in price. If you are wrong, your risk is limited.

■ Trade Four: Backspread (1 × 2 for Even)

The backspread works very well in many market and premium environments, but at blowoff levels you can get quite a bit of heartburn using it. You have a number of issues to deal with in the blowoff environment that weren't a problem when the market was in congestion and when it is trending.

You are buying two options and selling one, so you are long Vegas. Being long premium when the balloon is full of air is not a good idea. Earlier in the chapter, you observed what can happen if you buy premium in a contracting phase of the option market; you get hammered. Even if the market moves substantially when the fear or greed starts to be accounted for, sellers that had the capital to survive the combination of negative price movement and the escalating premium will be waiting, and they will be selling it with both hands. In addition, the traders that were long air during the explosion are going to want to take profit, and they also know that the current premium levels probably will not support the underlying asset's price movement. They will join their former adversaries and become sellers in the new market.

The second problem is an extension of the first one. In order to do the trade anywhere near Vega neutral, you are going to need to split your strikes quite a bit, and this can create an ugly problem near expiration. Unlike the low premium environments where the tight strikes prices offset almost all of the expiration risk in a high-Vega environment, they do the opposite; they create a huge risk. As an example, if you had to split your strikes by 3 or 4 to get a proper Vega fit, and the market decides to pin on expiration at your long strike, there is no defense for this type of price movement. Your short strike will now be near parity, and even though your long strike will contain two options with some air in them, the trade will blow up on you.

The third problem will be if the market remains close to your short strike on expiration. It will be the ATM and the trend will rotate around that mean, most likely $+/-1\sigma$. Your two long options will be too far away from your short to help, and you will be tortured by the short strike until the last few minutes. Of course, if you are dead right about price, then the trade works very well, but if you are correct in predicting the price movement, the risk reversal works much better. You are buying two options in that trade and selling one, so you are long an extra option. However, much of the Vega risk is alleviated because you buy and sell the same amount of Vega in your two ATM $+1/-1$ options. You will own much less Vega in the out-of-the-money put/call and so a complete collapse of premium will not hurt you nearly as much. On the other hand, if you are wrong about price, you don't have any pin risk, only the market risk, as in all trades.

In a blowoff market, don't use 1×2 backspreads unless you can get touching strikes. Employ either credit spreads or risk reversals.

Summary

This chapter married the trades with the blowoff phase of the market. Not all trades get the best results when the fear is at its greatest. You can use any trade in this market, but buying options outright is very risky, particularly buying puts when the market is at extremes. The next chapter will be on how to select a portfolio, but before that there is a quiz on the principles of this chapter.

Chapter 15 Quiz

All the questions refer to trades made in the blowoff phase of the market, whether stated or not.

1) In the blowoff phase of the market, when can buying a call be initiated?
    a) Buy the call anytime the technical signals are bullish.
    b) Buy the call when the shortest time frame you are observing turns positive.
    c) Buy the call when the market breaks out above 3σ.
    d) Buying a call in blowoff is not suggested.

2) In the blowoff phase of the market, when can buying a put be initiated?
    a) Buy the put anytime technical signals are bearish.
    b) Buy when the shortest time frame you are observing turns negative.
    c) Buy when your technical indicators turn negative.
    d) None of the above is correct.

3) In the blowoff phase of the market, volatility will be:
    a) low, as price is not moving between $+/- 2, 3\sigma$
    b) high, if the market is rallying
    c) at extremes, particularly if the market is breaking
    d) none of the above

4) In the blowoff phase of the market, buying options outright is usually:
   a) the first choice of most traders
   b) a safe bet, as the risk is limited and the reward is unlimited
   c) dangerous, as you might be right with price direction but still suffer premium losses
   d) none of the above

5) As a general rule, in the blowoff phase of the market, buying options:
   a) is not a good trade, if the market is rallying
   b) can make money even if the price goes down slightly
   c) is no longer a safe trade
   d) is difficult to overcome the premium levels

6) When should a bull credit spread (vertical) be initiated?
   a) The market goes through your longest strike.
   b) Your shortest technical indicator turns positive.
   c) Volatility is dropping.
   d) Both a and b.

7) In a blowoff market, a bull ATM credit spread (vertical) can make money even if:
   a) the market remains at the same price
   b) the market rallies strongly
   c) volatility collapses
   d) all of the above

8) In a blowoff market, a bear ATM credit spread (vertical) can make money even if:
   a) the market remains at the same price
   b) the market rallies slightly
   c) the market breaks
   d) all of the above

9) In a blowoff market, a 60/40 bull credit spread:
   a) has more reward possible than a 60/40 bear spread
   b) has a greater reward than an ATM bull credit spread
   c) can only make money if you are correct in predicting price
   d) only b and c

10) In a blowoff market, never use a credit spread
   a) when volatility is rising
   b) when you can buy an outright option for the same risk
   c) A credit spread can always be used in any market condition
   d) all of the above

11) In a blowoff market, profit can be taken on a credit spread:
   a) when price goes through the long strike
   b) when your shortest-term signal gives you a reversal
   c) on any Friday
   d) when it expires

12) In a blowoff market, how can an ATM credit spread be defended?
   a) Stop yourself out and reverse to the opposite credit spread.
   b) Turn it into an iron condor.
   c) You have limited risk; don't defend it.
   d) None of the above is correct.

13) In a blowoff market, if you turn an ATM credit spread into an iron condor, you can:
   a) never lose more than the net credit no matter what price does
   b) cash one side of the trade if you don't readjust
   c) cash both sides of the trade if price expires between your short strikes
   d) both b and c

14) During a blowoff market, a risk reversal should be initiated:
   a) when the shortest time frame you are observing turns bearish
   b) when the shortest time frame you are observing turns positive
   c) when your technical indicators turn positive
   d) all of the above

15) A bullish risk reversal resembles a call in that:
   a) both have unlimited reward and limited risk
   b) both should be initiated in a low-volatility environment
   c) both can make money even if the price goes slightly lower
   d) both b and c

16) A bearish risk reversal in a blowoff market resembles a put in that:
   a) both have unlimited reward and limited risk
   b) both should be initiated in a high-volatility environment
   c) both can make money, even if the price goes slightly lower
   d) both b and c

17) In a blowoff market, when should a bullish risk reversal be rolled up?
   a) The underlying asset begins to break.
   b) The long strike goes at least to an ATM +2.
   c) Never let the winner run.
   d) You don't need to roll up if you want to accept the intratrade risk.

18) When should a bearish risk reversal be rolled down?
   a) The underlying asset begins to break.

b) The long strike goes at least to an ATM −2.

c) The volatility suddenly rises.

d) You don't need to roll down if you want to accept the intratrade risk.

19) In a blowoff market, when should you roll back a winning bullish risk reversal?

a) anytime the long strike goes to ATM +2

b) when you reach a double top

c) on Friday, before the close of expiration

d) never

20) When should you roll back a winning bearish risk reversal?

a) anytime, as long as the market is not rallying

b) when you reach a double bottom

c) on Friday, before the close of expiration

d) only a and b

21) In a blowoff market, when does a 1 × 2 bullish backspread work best?

a) The trend continues in the direction in which you initiated the trade.

b) Don't use bullish backspreads in blowoff market; there are better trades.

c) Both a and d are correct.

d) It is initiated in a high-volatility environment.

22) During a bullish market, when does a 1 × 2 bearish backspread work best?

a) at double tops

b) when the market is rallying

c) in a low-volatility environment

d) in a high-volatility environment

23) Splitting strikes in a 1 × 2 backspread:

a) increases risk

b) decreases risk

c) has greater profit potential than touching strikes

d) works best in a low-volatility environment

24) In a blowoff market, rolling up a bullish 1 × 2 backspread:

a) decreases intratrade risk

b) is not necessary if you are not concerned about intratrade risk

c) should only be done in a low-volatility environment

d) only a and b

25) In a bearish blowoff market, rolling back a 1 × 2 bearish backspread:

a) is not necessary if you want to take profit

b) should be done on Friday

c) decreases intratrade risk

d) can be done at anytime

Selecting a Portfolio to Trade

So far, you have learned how to do many things trading weekly options. The book started with a section on market psychology, understanding how your opponent thinks and why that is important. It examined how markets are organized and how they trade, identified the various market participants and how they sculpt the market results. It explained why it is important to always trade in liquid markets and how to recognize the characteristics that constitute liquidity. The phases of the market were identified and a mathematical explanation was given to describe how and why they rotate around the mean. The option model was dissected, and you were taught how to price it like a professional market maker. Simple trades were suggested that would allow you to successfully trade in any market conditions. Finally, the trades were married to the market conditions and the ones that work best when it is in any of the market phases.

All of the preliminary information is now in place, and it is time to learn how to organize and trade a portfolio.

All of the technical work that has been done so far will not help you if you don't know how to organize a portfolio of stocks. **This is one of the most important aspects of trading, because your portfolio represents all of your liquid assets, cash!** If you don't know where to invest your money, the chances of beating the market will go to zero. The portfolio that you select must be in proportion to the amount of risk capital that you have to work with; in addition, the diversification of the portfolio is vitally important.

The selection process will be done in four steps, and it is a screening process that is universal. By that, it means that the only thing that changes is the amount of risk capital that you have to trade. The principles remain the same.

Liquidity

By now, you are probably tired of hearing about liquidity, but recognizing liquidity in a portfolio is slightly different than liquidity in an individual trade. Figure 16.1 is an option chain from Bank of America, which has been one of the most liquid stocks since the beginning of the Great Recession six years ago. By that, I mean that the number of shares that are traded each day and the tightness of the bid–offer spread make it ideally suited for all of the high-frequency traders. They don't pay any commission, and, in fact, they are paid a commission for providing liquidity; the spreads are 1c wide so no problem there. At first glance, this would seem to be an ideal candidate for a small trader to get involved in, but when you examine the option chain, you can see that there are some problems to overcome.

First is the absolute size of the stock. It is priced at around $15 a share and barely moves off of that number. The expected range is less than 0.75 a week, and the entire value is only $1,500. Because of the absolute dollar size of the underlying stock, it is not tradable. The credit spreads are so small that it is a waste of time to trade, and the commissions don't shrink because of the size of the underlying stock. This type of stock cannot go in your portfolio.

So, although at first glance this stock is liquid, when you dig deeper into the underlying issues, it can't be traded.

Figure 16.2 is an option chain of Caterpillar Inc. It is also a very liquid stock, and on first glance, it appears to have all of the characteristics that a trader could want. Good bid–offer spreads, a much wider expected price range, almost $4, and the credit spreads have enough meat to enable you to trade them. The total value of the underlying stock is a little over $10,300. This is an ideal candidate for any trader and should be included in your portfolio.

UNDERLYING								
Last X	Net Chng	Bid X	Ask X	Size	Volume	Open	High	Low
15.24 N	+.29	15.20 K	15.21 Q	159 x 15	155,338,090	15.04	15.30	14.9

TRADE GRID

OPTION CHAIN Spread: Single Layout: Volume, Open Interest Exchange: Composite

CALLS				Strikes: 14		PUTS			
Volume	Open Int	Bid X	Ask X	Exp	Strike	Bid X	Ask X	Volume	Open Int
MAY1 14 (3) 100 (Weeklys)								29.50% (±0.3	
5	5	3.15 C	3.25 Q	MAY1 14	12	0 B	.01 H	0	0
0	8	2.66 I	2.76 I	MAY1 14	12.5	0 T	.01 N	0	0
0	0	2.18 I	2.25 I	MAY1 14	13	0 B	.01 M	10	477
0	104	1.67 X	1.74 Q	MAY1 14	13.5	0 B	.01 X	0	5
268	346	1.23 Q	1.24 Q	MAY1 14	14	0 B	.01 M	93	2,542
2,891	4,104	.74 Q	.76 Q	MAY1 14	14.5	.01 Q	.02 M	5,620	6,315
10,708	17,346	.30 H	.31 Q	MAY1 14	15	.07 I	.08 C	9,590	14,633
19,555	15,249	.04 X	.05 Q	MAY1 14	15.5	.31 Q	.32 Q	5,115	6,585
771	12,984	0 B	.01 M	MAY1 14	16	.76 I	.77 Q	2,953	10,651
1,065	18,607	0 B	.01 X	MAY1 14	16.5	1.25 M	1.31 X	632	2,556
41	11,189	0 X	.01 X	MAY1 14	17	1.75 I	1.81 X	143	822
52	5,880	0 Z	.01 M	MAY1 14	17.5	2.25 I	2.31 I	24	282
10	8,683	0 Z	.01 M	MAY1 14	18	2.76 I	2.80 I	0	219
230	2,139	0 M	.01 M	MAY1 14	18.5	3.25 Q	3.35 Q	0	4

FIGURE 16.1 (BAC) Bank of America Three-Day Option Chain

FIGURE 16.2 (CAT) Caterpillar Inc. Three-Day Option Chain

UNDERLYING

	Last X	Net Chng	Bid X	Ask X	Size	Volume	Open	High	Low
▷	103.69 N	+1.05	103.52 P	103.69 P	4 x 3	4,533,140	102.78	104.1362	102.76

TRADE GRID

OPTION CHAIN Spread: Single Layout: Last X, Net Change Exchange: Composite

	CALLS			Strikes: 14			PUTS		
Last X	Net Chng	Bid X	Ask X	Exp	Strike	Bid X	Ask X	Last X	Net Chng
APR4 14 (3) 100 (Weekly)									45.23% (±3.73)
6.95 M	+.55	6.75 X	7.06 X	APR4 14	97	.19 Z	.23 C	.18 Z	-.05
5.31 C	0	5.90 X	6.25 X	APR4 14	98	.28 Q	.31 A	.27 C	-.07
5.17 B	+1.77	5.05 X	5.20 A	APR4 14	99	.41 Q	.44 A	.40 I	-.07
4.36 C	+1.21	4.25 A	4.40 X	APR4 14	100	.59 Q	.62 Q	.56 C	-.14
3.60 Q	+1.12	3.50 C	3.60 C	APR4 14	101	.83 Z	.87 A	.84 X	-.13
3.10 N	+1.15	2.82 Z	2.89 C	APR4 14	102	1.13 C	1.18 C	1.14 Z	-.24
2.39 I	+.99	2.21 M	2.28 C	APR4 14	103	1.52 X	1.55 A	1.53 A	-.36
1.77 N	+.82	1.68 Q	1.73 A	APR4 14	104	1.97 C	2.03 A	1.99 Q	-.67
1.28 I	+.63	1.23 I	1.26 Q	APR4 14	105	2.51 X	2.59 C	2.41 C	-1.39
.89 I	+.50	.87 C	.91 C	APR4 14	106	3.05 X	3.25 C	3.06 C	-.69
.72 Z	+.48	.59 C	.64 Q	APR4 14	107	3.55 X	4.00 C	3.55 A	N/A
.49 N	+.35	.39 I	.42 Q	APR4 14	108	4.40 X	4.80 X	4.62 C	N/A
.25 X	+.18	.25 Q	.27 H	APR4 14	109	5.15 X	5.65 X	5.40 X	N/A

FIGURE 16.2 (CAT) Caterpillar Inc. Three-Day Option Chain

UNDERLYING

	Last X	Net Chng	Bid X	Ask X	Size	Volume	Open	High	Low
▷	1230.00 D	+8.96	1229.50 P	1231.50 P	2 x 1	669,764	1222.01	1237.15	1220.15

TRADE GRID

OPTION CHAIN Spread: Single Layout: Last X, Net Change Exchange: Composite

	CALLS			Strikes: 14			PUTS		
Last X	Net Chng	Bid X	Ask X	Exp	Strike	Bid X	Ask X	Last X	Net Chng
APR4 14 (3) 100 (Weekly)									25.17% (±24.635)
22.00 Q	+5.00	20.40 X	21.70 X	APR4 14	1215	5.60 X	6.40 W	6.10 Z	-6.10
20.00 C	+4.30	18.70 W	20.40 X	APR4 14	1217.5	6.30 X	7.20 X	6.61 C	-9.29
17.01 I	+2.91	17.10 W	18.30 X	APR4 14	1220	7.10 X	8.10 X	8.10 Z	-6.30
15.50 C	+3.15	15.60 I	16.80 X	APR4 14	1222.5	8.10 X	9.20 X	8.39 W	-9.81
15.00 Z	+3.70	14.10 X	15.00 I	APR4 14	1225	9.20 H	10.10 X	9.80 Z	-8.00
13.00 C	+2.80	12.60 X	13.80 X	APR4 14	1227.5	10.30 X	11.10 H	10.61 W	-8.79
12.00 Z	+2.70	11.50 X	12.50 W	APR4 14	1230	11.40 X	12.30 X	12.00 A	-10.20
11.00 X	+3.19	10.40 W	11.30 X	APR4 14	1232.5	12.80 X	13.60 X	13.40 A	-10.17
9.30 X	+1.50	9.30 W	10.10 X	APR4 14	1235	14.10 X	15.00 X	14.80 N	-7.80
8.50 Q	+1.75	8.30 X	9.10 X	APR4 14	1237.5	15.60 X	16.40 X	16.30 X	-13.90
7.30 Q	+1.30	7.30 X	8.00 Z	APR4 14	1240	17.10 X	18.00 X	17.70 N	-12.40
8.52 C	+3.52	6.50 X	7.20 X	APR4 14	1242.5	18.80 X	19.60 X	20.50 N	-10.60
6.20 Q	+1.10	5.70 X	6.20 Q	APR4 14	1245	20.50 X	21.30 X	21.50 Z	-16.30

FIGURE 16.3 (PCLN) Priceline Inc. Day Option Chain

Figure 16.3 is Priceline, and you should be able to immediately see the difference. The bid–offer spread is getting much wider. The market makers are not willing to keep the spreads 1 to 5 cents wide; they need some room to maneuver. The expected range is over $24 and the total price for the stock is $123,000. This is the opposite extreme of BAC. This stock is tradable, but you need to have a very large amount of risk capital to even think about trading this stock.

When establishing a portfolio the three factors concerning liquidity are: the bid–offer spread, the expected range of the stock, and the size of the underlying security.

You will be looking for stocks that are somewhere in between Priceline and Bank of America. There are hundreds of stocks that fit that mold, and they are constantly changing. Three years ago, Facebook didn't exist as a public company, and now it is one of the most liquid in the world. Tight spreads, price of over $50 a share, and good ranges. Look for stocks that are priced at $50 or higher or have a good history of volatility.

Volatility

Liquidity was the first trait that we looked at; the second trait is volatility. **Volatility is the amount of air in the balloon in relation to the underlying stock price**. As an example, two stocks can be priced at $50. One is a utility that has been trading in a $5 range for the past year. It is a dividend stock and is very stable. It is possible something could happen that would change the price of the stock suddenly, but the chances are slim. The average expected range for a weekly option would probably be in the $1 range.

The second stock that we are looking at is a green energy stock that went public last year at $11 a share but is now trading at $50 a share. This segment of the market has a great degree of uncertainty. The stock has more than quadrupled in price in the past year, and you would think that it would have a much wider expected range; based on history, you can be sure that the expected range will be at least $4 and probably more.

When we price a portfolio, in addition to liquidity you need to factor in volatility. If you are choosing between two stocks with similar dollar prices, **the more volatile stock is the one you want in your portfolio**.

If you are an investor, you like to have a very smooth ride in which you very rarely trade in the marketplace; you don't care if you get a lot of price movement, you just want long-term return. A trader needs to a lot of price movement to make up for the slippage that is lost in bid–offer spreads and commissions.

Diversification by Product

Diversification by product is the next step in the process of establishing your portfolio. You want to make sure that the stocks that you are picking are all not from the same group (duplication). This should be logical; you want to make sure that if one segment of the market is bullish and another is bearish you balance your portfolio between the two segments.

As an example, if you decide that you want to trade a financial stock, you can look at a number of them and put the first two steps, liquidity and volatility, to the test. You then can decide from your technical indicators which one appears to give you the best chance currently to cash a ticket. Place that stock in your portfolio and then go on to the next group. **When you have at least five stocks from different groups in place, you are ready to begin trading**.

In addition to trading your portfolio, you must watch additional stocks in the groupings to make sure that you are keeping your portfolio up to date. If you are trading at the maximum portfolio size of $100,000+ you should be observing at least 50 stocks that fit the criteria of liquidity and volatility at all times. Even if you are trading at the minimum size of $1,000, you need at least 10 stocks in your observation list.

Diversification by Dollar Risk

This is an extremely important concept, and one that is commonly misused not only by first time traders, but by many veterans as well. **Dollar diversification is used to offset probability risk**.

Here is how it works.

We are back in the casino again, playing blackjack. This time we are the house, and there are two players against us. One is betting $500 a hand and one is betting $5 a hand. We know the odds are slightly in our favor, as we have the mathematical edge, so in the long run, we should expect the same results no matter which player wins. As a matter of fact, we are happy to see the big shooter, because, in theory, he should lose more to us in the long run. But here is where the problem comes in. Suppose the big shooter is an expert card counter and the $5 player is having fun. The $5 player is there to enjoy the thrill. If he loses his $50 bankroll, he is out the door; it doesn't have any effect on him. The $500 player is trying to beat the house, and in the long run, maybe he is good enough to do it. Since the players are so unbalanced, the casino could win its theoretical drop but lose money—not a good situation to be in.

This is the same problem that you will encounter if you don't account for the dollar difference in your portfolio. The reason I used the $50 stocks earlier was to show you that diversification by price and group is not enough. Suppose that your portfolio holds 100 shares of the $50 utility stock that has an average weekly move of $1 and 100 shares of the $50 green energy stock that has an average range of about $4. You should be able to see that you are not balanced; you would need to win four times as much in the utility stock on average to offset one theoretical loss in the green stock, assuming the loss was realized at the expected move.

In other words, you could win 75 percent of your trades and still lose money! An unbalanced dollar portfolio is more dangerous than one containing too many stocks of the same grouping. One hundred shares of Caterpillar is not the same as trading 100 shares of Netflix, and you must accommodate this in order to dollar balance your portfolio.

Table 16.1 is an example of a balanced portfolio. It contains five stocks that were taken from the "**Days until Expiration**" table in the back of the book. The stocks

TABLE 16.1	Sample Portfolio	
Stock symbol	**Current price**	**+/−3σ (Weekly EV)**
FB 2.32	72.30	2.32
GMCR 4.16	117.74	4.12
GS 3.18	169.42	3.18
SPY 2.21	192.65	2.21
LVS 2.35	71.86	2.35

are from five different underlying groups and represent a good cross section of what you can expect from any portfolio. Dollar balancing your portfolio is done in steps.

Step one

Take the stock with the highest Weekly EV and assign it a value of 1.

Step two

Divide the EV of all other stocks buy the EV in the highest stock.

Step three

Trade the remainder of step two and assign it the proper number or contracts.

In this example, GMCR has the highest EV of 4.12. It receives an assignment of 1. FB has an EV if 2.32. When you divide that by 1, you get 2.32 contracts. Always round to the nearest number of contracts; don't be concerned if your ratios are slightly off; unless you are trading hundreds of contracts, the rounding will have no effect. The idea is to balance the dollars in the portfolio as close as you can to the current EV levels.

Notice in Table 16.2 that the correlation between price and volatility doesn't hold as much weight as you would think. GMCR is the third highest priced underlying stock, but it is almost twice as volatile as the top dollar-weighted stock, SPY. **If you were only looking at the nominal price, you would think that you would want to trade roughly two contracts of SPY for every one you traded in GMCR—the exact opposite of what you want to do!**

■ Summary

This is a very important chapter, as it is the foundation of how you create and manage your portfolio. Managing cash is the most important part of trading. If you want to compete with professional traders, you need to know how they look at the market. They are always trying to figure out a way to reduce their exposure. Unless it is a market-making function where they are the house, they are not going to get

Stock symbol	Current price	+/−3σ (Weekly EV)	# of Contracts /Spreads
FB 2.32	72.30	2.32	2
GMCR 4.16	117.74	4.12	1
GS 3.18	169.42	3.18	1 or 2
SPY 2.21	192.65	2.21	2
LVS 2.35	71.86	2.35	2

TABLE 16.2 Weekly Days until Expiration Table

involved in illiquid markets. They will trade a balanced portfolio, and you should also trade one.

▪ Chapter 16 Quiz

1) What is true about creating a tradable portfolio?
   a) It is a must if you want to be successful.
   b) It protects cash, your most important asset.
   c) It is important to trading efficiently.
   d) All of the above are true.

2) When choosing a portfolio, liquidity is:
   a) the most important property
   b) not as important as price
   c) variable from group to group
   d) all of the above

3) Liquidity is defined by:
   a) the price of the underlying stock
   b) the bid–offer spread
   c) commission rates
   d) all of the above

4) Stocks under $20 a share generally:
   a) lack liquidity for a retail trader
   b) are a good trade for the retail trader
   c) are much less risky than higher-priced stocks
   d) are a good place to trade while learning options

5) How do weekly expected ranges (EV) influence picking a stock for trading purposes?
   a) The smaller the EV, the better, because they are less risky.
   b) EV has no effect on trading weekly options.

c) EVs are very important in choosing a stock to trade.

d) Bigger EVs make the stock more liquid.

6) What is true about selling credit spreads in a low EV trading environment?

    a) It is a good learning tool with low risk.

    b) It is impossible to overcome the commissions in the long run.

    c) Selling credit spreads is profitable if the price of the stock is high enough.

    d) Only a and c are true.

7) If you have a choice of two stocks in the same grouping:

    a) Trade the one with the highest EV.

    b) Trade the one with the lowest EV.

    c) Trade the one with the highest price.

    d) Trade the one with the lowest price.

8) What is the minimum number of stocks necessary to trade a portfolio?

    a) no minimum

    b) 3

    c) 5

    d) 12

9) If you are a 100K trader, how many stocks should you observe?

    a) 10

    b) 20

    c) 30

    d) 50

10) How many stock groups should you observe as a minimum?

    a) 3

    b) 5

    c) 20

    d) 50

11) Stocks in the same grouping are priced at $37 and $60. Which should you trade?

    a) the higher-priced stock

    b) the lower-priced stock

    c) the lowest EV stock

    d) the highest EV stock

12) What is dollar diversification used for?

    a) offsetting an imbalance of dollar risk when comparing stocks

    b) ensuring that one winner is the same as the other

    c) balancing your portfolio by EV

    d) all of the above

13) The first step to diversification by dollar risk is:
   a) assign the highest EV stock a value of 1
   b) assign the lowest EV stock a value of 1
   c) pick the median stock and supply it a value of 1
   d) none of the above

14) The second step to diversification by dollar risk is:
   a) divide the EV of all possible stocks by the EV of the highest ranked
   b) multiply the EV of all possible stocks by the EV of the highest ranked
   c) take the ratio of EVs and divide it by 2
   d) none of the above

15) What is true about comparing the nominal price of two stocks?
   a) It might not be relevant to their respective EVs.
   b) It might help to derive expected EVs.
   c) It will help to decide which stock has the lowest EV.
   d) It might help to dollar diversify.

Managing Your Equity

Most of the work so far has centered on how to view and execute trades in the weekly options market. The previous chapter examined how to take those trades and turn them into a workable portfolio. Once you have the portfolio in place, it is necessary to learn how to manage it in relation to your capital base. Understanding risk and the management of that risk will be vital to your success. Your danger in trading will vary, depending on what type of trade you are using. If you are using vertical credit spreads exclusively, both the risk and reward are clearly defined and you can develop a strategy that will accommodate the level of risk you can absorb. If you want to be more aggressive and use strategies that allow for unlimited reward and limited risk, you must have more capital available. This chapter will be devoted to how you calculate risk and how that translates into what type of trading you can afford to enter into.

■ Risk of Ruin

The risk of ruin is a concept that relates to all forms of gambling, insurance, and finance. Earlier in the book, examples were given about games of chance and how a single event could ruin your chances of winning a specific hand or game. It showed that games are divided into two categories—favorable and unfavorable. Favorable games are ones that give you a very strong probability of winning in the long run. Unfavorable games are just the opposite; the chances of winning in the long run are very slim at best. Trading weekly options within the parameters of this book is a favorable game. In the long run, you are much more likely to win than you are to lose, but you must make sure that you are around to be involved in the long run.

Your trading will run in a series of streaks commonly known as the variance. Sometimes it will be in a congestion pattern that will vacillate around the mean of your risk capital. It may last for days or weeks or even longer before it breaks out. When you are winning, everything will go your way. If the market is in congestion, you will be buying the double bottoms and selling the double tops, and it will be magical. When the market is trending, you will hit it perfectly, taking profit on retracements and then reentering to stay with the trend. When the conditions favor a blowoff trade and your short-term technical indicates an entry point, the market will magically turn for you on a dime. When things are going wrong, the opposite will happen: Double tops and bottoms will fail to hold and the market will break out to the trend just in time to reverse your position at a false breakout. When the blowoffs occur, they will move just far enough to get you out of your position before reversing.

If you are trading correctly, you will begin to notice that your capital resembles a bull market—it will have a positive slope but will also have retracements where it will dip below the mean, recover, and then go higher.

In order to ensure your success, your capital must be managed prudently. The big question is, what is sensible when it comes to your capital?

Every trader has a different idea of what is rational. Some traders believe that they are being conservative, while actually they are wildly aggressive. Others think that they are aggressive, while in actuality they are just the opposite. In this next section, the mathematics of risk will be discussed. If you learn this concept, it will be very useful to you not only when you are trading weekly options but also when you must make other decisions that involve probability and odds.

Our calculations to determine risk will take three factors into consideration: risk capital, volatility, and win rate.

■ Risk Capital

The term **risk capital** means exactly that—it is money that, if it is lost will not affect the way you live. It doesn't mean it will be like the blackjack player with $50 who wants to experience the thrill of trying to beat the house. It will be more important to you than that, but if everything goes wrong in your trading, it will not change your lifestyle. If you place too much capital at risk, the markets will beat you. Your decisions will be influenced by the risk and you will not be able to handle the pressure. All traders reach a point where they can no longer effectively handle the risk, and if you have too much of personal net worth at risk, the pressure will get the best of you.

Volatility

The amount of air in the balloon is a major factor, and later you will see how it affects your risk capital mathematically. Basically, the higher the volatility, the less risk capital you have to play with. The reason is the amount of noise or the rotation around the mean will become greater; the market will still fluctuate within 1σ, but the difference is that if the current 1σ is $+/-3.00$, it could double or triple as the uncertainty increases. That will place additional strain on your capital base, and that means more fluctuation in your trading profits.

Win Rate

The percentage of trades that are winners will also have a strong effect on your ability to trade. Here are a couple of examples of what it can mean.

Assume that you have two possible methods to trade.

The first method picks 90 percent winners and has an average win of 0.25 percent with an average loss of 1 percent. In this case, the win rate is 0.90, and every 10 trades that you make will average .125 percent profit $(.90 \times .25 - 1.00) = 0.125$. If your risk capital is $1,000 after 10 trades, you will have made $125.00. It doesn't seem like much of an edge, but if you are making three trades a week, you will have more than doubled your bankroll with very little risk.

The second method picks 10 percent winners and it has an average win of 10.5 percent; the average loss is 1 percent. In this case, your average win is higher. That is, 0.150 percent versus 0.125 percent $(.10 \times 10.5\%) - (-1 \times .90) = 0.150$. After 10 trades, you would have made $150 on average. If the second method of trading returns 20 percent more than method number one, which method should you choose?

If you took the higher return, you are risky trader, because even though on average you get a 20 percent higher return per trade, the **variance** is nine times as great. The first method has a very low variance and will make your trading much smoother. There is nothing wrong with the second method, but your losing streaks will be much worse and it will be more stressful. **The greater the variance, the longer the losing streaks will be when you are trading**. If you trade with a method that has a higher percentage of wins, you will be able to withstand losing streaks much better. In general, go with the method that gives you the highest percentage of winning trades.

Table 17.1 shows how this concept looks when you apply some statistical analysis to the problem. It assumes a constant win rate and then looks at the starting capital and how much it will be affected by a rise in volatility. The actual numbers are not that important, but as you can see, the lower the amount of capital you start

TABLE 17.1	Risk of Ruin		
Capital	Win Rate	VIX	Risk of Ruin
20×Win	.005%	10%	1.7%
40×Win	.005%	10%	0.5%
80×Win	.005%	10%	0.1%
Capital	Win Rate	VIX	Risk of Ruin
20×Win	.005%	20%	6.2%
40×Win	.005%	20%	1.8%
80×Win	.005%	20%	0.3%

with in relation to the volatility, the higher your chances of going broke become. The more equity that you start with, the better the cushion, even as volatility rises significantly.

Starting Capital

Starting capital is very important. If you have too much capital in reserve, you will not be able to get a very good rate of return; if you have too little, the chances of ruin are very high. **As a rule, you should never risk more than 3 to 4 percent of your capital in any trade**. If you have $1,000 to trade, you must pick strategies that lose no more than $30 to $40 a trade. As long as you don't duplicate your portfolio, you can have as many trades active as you would like. Theoretically, you could have as many as 30 different trades in action and still be within the risk parameters described in this chapter. Managing that many trades would be extremely difficult and it is not recommended, but if you can manage that many, it would be workable. In practice, if you are trading in the shorter time frames (swing trades), 5 to 10 simultaneous trades would probably be the most that you could manage.

Summary

This chapter dealt with some important concepts. First, it defined what the risk of ruin is, and how it changes as the amount of air going in and out of the balloon varies. Second, it named the components of risk, how each interacts with the portfolio and your starting capital. Finally, it set parameters for you as to how you should manage your risk in relation to your capital. The chapter was short and to the point, and that is the way you should manage your risk—keep it as simple as possible. The more moving parts you have, the harder it will be to manage your trades when the markets get frisky. The next chapter will deal with how to put things together and begin to trade.

■ Chapter 17 Quiz

1) The principle of risk of ruin applies to:
   a) trading weekly options
   b) all forms of trading
   c) all decision making
   d) all of the above

2) Weekly strategies that give you unlimited reward and limited risk require:
   a) more risk capital than credit spreads
   b) more risk per trade than credit spreads
   c) less risk per trade than risk reversals
   d) only a and b

3) The higher the variance, the greater:
   a) the length of winning streaks
   b) the length of losing streaks
   c) the amount of risk per trade
   d) the amount of loss per trade

4) The lower the variance, the greater:
   a) the length of winning streaks
   b) the length of losing streaks
   c) the amount of loss per trade
   d) the amount of risk per trade

5) If you are trading correctly, your equity curve should:
   a) always be going up
   b) resemble a bull market with a positive slope
   c) usually be in congestion
   d) never dip below its mean

6) Risk capital is money that:
   a) will not change your lifestyle if lost
   b) can be risked in investments
   c) is only used for trading
   d) all of the above

7) What is volatility?
   a) the amount of uncertainty in the market
   b) the amount of air in the balloon

     c) affects the amount of risk capital you have

     d) all of the above

8) What is the win rate?

     a) the percentage of winners you pick

     b) the average size of the winning trade

     c) the average loss in any trade

     d) all of the above

9) As a rule of thumb regarding risk capital:

     a) You can risk as much as 10 percent in any trade if you are aggressive.

     b) You should never risk more than 15 percent in any one trade.

     c) You need to have capital of at least 30 times your risk in any one trade.

     d) All of the above are true.

10) How many trades can you have open versus your risk capital?

     a) as many as you can manage, as long as each one has risk limited to 3 percent

     b) no more than 10, because you cannot manage more than that

     c) no more than 3, because of SEC rules

     d) no more than 1, as long as your broker approves it

CHAPTER 18

Organizing Trades and FAQs

All of the information necessary to be a successful weekly options trader has now been presented. This chapter will go through the steps that should be used to find trades and then initiate them within the risk capital parameters that you have established.

■ Step One: Observing Your Portfolio

Chapter 16 dealt with the reason to create a portfolio that you must constantly observe because of continually fluctuating market conditions. Some stocks will follow the underlying indexes very closely (high beta correlation) and others will trade in their own pattern; volatility within groupings will be quite varied, so having a widely diversified portfolio is a must. **Even if you are a very small trader and never have more than one position on at any one time**, you want to have the best opportunity to pick winners. If you are not constantly monitoring your portfolio, you will be compromising your chance to be in that position.

Always concentrate on the stocks with the highest EV; those stocks will be the most liquid, and the more liquidity, the better the chance that you will be able to overcome the bid–offer spread and commissions. Remember, you don't get a commission discount because the price of the stock is lower. As the EV declines, it means that the commission dollars that you are spending increase in relation to the potential profit, even if you are trading a position that has limited risk and unlimited reward.

Step Two: Observing the Major Trend and Making a Trade

Once you have narrowed your selection of stocks down to a couple of candidates, you must match the trade with the market conditions. As an example, you have decided that you want to trade either AAPL or GS or both, but you are not sure which one gives you the best chance to have a winner. Look at the major indexes to see what phase they are trading. Is the market in congestion, is it trending, or is it in a blowoff pattern?

Suppose the NASDAQ has been in congestion and is nearing a double top. Most likely, AAPL will be in a very similar pattern. GS is in an uptrend, but the S&P 500 is also in congestion and nearing a double top. Both of these stocks are now very good candidates, but you still need to observe them until you get a signal in the individual stock. When your shortest-term indicator turns negative at the double top, initiate the trade.

If the major indexes were in a different pattern, you would use that as a guide until your selected stocks meet the requirements and you can enter the trade. The higher the correlation between the individual stock that you are trading and the index that it is associated with, the better the chance that you will cash the trade.

Step Three: The Amount of Equity Needed to Trade Each Strategy

Earlier chapters dealt with the risk associated with any trade; the higher the risk, the higher the reward should be. However, depending on your risk capital, the number and quality of the trades will vary significantly. Table 18.1 shows you how much equity you need to trade a specific strategy, given the fact that you cannot risk more than 3 to 4 percent of your risk capital on any one trade and still be successful. There is a minimum amount of capital necessary to trade below that critical mass. It is very difficult to win because it becomes impossible to keep the risk/reward ratio in line.

For purposes of this book, the minimum amount that is necessary to trade weekly options is around $1,000. At that level, you can trade one $0.50 wide vertical credit spread. If you get your proper ratio of 2/3, your maximum risk is about $30 a trade, which is in line with the overall risk strategy. If you have $2,000 in risk capital, you can go to the stocks that have $1.00 strikes and your 2/3 ratio is again in line, as you only risk $60. The chart shows that the more risk capital that you have at your disposal, the more aggressive your strategy can become and still be within the risk tolerances of the book.

Once you have more than 5K in your account, you can begin to expand your strategies to include limited risk, unlimited reward trades. When you reach the top

TABLE 18.1	Amount of Equity Needed to Trade Each Strategy			
Risk Capital	Credit Spreads	Outright Buys	Risk Reversals	1 × 2
1K	X			
2K	X			
3K	X			
5K	X			
8K	X	X	X	
10K	X	X	X	X
15K	X	X	X	X
20K	X	X	X	X
25K	X	X	X	X
50K	X	X	X	X
75K	X	X	X	X
100K	X	X	X	X

bracket of $100,000, not only can you trade all of the strategies but you should probably be trading multiple stocks and multiple contracts within those stocks.

Once you have phased into the cycle, it is a matter of repeating the trades each time the market conditions are met.

■ Frequently Asked Questions

When I give a seminar or work with students one on one, several questions come up often. Many of the questions have very little merit, but some of them are vitally important, and I would like to address them.

How much money can I expect to make?

The first question is frequently how much they can expect to make trading weekly options. I believe that it is the wrong question to ask initially. The opening question should be what my risk is, but very few retail traders have that mind-set to begin with. Weekly options are a new vehicle, and they represent the best chance for retail option traders to compete with professionals. When I entered the business 30-plus years ago, there were only four expirations per year. Now you have 52. The growth of the weekly option volume and open interest is telling you that this new way to trade options is offering great opportunities. Instead of selling a $5 vertical credit spread for $3 in the hope of collecting the credit a year from now, you can sell the same spread 52 times a year for around $2 and collect $104. That edge alone should allow you to earn a positive return.

How much capital do I need?

The second question is, how much capital do I need to be a professional options trader? The answer to that one is not as hard. When you are a professional trader, you have to look at it like any other business venture. You have to control your inventory (equity and open trades), manage your cost of goods sold (commission and slippage), and generate sales (positive trading results). In addition, you must pay your employees (you and any assistants). Is it possible to a buy a business or a franchise with $1,000? It is possible, but highly unlikely that it will make any money. If you start with a small amount of risk capital, you will need to keep the day job until you learn how to compete in the marketplace. You can then grow your capital organically and eventually become a full-time trader.

How bad will my losing streaks be?

In general, if you are trading only credit spreads, your losing streaks should be very mild. However, from time to time, market conditions will meet extremes and the losing streaks can become severe. As an example, during the past 30 years I have made over 95 percent of my income trading options, stock, and future contracts, either through my own personal trades or in partnerships where I worked with experienced traders. On the other hand, depending on the time frame you were observing me trade, I was either a genius or was totally incompetent. I have had many losing streaks extend for months and it is brutal—that is why you need to keep your risk capital in line with the possible reward. If you are undercapitalized, most likely your trading will be compromised and it will be difficult to turn a profit. Leverage is a two-way sword, and you must realize that. The chance of turning $1,000 into $1 million is very small, but the chance of learning how to trade and turn a profit is very realistic.

Can I average up/down my price?

Many highly successful traders average their price up/down when a trade is going against them after it is initiated. They might have picked an initial buy or sell point that wasn't the optimum, and they like to average in price. In order to trade like this, you need to have sufficient capital in reserve to add to the trade. In addition, I believe that you need very good trading skills to successfully average in price. The main problem is, where does averaging become "cannonballing" (continually adding to losing trades until you blow out). I talk to many traders who have extreme trouble with ending the trade when they average up/down, and some of them have had catastrophic results. If you want to average in price, I suggest that you do it only once, and that you place a hard stop if you do use this technique.

How do I get my technical indicators?

There are many good sources to get technical indicators; I personally have used **Ablesys Corporation** for the past 17 years to manage trades both on and off of the floor. Their software gives very concise signals, and if you use them, combined with the equity management skills presented in this book, there is an excellent chance to make money. There is no magic bullet. If there was one, no one would sell it. Trading takes discipline and hard work, but good software will help you to win the battle.

Summary

This chapter concludes the book.

Many principles of trading weekly options have been introduced and discussed. Certain points are the key to success, and they have been emphasized in many chapters. The most important recipe for winning is to realize that you can only make money if you trade in liquid markets. Second, you must accept that the markets never change, they will repeat, and the ability to recognize those patterns is vital. Third, you must constantly observe your portfolio, as it will be in recurring instability, and, finally, you must able to control your emotions when things go wrong. If you want to be a trader, you better believe in Murphy's law!

A 100-question final exam is included. It has many of the questions that you have already answered in previous chapters. Before you employ these principles and begin to trade your risk capital, you should get a score of 270 or better.

Good luck to you in your personal life, and also in your trading!

Final Exam: 100 Questions

1) Why did Sir Isaac Newton lose his fortune in the South Sea bubble?
   a) The South Sea stock was allowed to trade freely.
   b) The Crown lost a great deal of money developing the trade routes to the South Seas.
   c) Land companies drove up the price of the trade routes.
   d) He was greedy.

2) What caused the Cotton Panic of 1837?
   a) Andrew Jackson's feud with Nicholas Biddle
   b) the move to a bimetal system and the end of a central bank
   c) the overexpansion to the Western territories
   d) greed

3) What was the bitcoin bubble of 2014?
    a) a classic example of a new technology that had no upper limit
    b) an event caused by the collapse of the Mt. Gox Exchange
    c) an event caused by government corruption
    d) a classic example of greed

4) All the bubbles reviewed had which of the following common characteristics?
    a) Technology had produced a product that had no upper limit.
    b) Government regulations contributed to the problem.
    c) Inflation caused the markets to collapse.
    d) Greed or fear overwhelmed reason.

5) Stock indexes rallying after a bad unemployment number is:
    a) highly unusual and is generally a selling opportunity
    b) caused by high-frequency traders
    c) called market expectation
    d) all of the above

6) Fundamental traders generally:
    a) only look at supply and demand for a stock
    b) are predictive in nature
    c) are reactive in nature
    d) never consider technical factors

7) Fundamental traders:
    a) examine balance sheets
    b) watch EPS levels
    c) watch inventory levels
    d) all of the above

8) Fundamental traders never take into consideration:
    a) overbought or oversold indicators
    b) high-frequency trading volume
    c) moving averages
    d) media buying or selling advice

9) Technical traders never take into consideration:
    a) P/E ratios of stocks they are looking to buy
    b) overbought or oversold conditions
    c) price retracement levels
    d) media buying or selling advice

10) Technical traders always:
    a) follow the trend
    b) look at key levels to trade

c) countertrend trade media advice

d) take profits too early

11) Technical traders usually buy:
a) double bottoms
b) breakouts from congestion
c) blowoff bottoms
d) all of the above

12) Even in a bull market of 45 degrees:
a) The weak hands will push the market down.
b) There can be a congestion phase.
c) The strong hands can become the weak hands.
d) All of the above are correct.

13) All bear trending markets are controlled by:
a) the weak hands
b) the strong hands
c) new money
d) none of the above

14) All bull markets have which characteristic?
a) They are controlled by the strong hands.
b) Stubborn weak hands will be hurt financially.
c) It will make a series of higher highs.
d) All of the above.

15) The deferred serial will always have:
a) more air in the balloon, as it has more uncertainty
b) more air in the out-of-the-money options
c) parity options and teenies
d) all of the above

16) What will happen if volatility doubles in the expiring month?
a) The at-the-money options will double in price.
b) The differed serial expirations will double.
c) There will no longer be parity options.
d) Volatility cannot double in the front month.

17) Which of the following is true about in-the-money options?
a) They all expire in the money.
b) They will have no premium at expiration.
c) They always have intrinsic value at expiration.
d) It cannot be determined from this information.

18) An expiring option can:
   a) never have more premium than a differed option at the same strike price
   b) always be exercised
   c) be assigned
   d) all of the above

19) A lower-priced stock can never have
   a) more premium than a higher-priced stock
   b) more volatility than a higher-priced stock
   c) more price movement than a higher-priced stock
   d) none of the above

20) Buying a call to open:
   a) has premium risk in addition to market risk
   b) is a poor trading strategy
   c) has defined risk and reward
   d) both a and c

21) Call buyers have:
   a) assignment risk
   b) exercise rights
   c) rights but no obligations
   d) both b and c

22) A credit spread:
   a) sells air and therefore has unlimited risk
   b) has little upside in relation to its risk
   c) is selling one option and buying another
   d) both a and b

23) A bearish call credit spread is initiated by:
   a) selling a call nearer to the ATM and buying an in-the-money call
   b) buying a call that is out of the money and selling a call in the money
   c) selling any call and buying a call at another strike
   d) both a and b

24) The conversion and reversal formula allows a trader to do which of the following?
   a) tell how much of an ITM put is intrinsic
   b) tell how much of an ITM call is air
   c) compute where the underlying price should be
   d) all of the above

25) The amount of premium in any strike in the same serial:
   a) is constant and will be the same in a put as well as a call
   b) can vary depending on what option model is being traded

c) can't be calculated until expiration

d) both a and c

26) Weekly option credit spreads offer:
   a) liquidity
   b) the opportunity to cash a trade each week as opposed to once a month
   c) limited risk, limited reward trades with a high percentage of wins
   d) all of the above

27) Priceline (PCLN) priced at over $1,000 a share is a good candidate for which of the following?
   a) 1 × 2 backspreads
   b) outright purchase of a call or put
   c) synthetic long or short through a risk reversal
   d) all of the above

28) Delta is a Greek term that is:
   a) the rate of change of the option to the underlying price of an asset
   b) a positive number for calls
   c) a negative number for puts
   d) all of the above

29) Gamma is a Greek term that describes:
   a) the change in premium as volatility increases
   b) a negative for calls
   c) the speed at which the delta changes for a one-point change in the underlying asset
   d) all of the above

30) The Black–Scholes option model:
   a) was the first option model
   b) has changed because of high-frequency traders
   c) is not reliable in volatile markets
   d) none of the above

31) The option model has the most uncertainty:
   a) at the current price of the underlying asset
   b) when an option reaches parity
   c) when an option becomes a teenie
   d) none of the above

32) Which of the following is true about theta?
   a) It is the loss of premium as options move closer to expiration.
   b) It is the increase of premium when there is more uncertainty in the market.

c) It is the decrease of premium as uncertainty diminishes.

d) Theta is not a term associated with options.

33) An option that reaches parity is synonymous with:

    a) an option that currently has no premium

    b) an option that can be exercised

    c) an option that can be assigned

    d) all of the above

34) The standard contract size for all US exchange-traded stocks:

    a) is 100 shares

    b) is regulated by the OCC and SEC

    c) expires on Friday after the close

    d) all of the above

35) If the at-the-money option has premium expanding, what is most likely true?

    a) The out-of-the-money options will have more air.

    b) The in-the-money options will have more air.

    c) Volatility of the underlying asset is probably increasing.

    d) All of the above are true.

36) At expiration, which option will have the most premium?

    a) the at the money

    b) the 40 delta put

    c) the 40 delta call

    d) none of the above

37) Once an option reaches parity, what happens if the volatility doesn't change?

    a) It will remain at parity.

    b) It will mimic the underlying stock 100 percent.

    c) It can never end up as a teenie.

    d) It is always at risk for market direction.

38) In the congestion phase of the market, buying a put can be initiated:

    a) at a double top

    b) when the shortest time frame you are observing turns negative

    c) when your technical indicators turn negative

    d) all of the above

39) In the congestion phase of the market, what is true about volatility?

    a) It is low, as price is not moving more than $+1/-1\sigma$.

    b) It is high, as there will be maximum uncertainty as to future price direction.

c) It is impossible to tell what volatility will be at any point in the market cycle.

d) Volatility is not important in the congestion phase of the market.

40) In the congestion phase of the market, what is true about buying options outright?

   a) It is always dependent on the uncertainty in the market (volatility).

   b) It is always a safe play, as the risk is limited and the reward is unlimited.

   c) It should only be done in a low-volatility environment.

   d) It should only be done in a high-volatility environment.

41) Buying calls in a rising volatility environment generally:

   a) is not a good trade; if the market is rallying volatility will be dropping

   b) can make money even if the price goes down slightly

   c) is no longer a safe trade

   d) none of the above

42) If you turn an ATM credit spread into an iron condor, you can:

   a) never lose more than the net credit no matter what price does

   b) cash one side of the trade if you don't readjust

   c) cash both sides of the trade if price expires between your short strikes

   d) both b and c

43) When should a bullish risk reversal be initiated in congestion?

   a) when the market is within 5 percent of a double bottom

   b) when the shortest time frame you are observing turns positive

   c) when your technical indicators turn positive

   d) all of the above

44) When should a bearish risk reversal be rolled down?

   a) The underlying asset begins to break.

   b) The long strike goes at least to an ATM -2.

   c) The volatility suddenly rises.

   d) You don't need to roll down if you want to accept the intratrade risk.

45) When should you roll back a winning bullish risk reversal?

   a) anytime the long strike goes to ATM $+2$

   b) when you reach a double top

   c) on Friday, before the close of expiration

   d) never

46) A 1 × 2 bullish backspread works best at

   a) double bottoms

   b) double tops

c) a low-volatility environment

d) a high-volatility environment

47) Splitting strikes in a 1 × 2 backspread

    a) increases risk

    b) decreases risk

    c) has greater profit potential than touching strikes

    d) works best in a low-volatility environment

48) A bullish credit spread should never be used:

    a) when volatility is rising

    b) when you can buy an outright option for the same risk

    c) A credit spread can always be used in any market condition

    d) all of the above

49) In a trending market, profit can be taken on a credit spread when:

    a) price goes through the long strike

    b) your shortest-term signal gives you a reversal

    c) on any Friday

    d) only b and c

50) How does a bearish risk reversal in a blowoff market resemble a put?

    a) Both have unlimited reward and limited risk.

    b) Both should be initiated in a high-volatility environment.

    c) Both can make money even if the price goes slightly lower.

    d) Both b and c.

51) In a blowoff market, when should a bullish risk reversal be rolled up?

    a) The underlying asset begins to break.

    b) The long strike goes at least to an ATM +2.

    c) Never let the winner run.

    d) You don't need to roll up if you want to accept the intratrade risk.

52) When should a bearish risk reversal be rolled down?

    a) The underlying asset begins to break.

    b) The long strike goes at least to an ATM −2.

    c) If the volatility suddenly rises.

    d) You don't need to roll down if you want to accept the intratrade risk.

53) In a blowoff market, when should you roll back a winning bullish risk reversal?

    a) anytime the long strike goes to ATM +2

    b) when you reach a double top

    c) on Friday, before the close of expiration

    d) never

54) What is true about creating a tradable portfolio?
   a) It is a must if you want to be successful.
   b) It protects cash, your most important asset.
   c) It is important to trading efficiently.
   d) All of the above are true.

55) When choosing a portfolio, liquidity is:
   a) the most important property
   b) not as important as price
   c) variable from group to group
   d) all of the above

56) Liquidity is defined by:
   a) the price of the underlying stock
   b) the bid–offer spread
   c) commission rates
   d) all of the above

57) Stocks under $20 a share generally:
   a) lack liquidity for a retail trader
   b) are a good trade for the retail trader
   c) are much less risky than higher-priced stocks
   d) are a good place to trade while learning options

58) How do weekly expected ranges (EV) influence picking a stock for trading?
   a) The smaller the EV, the better, because they are less risky.
   b) EV has no effect on trading weekly options.
   c) EVs are very important in choosing a stock to trade.
   d) Bigger EVs make the stock more liquid.

59) Stocks in the same grouping are priced at $37 and $60. Which should you trade?
   a) the higher-priced stock
   b) the lower-priced stock
   c) the lowest EV stock
   d) the highest EV stock

60) What is dollar diversification used for?
   a) offsetting an imbalance of dollar risk when comparing stocks
   b) ensuring that one winner is the same as the other
   c) balancing your portfolio by EV
   d) all of the above

61) The first step to diversification by dollar risk is:
   a) Assign the highest EV stock a value of 1.
   b) Assign an lowest EV stock a value of 1.

c) Pick the median stock and supply it a value of 1.

d) None of the above.

62) Intrinsic value is:

    a) the amount of premium in an option

    b) the opposite of extrinsic value

    c) the same as a credit

    d) none of the above

63) Buying options can create which of the following positions?

    a) The trader owns a call.

    b) The trader owns a put.

    c) The trader owns both a put and a call.

    d) All of the above.

64) Selling or writing options has which of the following characteristics?

    a) It gives the seller the right to exercise on or before expiration.

    b) It gives the seller the obligation to deliver the underlying asset at expiration.

    c) It gives the seller the right to assign options at expiration.

    d) None of the above is correct.

65) How is poker similar to options?

    a) Some information concerning the market is revealed.

    b) Both rely on probability models to succeed.

    c) Luck can play a part in the short run.

    d) All of the above.

66) How is blackjack similar to options?

    a) Your opponent has unlimited capital.

    b) Both rely on probability models and skill to succeed.

    c) Luck can overcome your opponent in the short run.

    d) All of the above are true.

67) When the at-the-money call is exactly where the underlying asset is trading:

    a) it has a 50 percent chance of ending up in the money

    b) it has less than a 50 percent chance if the market is in a bear trend

    c) it is impossible to say what its chances are of ending up in the money

    d) none of the above

68) The principle of risk of ruin applies to:

    a) trading weekly options

    b) all forms of trading

    c) all decision making

    d) all of the above

69) Weekly strategies that give you unlimited reward and limited risk require:
   a) more risk capital than credit spreads
   b) more risk per trade than credit spreads
   c) less risk per trade than risk reversals
   d) only a and b

70) The higher the variance, the greater:
   a) the length of winning streaks
   b) the length of losing streaks
   c) the amount of risk per trade
   d) the amount of loss per trade

71) The lower the variance, the greater:
   a) the length of winning streaks
   b) the length of losing streaks
   c) the amount of loss per trade
   d) the amount of risk per trade

72) Risk capital is money that:
   a) will not change your lifestyle if lost
   b) can be risked in investments
   c) is only used for trading
   d) all of the above

73) What is volatility?
   a) the amount of uncertainty in the market
   b) the amount of air in the balloon
   c) a factor that affects the amount of risk capital you have
   d) all of the above

74) The amount of premium in the at-the-money option is determined by
   a) the Black–Scholes model
   b) the rate at which the underlying stock is moving
   c) the supply and demand for the option in the specific expiration serial
   d) all of the above

75) The longest time frame is:
   a) not related to shorter time frames
   b) not valid if the market is blowing off
   c) the sum of all shorter time frames
   d) generally in congestion

76) Another name for the longest time frame is:
   a) the major trend that we are observing
   b) the strong hands running over the weak hands

c) new money entering a bear market

d) none of the above

77) In a bull market, the shorter time frames:

a) are always bullish

b) are not relevant

c) can be bearish

d) none of the above

78) A 60/40 credit spread has:

a) theta risk if the price remains constant to expiration

b) more potential profit than an ATM bear credit spread

c) more potential loss than an ATM bull credit spread

d) only b and c

79) What is the limit on the credit spread's risk?

a) It has no limit, as you are selling air.

b) The limit is the difference between the strikes used in the spread.

c) It has no limit on reward.

d) The limit is the difference between the strikes used minus the credit.

80) A pure risk reversal:

a) is buying or selling the underlying asset synthetically

b) has both unlimited risk and unlimited reward

c) has no theta risk

d) all of the above

81) What is true about an ITM risk reversal?

a) It requires that you buy an additional OTM option to limit the risk.

b) It has a small theta risk.

c) It has unlimited reward.

d) All of the above are true.

82) The first step to choosing a trade is:

a) observing your own stock portfolio

b) concentrating on trades within your portfolio that have the highest EV

c) looking for stocks that display liquidity

d) all of the above

83) What is step two in choosing a trade?

a) Observe the major trend.

b) Select stocks in your portfolio and use those that are in sync with the major trend.

c) Trade the highest correlation stocks with the major trend.

d) None of the above.

84) Your risk capital determines:
   a) the kind of strategy you can use
   b) if you can trade multiple contracts
   c) your risk of ruin
   d) all of the above

85) The minimum amount of capital needed to trade weekly options is:
   a) at least $1,000 to trade the most conservative strategy
   b) more than $5,000 to trade outright buys and risk reversals
   c) at least $10,000 to trade all strategies
   d) all of the above

86) When trading weekly options, when can you average up or down?
   a) You can average anytime, if you can handle the risk.
   b) Never; it can be a dangerous practice.
   c) You can average only when you are sure the market will reverse.
   d) You can average as many times as you like during a trade.

87) When the angle of the bull market approaches 60 degrees:
   a) The last of the weak hands will be getting forced out.
   b) Longs will be the strong hands.
   c) New money will come in on the long side of the market.
   d) None of the above.

88) Price discovery is:
   a) where value changes hands
   b) where price is in equilibrium
   c) not recognized by fundamental traders
   d) a and b

89) A rally in the market is caused by:
   a) a lack of sellers
   b) no strong hands to fight the buyers
   c) more buyers than sellers
   d) aggressive buyers

90) What condition creates an upside price gap?
   a) Buyers are active in the market.
   b) Sellers are active in the market.
   c) There are no sellers to meet buyer demand.
   d) Overnight geopolitical news shocks the market.

91) Futures markets are characterized by:
   a) different-sized contracts for each product
   b) an expiration date for trading

c) good-faith margin deposits

d) all of the above

92) Stock index futures:

    a) are a safe investment

    b) mirror the underlying cash index

    c) are settled in stock from the index

    d) have no specific expiration date

93) What is true about the Forex market?

    a) It is guaranteed by the Forex currency exchange.

    b) It is dominated by large banks.

    c) It has fixed expiration dates.

    d) It is liquid for small traders.

94) Congestion markets can extend for how long?

    a) Never more than six months; they then are known as a trend.

    b) They can extend until they break out to a trend.

    c) There is no time limit.

    d) All of the above.

95) What is a serial?

    a) another word for a near-term put

    b) the grouping of options that have the same expiration

    c) the order in which options are priced

    d) all of the above

96) What is the strike price?

    a) the value of a call at expiration

    b) the price at which a call must be delivered by the buyer

    c) the price at which the seller must buy or sell the underlying asset

    d) the at-the-money strike

97) The at-the-money option always:

    a) has the most amount of premium

    b) has the least amount of premium

    c) is closest to the underlying asset's current price

    d) both a and c

98) In terms of options, what is a tick?

    a) a small insect

    b) the smallest price change allowed in an option or underlying asset

    c) varies from stock to stock

    d) none of the above

99) What is true about debit spreads?
   a) They have a reward greater than any credit spread.
   b) They can be cashed if there is no price movement.
   c) They have unlimited reward, once the debit is paid for by price movement.
   d) None of the above.

100) What is true about markets?
   a) They can be confidently predicted from time and price charts.
   b) They can never be accurately predicted.
   c) They can be beaten even if they are illiquid.
   d) They are rigged by high-frequency traders.

Answers to the Chapter Quizzes

■ Chapter 1

1. a) 0   b) 1   c) 3   d) 0
2. a) 1   b) 0   c) 3   d) 0
3. a) 0   b) 0   c) 0   d) 3
4. a) 0   b) 0   c) 0   d) 3 Greed caused the panic.
5. a) 3   b) 0   c) 0   d) 0 Greed caused the panic.
6. a) 0   b) 0   c) 0   d) 3 Greed caused the panic.
7. a) 0   b) 0   c) 0   d) 3
8. a) 0   b) 0   c) 0   d) 3
9. a) 1   b) 0   c) 0   d) 3
10. a) 0   b) 0   c) 0   d) 3 If you missed this one, you have failed to comprehend the point of the first chapter!

There were 30 possible points for the quiz on Chapter 1.

■ Chapter 2

1. a) 1   b) 1   c) 0   d) 3
2. a) 3   b) 0   c) 0   d) 0
3. a) 1   b) 1   c) 1   d) 3
4. a) 0   b) 0   c) 0   d) 3

5. a) 0   b) 0   c) 0   d) 3
6. a) 0   b) 1   c) 1   d) 3
7. a) 0   b) 0   c) 3   d) 0 Overnight geopolitical news could be neutral!
8. a) 1   b) 1   c) 1   d) 3
9. a) 0   b) 3   c) 0   d) 0
10. a) 0   b) 3   c) 0   d) 0

There were 30 possible points for the quiz on Chapter 2.

■ Chapter 3

1. a) 0   b) 0   c) 3   d) 0
2. a) 0   b) 0   c) 3   d) 0
3. a) 0   b) 3   c) 0   d) 1
4. a) 1   b) 1   c) 1   d) 3
5. a) 0   b) 0   c) 0   d) 3 Fundamental traders use many technical analysis
   points to predict.
6. a) 1   b) 0   c) 0   d) 3
7. a) 0   b) 3   c) 0   d) 0
8. a) 1   b) 1   c) 1   d) 3
9. a) 1   b) 1   c) 0   d) 3
10. a) 0   b) 3   c) 0   d) 0

There were 30 possible points for the quiz on Chapter 3.

■ Chapter 4

1. a) 1   b) 1   c) 1   d) 3
2. a) 3   b) 0   c) 0   d) 0
3. a) 0   b) 3   c) 0   d) 0
4. a) 1   b) 1   c) 1   d) 3
5. a) 0   b) 0   c) 3   d) 0
6. a) 0   b) 3   c) 0   d) 0
7. a) 0   b) 3   c) 0   d) 0
8. a) 1   b) 1   c) 1   d) 3
9. a) 1   b) 1   c) 1   d) 3
10. a) 0   b) 3   c) 1   d) 0
11. a) 1   b) 2   c) 1   d) 3
12. a) 1   b) 3   c) 1   d) 0
13. a) 1   b) 1   c) 1   d) 3

14. a) 0   b) 0   c) 0   d) 3
15. a) 1   b) 1   c) 1   d) 3

There were 45 possible points for the quiz on Chapter 4.

■ Chapter 5

1. a) 3   b) 0   c) 0   d) 0
2. a) 3   b) 0   c) 1   d) 0
3. a) 3   b) 0   c) 0   d) 0
4. a) 0   b) 3   c) 0   d) 0
5. a) 3   b) 0   c) 0   d) 0
6. a) 0   b) 3   c) 0   d) 0
7. a) 0   b) 0   c) 3   d) 1
8. a) 3   b) 0   c) 0   d) 0
9. a) 0   b) 1   c) 1   d) 3
10. a) 0   b) 0   c) 3   d) 0

There were 30 possible points for the quiz on Chapter 5.

■ Chapter 6

1. a) 0   b) 0   c) 3   d) 0
2. a) 0   b) 0   c) 0   d) 3
3. a) 0   b) 3   c) 0   d) 0
4. a) 0   b) 0   c) 3   d) 0
5. a) 0   b) 0   c) 0   d) 3
6. a) 0   b) 0   c) 3   d) 0
7. a) 3   b) 0   c) 0   d) 0
8. a) 1   b) 1   c) 1   d) 3
9. a) 0   b) 3   c) 0   d) 0
10. a) 1   b) 1   c) 1   d) 3
11. a) 0   b) 3   c) 0   d) 0
12. a) 3   b) 0   c) 0   d) 0
13. a) 1   b) 3   c) 0   d) 0
14. a) 3   b) 0   c) 0   d) 0
15. a) 1   b) 1   c) 1   d) 3
16. a) 1   b) 1   c) 1   d) 3
17. a) 3   b) 0   c) 0   d) 0
18. a) 1   b) 0   c) 1   d) 3

19. a) 1   b) 1   c) 1   d) 3
20. a) 0   b) 0   c) 3   d) 0

There were 60 possible points for the quiz on Chapter 6.

■ Chapter 7

1. a) 3   b) 0   c) 0   d) 0
2. a) 1   b) 1   c) 0   d) 3
3. a) 3   b) 0   c) 0   d) 0
4. a) 1   b) 1   c) 1   d) 3
5. a) 1   b) 1   c) 1   d) 3
6. a) 3   b) 0   c) 0   d) 0
7. a) 1   b) 1   c) 1   d) 3
8. a) 0   b) 0   c) 0   d) 3 At expiration there is no premium.
9. a) 0   b) 0   c) 0   d) 3
10. a) 0   b) 0   c) 3   d) 0 The Black–Scholes model has nothing to do with the premium.

There were 30 possible points for the quiz on Chapter 7.

■ Chapter 8

1. a) 3   b) 0   c) 0   d) 0
2. a) 3   b) 0   c) 0   d) 0
3. a) 1   b) 1   c) 0   d) 3
4. a) 1   b) 1   c) 1   d) 3
5. a) 3   b) 0   c) 0   d) 0
6. a) 0   b) 3   c) 0   d) 0
7. a) 1   b) 1   c) 1   d) 3
8. a) 0   b) 0   c) 0   d) 3 Supply and demand will determine the premium.
9. a) 0   b) 0   c) 3   d) 0
10. a) 0   b) 0   c) 0   d) 3

There were 30 possible points for the quiz on Chapter 8.

■ Chapter 9

1. a) 0   b) 0   c) 3   d) 0
2. a) 1   b) 1   c) 1   d) 3

3. a) 1   b) 1   c) 0   d) 3
4. a) 3   b) 0   c) 0   d) 0
5. a) 3   b) 0   c) 0   d) 0
6. a) 0   b) 1   c) 1   d) 3
7. a) 0   b) 0   c) 3   d) 0
8. a) 0   b) 3   c) 0   d) 0
9. a) 0   b) 1   c) 1   d) 3
10. a) 1   b) 1   c) 1   d) 3
11. a) 1   b) 1   c) 1   d) 3
12. a) 3   b) 0   c) 0   d) 0
13. a) 1   b) 1   c) 1   d) 3
14. a) 3   b) 0   c) 0   d) 0 It will have no air but the call may end up in the money!
15. a) 0   b) 0   c) 0   d) 3
16. a) 1   b) 1   c) 0   d) 3
17. a) 0   b) 0   c) 0   d) 3
18. a) 1   b) 1   c) 1   d) 3
19. a) 0   b) 1   c) 1   d) 3
20. a) 0   b) 0   c) 0   d) 3
21. a) 1   b) 1   c) 1   d) 3
22. a) 1   b) 1   c) 1   d) 3
23. a) 0   b) 3   c) 0   d) 0
24. a) 1   b) 1   c) 1   d) 3
25. a) 1   b) 1   c) 1   d) 3

There were 75 possible points for the quiz on Chapter 9.

■ Chapter 10

1. a) 0   b) 1   c) 1   d) 3
2. a) 3   b) 0   c) 0   d) 0
3. a) 0   b) 1   c) 1   d) 3
4. a) 1   b) 1   c) 1   d) 3
5. a) 0   b) 0   c) 3   d) 0
6. a) 1   b) 1   c) 1   d) 3
7. a) 0   b) 1   c) 1   d) 3
8. a) 3   b) 0   c) 0   d) 0
9. a) 3   b) 0   c) 0   d) 0
10. a) 1   b) 1   c) 1   d) 3

There were 30 possible points for the quiz on Chapter 10.

Chapter 11 Midterm

1. a) 3   b) 0   c) 0   d) 0
2. a) 0   b) 3   c) 0   d) 0
3. a) 0   b) 3   c) 0   d) 0
4. a) 0   b) 0   c) 3   d) 0
5. a) 0   b) 0   c) 0   d) 3
6. a) 1   b) 1   c) 1   d) 3
7. a) 1   b) 1   c) 1   d) 3
8. a) 0   b) 3   c) 0   d) 0
9. a) 0   b) 3   c) 0   d) 0
10. a) 1   b) 3   c) 1   d) 0
11. a) 0   b) 1   c) 3   d) 1
12. a) 0   b) 0   c) 0   d) 3
13. a) 0   b) 0   c) 3   d) 0
14. a) 1   b) 1   c) 0   d) 3
15. a) 1   b) 1   c) 1   d) 3
16. a) 0   b) 0   c) 0   d) 3
17. a) 0   b) 0   c) 3   d) 0
18. a) 1   b) 1   c) 1   d) 3
19. a) 0   b) 3   c) 0   d) 0
20. a) 1   b) 3   c) 1   d) 0
21. a) 0   b) 1   c) 3   d) 0
22. a) 0   b) 3   c) 1   d) 0
23. a) 0   b) 0   c) 3   d) 0
24. a) 0   b) 3   c) 0   d) 0
25. a) 0   b) 0   c) 3   d) 0
26. a) 1   b) 1   c) 1   d) 3
27. a) 1   b) 0   c) 1   d) 3
28. a) 1   b) 1   c) 1   d) 3
29. a) 0   b) 0   c) 0   d) 3
30. a) 3   b) 0   c) 0   d) 0
31. a) 3   b) 0   c) 0   d) 0
32. a) 1   b) 1   c) 1   d) 3
33. a) 1   b) 1   c) 1   d) 3
34. a) 1   b) 3   c) 0   d) 0
35. a) 3   b) 0   c) 0   d) 0
36. a) 1   b) 1   c) 1   d) 3
37. a) 1   b) 1   c) 1   d) 3
38. a) 1   b) 1   c) 1   d) 3
39. a) 0   b) 0   c) 0   d) 3 At expiration, there is no premium left in the options.

40. a) 0   b) 0   c) 0   d) 3
41. a) 0   b) 0   c) 3   d) 0
42. a) 0   b) 0   c) 3   d) 1
43. a) 3   b) 0   c) 0   d) 0
44. a) 0   b) 0   c) 3   d) 0
45. a) 1   b) 1   c) 1   d) 3
46. a) 3   b) 0   c) 0   d) 0
47. a) 0   b) 3   c) 0   d) 0
48. a) 0   b) 3   c) 0   d) 0
49. a) 1   b) 1   c) 1   d) 3
50. a) 0   b) 3   c) 0   d) 0

There were 150 possible points for the quiz on Chapter 11.

Chapter 12

1. a) 3   b) 0   c) 0   d) 0
2. a) 1   b) 1   c) 1   d) 3
3. a) 1   b) 1   c) 1   d) 3
4. a) 3   b) 0   c) 0   d) 0
5. a) 3   b) 0   c) 0   d) 0
6. a) 0   b) 3   c) 0   d) 0
7. a) 3   b) 0   c) 0   d) 0
8. a) 1   b) 1   c) 1   d) 3
9. a) 1   b) 1   c) 0   d) 3
10. a) 1   b) 1   c) 0   d) 3

There were 30 possible points for the quiz on Chapter 12.

Chapter 13

1. a) 1   b) 1   c) 1   d) 3
2. a) 1   b) 1   c) 1   d) 3
3. a) 0   b) 0   c) 3   d) 0
4. a) 3   b) 0   c) 0   c) 0
5. a) 0   b) 3   c) 0   d) 0
6. a) 1   b) 1   c) 0   d) 3
7. a) 1   b) 1   c) 1   d) 3
8. a) 1   b) 1   c) 1   d) 3
9. a) 1   b) 1   c) 1   d) 3

10. a) 0   b) 0   c) 3   d) 0
11. a) 0   b) 1   c) 1   d) 3
12. a) 1   b) 3   c) 1   d) 0
13. a) 0   b) 1   c) 1   d) 3
14. a) 1   b) 1   c) 1   d) 3
15. a) 1   b) 1   c) 1   d) 3
16. a) 3   b) 0   c) 0   d) 0
17. a) 0   b) 3   c) 0   d) 1
18. a) 3   b) 0   c) 0   d) 0
19. a) 0   b) 3   c) 0   d) 0
20. a) 0   b) 3   c) 0   d) 0
21. a) 0   b) 0   c) 3   d) 0
22. a) 0   b) 0   c) 3   d) 0
23. a) 0   b) 0   c) 3   d) 0
24. a) 0   b) 0   c) 3   d) 0
25. a) 3   b) 0   c) 0   d) 0

There were 75 possible points for the quiz on Chapter 13.

■ Chapter 14

1. a) 1   b) 1   c) 1   d) 3
2. a) 1   b) 1   c) 1   d) 3
3. a) 0   b) 0   c) 3   d) 0
4. a) 1   b) 0   c) 0   d) 3
5. a) 0   b) 3   c) 0   d) 0
6. a) 1   b) 1   c) 0   d) 3
7. a) 1   b) 1   c) 1   c) 3
8. a) 1   b) 1   c) 1   d) 3
9. a) 1   b) 1   c) 1   d) 3
10. a) 0   b) 1   c) 3   d) 0
11. a) 0   b) 3   c) 1   d) 1
12. a) 0   b) 3   c) 1   d) 0
13. a) 0   b) 1   c) 1   d) 3
14. a) 1   b) 1   c) 1   d) 3
15. a) 3   b) 0   c) 0   d) 0
16. a) 3   b) 0   c) 0   d) 0
17. a) 0   b) 3   c) 0   d) 1
18. a) 0   b) 3   c) 0   d) 1

19. a) 0   b) 0   c) 3   d) 0
20. a) 0   b) 0   c) 3   d) 0
21. a) 1   b) 3   c) 1   d) 1
22. a) 0   b) 0   c) 3   d) 0
23. a) 3   b) 0   c) 1   d) 1
24. a) 1   b) 1   c) 0   d) 3
25. a) 0   b) 3   c) 0   d) 0

There were 75 possible points for the quiz on Chapter 14.

◼ Chapter 15

1. a) 0   b) 0   c) 0   d) 3
2. a) 0   b) 0   c) 0   d) 3
3. a) 0   b) 1   c) 3   d) 0
4. a) 0   b) 0   c) 3   d) 0
5. a) 1   b) 1   c) 1   d) 3
6. a) 0   b) 3   c) 0   d) 0
7. a) 1   b) 1   c) 1   d) 3
8. a) 1   b) 1   c) 1   d) 3
9. a) 0   b) 1   c) 1   d) 3
10. a) 0   b) 0   c) 3   d) 0
11. a) 0   b) 1   c) 1   d) 3
12. a) 1   b) 1   c) 3   d) 0
13. a) 0   b) 1   c) 1   d) 3
14. a) 1   b) 1   c) 1   d) 3
15. a) 3   b) 0   c) 0   d) 0
16. a) 3   b) 0   c) 0   d) 0
17. a) 0   b) 3   c) 0   d) 0
18. a) 0   b) 3   c) 0   c) 0
19. a) 0   b) 0   c) 3   c) 0
20. a) 0   b) 0   c) 3   c) 0
21. a) 1   b) 3   c) 0   d) 0
22. a) 0   b) 1   c) 3   d) 0
23. a) 3   b) 0   c) 0   d) 0
24. a) 1   b) 0   c) 3   d) 0
25. a) 0   b) 3   c) 0   c) 0

There were 75 possible points for the quiz on Chapter 15.

Chapter 16

1. a) 1   b) 1   c) 1   d) 3
2. a) 3   b) 0   c) 1   c) 0
3. a) 1   b) 1   c) 1   d) 3
4. a) 3   b) 0   c) 0   d) 0
5. a) 0   b) 0   c) 1   d) 3
6. a) 0   b) 3   c) 0   d) 0
7. a) 3   b) 0   c) 0   d) 0
8. a) 0   b) 0   c) 3   d) 0
9. a) 0   b) 0   c) 0   d) 3
10. a) 0   b) 3   c) 0   d) 0
11. a) 0   b) 0   c) 0   d) 3
12. a) 1   b) 1   c) 1   d) 3
13. a) 3   b) 0   c) 0   d) 0
14. a) 3   b) 0   c) 0   d) 0
15. a) 3   b) 0   c) 0   d) 0

There were 45 possible points for the quiz on Chapter 16.

Chapter 17

1. a) 0   b) 0   c) 3   d) 0
2. a) 1   b) 1   c) 0   d) 3
3. a) 0   b) 3   c) 0   d) 0
4. a) 3   b) 0   c) 0   d) 0
5. a) 0   b) 3   c) 0   d) 0
6. a) 1   b) 1   c) 1   d) 3
7. a) 1   b) 1   c) 1   d) 3
8. a) 1   b) 1   c) 1   d) 3
9. a) 0   b) 0   c) 3   d) 0
10. a) 3   b) 0   c) 0   d) 0

There were 30 possible points for the quiz on Chapter 17.

Chapter 18 Final

1. a) 0   b) 0   c) 0   d) 3
2. a) 0   b) 1   c) 0   d) 3
3. a) 1   b) 0   c) 0   d) 3

4. a) 0   b) 0   c) 0   d) 3
5. a) 0   b) 0   c) 3   d) 0
6. a) 0   b) 3   c) 0   d) 0
7. a) 1   b) 1   c) 1   d) 3
8. a) 1   b) 1   c) 1   d) 3
9. a) 1   b) 1   c) 1   d) 3
10. a) 0   b) 3   c) 0   d) 0
11. a) 1   b) 1   c) 1   d) 3
12. a) 1   b) 1   c) 1   d) 3
13. a) 0   b) 3   c) 0   d) 0
14. a) 1   b) 1   c) 1   d) 3
15. a) 1   b) 1   c) 1   d) 3
16. a) 3   b) 0   c) 0   d) 0
17. a) 0   b) 3   c) 0   d) 0
18. a) 1   b) 1   c) 1   d) 3
19. a) 0   b) 0   c) 0   d) 3
20. a) 1   b) 0   c) 1   c) 3
21. a) 0   b) 1   c) 1   d) 3
22. a) 0   b) 0   c) 3   d) 0
23. a) 1   b) 1   c) 0   d) 3
24. a) 1   b) 1   c) 1   d) 3
25. a) 3   b) 0   c) 0   d) 0
26. a) 1   b) 1   c) 1   d) 3
27. a) 0   b) 0   c) 3   d) 0
28. a) 1   b) 1   c) 1   d) 3
29. a) 0   b) 0   c) 3   d) 0
30. a) 3   b) 0   c) 0   d) 0
31. a) 3   b) 0   c) 0   d) 0
32. a) 3   b) 0   c) 0   d) 0
33. a) 1   b) 1   c) 1   d) 3
34. a) 1   b) 1   c) 1   d) 3
35. a) 1   b) 1   c) 1   d) 3
36. a) 0   b) 0   c) 0   d) 0
37. a) 0   b) 0   c) 0   d) 3
38. a) 1   b) 1   c) 1   d) 3
39. a) 0   b) 0   c) 3   d) 0
40. a) 3   b) 0   c) 0   d) 0
41. a) 0   b) 3   c) 0   d) 0
42. a) 0   b) 1   b) 1   d) 3
43. a) 1   b) 1   c) 1   d) 3
44. a) 0   b) 3   c) 0   d) 1

45. a) 0   b) 0   c) 3   d) 0
46. a) 0   b) 0   c) 3   d) 0
47. a) 3   b) 0   c) 3   d) 0
48. a) 0   b) 0   c) 0   d) 3
49. a) 0   b) 1   c) 1   c) 3
50. a) 3   b) 0   c) 0   d) 0
51. a) 0   b) 1   c) 0   d) 3
52. a) 0   b) 1   c) 0   d) 3
53. a) 0   b) 0   c) 3   d) 0
54. a) 1   b) 1   c) 1   d) 3
55. a) 3   b) 0   c) 1   d) 0
56. a) 1   b) 1   c) 1   d) 3
57. a) 3   b) 0   c) 0   d) 0
58. a) 0   b) 0   c) 3   d) 1
59. a) 0   b) 0   c) 0   d) 1
60. a) 1   b) 1   c) 1   d) 3
61. a) 3   b) 0   c) 0   d) 0
62. a) 0   b) 3   c) 0   d) 0
63. a) a   b) 1   c) 1   d) 3
64. a) 0   b) 3   c) 0   d) 0
65. a) 1   b) 1   c) 1   d) 3
66. a) 1   b) 1   c) 1   d) 3
67. a) 3   b) 0   c) 0   d) 0
68. a) 1   b) 1   c) 1   d) 3
69. a) 1   b) 1   c) 0   d) 3
70. a) 0   b) 3   c) 1   d) 1
71. a) 3   b) 0   c) 0   d) 0
72. a) 1   b) 1   c) 1   d) 3
73. a) 1   b) 1   c) 1   d) 3
74. a) 0   b) 1   c) 3   d) 0
75. a) 0   b) 0   c) 3   d) 0
76. a) 3   b) 0   c) 0   d) 0
77. a) 0   b) 0   c) 3   d) 0
78. a) 0   b) 3   c) 0   c) 0
79. a) 0   b) 0   c) 0   d) 3
80. a) 1   b) 1   c) 1   d) 3
81. a) 1   b) 1   c) 1   d) 3
82. a) 1   b) 1   c) 1   d) 3
83. a) 1   b) 1   c) 1   d) 3
84. a) 1   b) 1   c) 1   d) 3
85. a) 1   b) 1   c) 1   d) 3

86. a) 3   b) 0   c) 0   d) 0
87. a) 0   b) 3   c) 0   d) 0
88. a) 1   b) 1   c) 0   d) 3
89. a) 0   b) 0   c) 0   d) 3
90. a) 0   b) 0   c) 3   d) 0
91. a) 1   b) 1   c) 1   d) 3
92. a) 0   b) 3   c) 0   d) 0
93. a) 9   b) 3   c) 1   d) 0
94. a) 0   b) 0   c) 3   d) 0
95. a) 0   b) 3   c) 0   d) 0
96. a) 0   b) 0   c) 3   d) 0
97. a) 1   b) 0   c) 1   d) 3
98. a) 1   b) 3   c) 0   d) 0
99. a) 3   b) 0   c) 0   d) 0
100. a) 0   b) 3   c) 0   d) 0

There were 300 possible points for the final exam.

Days until Expiration Straddle Values

Bold Indicates a Weekend

Stock	1	2	3	4	5	6	7	8	9	10	11	12	13	14
AAPL	5.91	7.88	9.72	*11.01*	*11.01*	*11.01*	11.44	12.1	13.69	14.56	*18.01*	*18.01*	*18.01*	18.1
AMZN	5.87	7.54	8.9	*8.56*	*8.56*	*8.56*	9.35	10.38	11.35	12.13	*12.2*	*12.2*	*12.2*	13.22
AXP	1.04	1.27	1.4	*1.36*	*1.36*	*1.36*	1.57	1.78	1.99	2.11	*2.11*	*2.11*	*2.11*	2.35
BA	1.49	1.96	2.32	*2.02*	*2.02*	*2.02*	2.46	2.82	3	3.34	*3.24*	*3.24*	*3.24*	3.57
BIDU	3.88	4.46	4.98	*5.31*	*5.31*	*5.31*	6.13	6.57	7.03	7.43	*7.9*	*7.9*	*7.9*	8.59
CAT	1.23	1.59	1.54	*1.7*	*1.7*	*1.7*	1.96	2.22	2.37	2.53	*2.46*	*2.46*	*2.46*	2.63
CMG	7.65	10.21	11.74	*12.79*	*12.79*	*12.79*	15.11	14.79	16.76	18.19	*19.11*	*19.11*	*19.11*	20.25
CMCSA	0.5	0.65	0.69	*0.75*	*0.75*	*0.75*	0.83	0.87	0.98	1.08	*1.13*	*1.13*	*1.13*	1.18
COST	1.2	1.34	1.37	*2.73*	*2.73*	*2.73*	2.83	3.01	3.15	3.17	*3.3*	*3.3*	*3.3*	3.4
DDD	1.6	1.98	2.25	*2.79*	*2.79*	*2.79*	3.18	2.91	3.15	3.42	*3.95*	*3.95*	*3.95*	4.31
DG	0.74	0.83	1.04	*1.07*	*1.07*	*1.07*	1.22	1.33	1.39	1.52	*2.78*	*2.78*	*2.78*	2.81
DIA	1.03	1.49	1.53	*1.52*	*1.52*	*1.52*	1.87	2.05	2.46	2.4	*2.56*	*2.56*	*2.56*	2.79

(continued)

Stock	1	2	3	4	5	6	7	8	9	10	11	12	13	14
EBAY	0.83	1.05	1.3	*0.97*	*0.97*	*0.97*	1.16	1.42	1.6	1.84	*1.62*	*1.62*	*1.62*	1.75
FB	1.47	1.72	1.92	*1.94*	*1.94*	*1.94*	2.32	2.6	2.81	2.8	*3.09*	*3.09*	*3.09*	3.32
FAS	2.06	2.72	2.98	*2.88*	*2.88*	*2.88*	3.6	3.87	4.33	4.56	*4.53*	*4.53*	*4.53*	4.97
FSLR	1.79	2.25	2.6	*2.47*	*2.47*	*2.47*	2.86	3.28	3.46	3.88	*3.99*	*3.99*	*3.99*	4.23
GILD	1.36	1.69	1.83	*2.33*	*2.33*	*2.33*	2.27	2.58	2.66	2.95	*3.61*	*3.61*	*3.61*	3.41
GLD	1.3	1.4	1.68	*1.93*	*1.93*	*1.93*	2.11	2.34	2.2	2.41	*2.76*	*2.76*	*2.76*	2.78
GMCR	2.49	3.1	3.64	*3.5*	*3.5*	*3.5*	4.11	4.51	4.94	5.37	*5.57*	*5.57*	*5.57*	5.98
GOOG	6.56	8.51	9.33	*9.63*	*9.63*	*9.63*	10.95	11.92	13.34	13.63	*14.37*	*14.37*	*14.37*	15.15
GS	2.1	2.53	2.66	*2.84*	*2.84*	*2.84*	3.18	3.46	3.85	3.88	*4.06*	*4.06*	*4.06*	4.28
HD	0.88	1.21	2.26	*1.21*	*1.21*	*1.21*	1.4	1.45	1.71	2.67	*1.86*	*1.86*	*1.86*	1.96
HLF	1.42	1.69	2.06	*1.96*	*1.96*	*1.96*	2.55	2.76	2.84	3.42	*3.26*	*3.26*	*3.26*	3.88
IBM	1.98	2.58	2.83	*2.77*	*2.77*	*2.77*	3.15	3.41	3.88	4.01	*3.96*	*3.96*	*3.96*	4.34
IWM	1.35	1.74	1.82	*1.95*	*1.95*	*1.95*	2.31	2.53	2.79	2.73	*3.02*	*3.02*	*3.02*	3.27
JPM	0.58	0.7	0.75	*0.81*	*0.81*	*0.81*	0.94	1.05	1.15	1.16	*1.24*	*1.24*	*1.24*	1.33
KORS	1.68	2.06	2.49	*7.31*	*7.31*	*7.31*	7.2	7.26	7.1	7.28	*8.29*	*8.29*	*8.29*	8
LNKD	4.19	5.23	6.1	*5.77*	*5.77*	*5.77*	6.75	7.61	8.37	8.99	*9.03*	*9.03*	*9.03*	9.67
LVS	1.28	1.83	2.01	*2.01*	*2.01*	*2.01*	2.35	2.63	3	3.16	*3.13*	*3.13*	*3.13*	3.33
MA	0.95	1.22	1.37	*1.39*	*1.39*	*1.39*	1.55	1.75	1.96	2.03	*2.08*	*2.08*	*2.08*	2.2
MCD	1.01	1.18	1.3	*1.93*	*1.93*	*1.93*	2.07	2.15	2.09	2.17	*2.38*	*2.38*	*2.38*	2.48
MSFT	0.45	0.53	0.59	*0.62*	*0.62*	*0.62*	0.68	0.73	0.84	0.89	*0.94*	*0.94*	*0.94*	0.96
NFLX	10.81	12.87	14.98	*14.66*	*14.66*	*14.66*	17.76	19.25	19.95	21.51	*22.72*	*22.72*	*22.72*	23.91
PCLN	18.06	23.1	27.72	*28.02*	*28.02*	*28.02*	31.59	34.09	39.54	42.62	*44.8*	*44.8*	*44.8*	46.61
QCOM	0.76	0.94	0.98	*1.08*	*1.08*	*1.08*	1.23	1.34	1.49	1.54	*1.58*	*1.58*	*1.58*	1.74
QQQ	0.77	1.09	1.12	*1.09*	*1.09*	*1.09*	1.32	1.49	1.69	1.74	*1.77*	*1.77*	*1.77*	1.97
SPY	1.27	1.78	1.83	*1.91*	*1.91*	*1.91*	2.21	2.43	2.91	2.83	*3.04*	*3.04*	*3.04*	3.41
TBT	0.87	1.13	1.27	*1.15*	*1.15*	*1.15*	1.33	1.53	1.75	1.85	*2.01*	*2.01*	*2.01*	2.14
TGT	0.83	2.38	2.02	*0.96*	*0.96*	*0.96*	1.14	1.37	2.58	2.3	*1.35*	*1.35*	*1.35*	1.51
TLT	0.79	1.05	1.17	*1.06*	*1.06*	*1.06*	1.22	1.41	1.64	1.69	*1.85*	*1.85*	*1.85*	1.96
TSLA	5.28	6.25	7.93	*8.1*	*8.1*	*8.1*	9.54	9.96	10.51	11.94	*12.89*	*12.89*	*12.89*	13.9
TWTR	0.95	1.25	1.35	*1.53*	*1.53*	*1.53*	1.62	1.69	1.94	2.01	*2.2*	*2.2*	*2.2*	2.28
V	2.43	3.13	3.48	*3.52*	*3.52*	*3.52*	4.08	4.46	4.96	4.89	*5.27*	*5.27*	*5.27*	5.63
VZ	0.46	0.55	0.58	*0.61*	*0.61*	*0.61*	0.71	0.83	0.89	0.96	*0.93*	*0.93*	*0.93*	1.03
WAG	1.06	1.29	1.49	*1.44*	*1.44*	*1.44*	1.67	1.81	2.01	2.28	*2.2*	*2.2*	*2.2*	2.36
WFC	0.45	0.6	0.68	*0.71*	*0.71*	*0.71*	0.77	0.85	0.96	0.97	*0.98*	*0.98*	*0.98*	1.04
WMT	0.59	0.72	0.91	*0.85*	*0.85*	*0.85*	0.98	1.07	1.17	1.26	*1.3*	*1.3*	*1.3*	1.43
WYNN	3.99	5.56	6.37	*0.65*	*0.65*	*0.65*	7.46	8.28	9.18	9.94	*9.73*	*9.73*	*9.73*	10.52
XLE	0.74	1.09	1.21	*1.26*	*1.26*	*1.26*	1.38	1.49	1.71	1.83	*1.91*	*1.91*	*1.91*	1.99
XOM	0.91	1.09	1.25	*1.33*	*1.33*	*1.33*	1.48	1.59	1.74	1.88	*1.98*	*1.98*	*1.98*	2.13

ALL OR NONE (AON) ORDER   An order in which the quantity must be completely filled or it will be canceled.

AMERICAN-STYLE OPTION   A call or put option contract that can be exercised at any time before the expiration of the contract.

ASK, ASKED PRICE   The price at which the trader making the price is willing to sell an option or security.

ASSIGNMENT   Notification by the **Options Clearing Corporation (OCC)** to a clearing member and the writer of an option that an owner of the option has exercised the option and that the terms of settlement must be met. Assignments are made on a random basis by the **OCC**. The writer of a call option is obligated to sell the underlying asset at the strike price of the call option; the writer of a put option is obligated to buy the underlying at the strike price of the put option.

AT-THE-MONEY (ATM)   An option whose strike price is equal to (or, in practice, very close to) the current price of the underlying.

BACK MONTH   Any exchange-traded derivatives contract for a future period beyond the front month contract. Also known as a **LEAP** if it extends beyond the current calendar year.

BEAR CALL SPREAD   (Vertical spread) A net credit transaction established by selling a call and buying another call at a higher strike price, on the same underlying, in the same expiration. It is a directional trade where the maximum loss equals the difference between the strike prices less the credit received, and the maximum profit equals the credit received.

BEAR PUT SPREAD   (Vertical spread) A trade initiated by selling a put and buying a put at a higher strike; it is a debit spread. The price must go lower in order to cash this trade.

BETA   A prediction of what percentage a position will move in relation to an index. If a position has a beta of 1, then the position will tend to move in line with the index. If the beta is 0.5, this suggests that a 1 percent move in the index will cause the position price to move by 0.5 percent. Beta should not be confused with volatility.

BID   The price that the trader making the price is willing to buy an option or security for.

BID–ASK SPREAD   The difference between the bid and ask prices of a security. The wider (i.e., larger) the spread is, the less liquid the market and the greater the slippage.

BINOMIAL PRICING MODEL   Methodology employed in some option pricing models that assumes that the price of the underlying can either rise or fall by a certain amount at each predetermined interval until expiration.

BLACK–SCHOLES PRICING MODEL   A formula used to compute the value of European-style call and put options, invented by Fischer Black and Myron Scholes.

BULL, BULLISH   A bull is someone with an optimistic view on a market or particular asset (e.g., believes that the price will rise). Such views are often described as bullish.

BULL CALL SPREAD   A net debit transaction established by buying a call and selling another call at a higher strike price, on the same underlying, in the same expiration. It is a directional trade where the maximum loss equals the debit paid, and the maximum profit equals the difference between the strike prices, less the debit. No margin is required.

BULL PUT SPREAD   A net credit transaction established by buying a put and selling another put at a higher strike price, on the same underlying, in the same expiration. It is a directional trade where the maximum loss equals the difference between the strike prices, less the credit, and the maximum profit equals the credit received.

BUTTERFLY SPREAD   A strategy involving four contracts of the same type at three different strike prices. A long (short) butterfly involves buying (selling) the lowest strike price, selling (buying) double the quantity at the central strike price, and buying (selling) the highest strike price. All options are on the same underlying, in the same expiration.

CALENDAR SPREAD   (Horizontal spread) The simultaneous purchase and sale of options of the same type, but with different expiration dates. This would include horizontal debit spreads, horizontal credit spreads, diagonal debit spreads, and diagonal credit spreads.

CALL   This option contract conveys the right to buy a standard quantity of a specified asset at a fixed price per unit (the strike price) for a limited length of time (until expiration).

CALL RATIO BACKSPREAD   A long backspread using calls only.

CLOSING TRANSACTION To sell a previously purchased position or to buy back a previously purchased position, effectively canceling out the position.

COLLAR A trade that establishes both a maximum profit (the ceiling) and minimum loss (the floor) when holding the underlying asset. The premium received from the sale of the ceiling reduces that due from the purchase of the floor. Strike prices are often chosen at the level at which the premiums net out. An example would be: owning 100 shares of a stock, while simultaneously selling a call, and buying a put.

COMMISSION The charge paid to a broker for transacting the purchase or the sale of stock, options, or any other security.

COMMODITY A raw material or primary product used in manufacturing or industrial processing or consumed in its natural form.

CONDOR A strategy similar to the butterfly involving four contracts of the same type at four different strike prices. A long (short) condor involves buying (selling) the lowest strike price, selling (buying) two different central strike prices, and buying (selling) the highest strike price. All contracts are on the same underlying, in the same expiration.

CONTRACT SIZE The number of units of an underlying specified in a contract. In stock options, the standard contract size is 100 shares of stock. In futures options, the contract size is one futures contract. In index options, the contract size is an amount of cash equal to parity times the multiplier. In the case of currency options, it varies.

COST OF CARRY The interest cost of holding an asset for a period of time. It is either the cost of funds to finance the purchase (real cost) or the loss of income because funds are diverted from one investment to another (opportunity cost).

COVERED A covered option strategy is an investment in which all short options are completely offset with a position in the underlying or a long option in the same asset. The loss potential with such a strategy is therefore limited.

COVERED CALL Both long the underlying and short a call. The sale of a call by investors who own the underlying is a common strategy and is used to enhance their return on investment.

COVERED COMBO A strategy in which you are long the underlying, short a call, and short a put. Often used by those wishing to own the underlying at a price less than today's price.

COX–ROSS–RUBINSTEIN A binomial option-pricing model invented by John Cox, Stephen Ross, and Mark Rubinstein.

CREDIT The amount you receive for placing a trade. This is the net inflow of cash into your account as the result of a trade.

DAY ORDER An order to purchase or sell a security, usually at a specified price, that is good for just the trading session on which it is given. It is automatically canceled on the close of the session if it is not executed.

DEBIT   The amount you pay for placing a trade.

DELTA   Measures the rate of change in an option's theoretical value for a one-unit change in the underlying. Calls have positive deltas and puts have negative deltas.

DELTA NEUTRAL   A strategy in which the delta-adjusted values of the options (plus any position in the underlying) offset one another.

DIAGONAL CREDIT SPREAD   A type of calendar spread. It is a debit transaction where options are purchased in a nearer expiration and options of the same type are sold in a farther expiration, on the same underlying. It is diagonal because the options have different strike prices.

DIAGONAL DEBIT SPREAD   Type of calendar spread. It is a credit transaction where options are sold in a nearer expiration and options of the same type are purchased in a farther expiration, on the same underlying. It is diagonal because the options have different strike prices.

DIRECTIONAL TRADE   A trade designed to take advantage of an expected movement in price.

EARLY EXERCISE   (American style) Allows the owner of an option the right to exercise and accept the stock at the strike price at any time during the option cycle.

EQUITY OPTION   An option on shares of an individual common stock, this is more commonly known as a stock option.

EUROPEAN-STYLE OPTION   An option that can only be exercised on the expiration date of the contract.

EXCHANGE TRADED   The generic term used to describe futures, options, and other derivative instruments that are traded on an organized exchange.

EXERCISE   The act by which the holder of an option has the right but not the obligation to take delivery of the underlying at the strike price of the option.

EXPIRATION, EXPIRATION DATE, EXPIRATION MONTH   The date by which an option contract must be exercised or it becomes void and the holder of the option ceases to have any rights under the contract. All stock and index option contracts expire on the Saturday following the third Friday of the month specified.

FILL   When an order has been completely executed, it is described as filled.

FILL OR KILL (FOK) ORDER   This means do it now if the option (or stock) is available in the crowd or from the specialist; otherwise, kill the order altogether. Similar to an all-or-none (**AON**) order, except it is "killed" immediately if it cannot be completely executed as soon as it is announced. Unlike an **AON** order, the **FOK** order cannot be used as part of a **GTC** order.

FRONT MONTH   The first month of those listed by an exchange, this is usually the most actively traded contract, but liquidity will move from this to the second month contract as the front month nears expiration, also known as the "front step" or "top step" expiration serial.

FUTURES, FUTURES CONTRACT A standardized, exchange-traded agreement specifying a quantity and price of a particular type of commodity (soybeans, gold, oil, etc.) to be purchased or sold at a predetermined date in the future. On contract date, delivery and physical possession take place unless the contract has been closed out. Futures are also available on various financial products and indexes today.

GAMMA Gamma expresses how fast delta changes with a one-point increase in the price of the underlying. Gamma is positive for all options. If an option has a delta of 45 and a gamma of 10, then the option's expected delta will be 55 if the underlying goes up one point. If we consider delta to be the velocity of an option, then gamma is the acceleration.

GOOD 'TIL CANCELED (GTC) ORDER An order that is effective until it is either filled by the broker or canceled by the investor. This order will automatically cancel at the option's expiration.

GREEKS The Greek letters used to describe various measures of the sensitivity of the value of an option with respect to different factors. They include delta, gamma, theta, rho, and Vega.

HISTORIC VOLATILITY The measure of the actual price fluctuations of the underlying asset over a specific period of time.

HORIZONTAL CREDIT SPREAD A type of calendar spread. It is a credit transaction where you buy an option in a nearer expiration month and sell an option of the same type in a farther expiration month, with the same strike price, and in the same underlying asset.

HORIZONTAL DEBIT SPREAD A type of calendar spread. It is a debit transaction where you sell an option in a nearer expiration month and buy an option of the same type in a farther expiration month, with the same strike price, and in the same underlying asset.

ILLIQUID An illiquid market is one that cannot be easily traded without the dislocation of price. Usually it is caused by a lack of active market participants.

IMPLIED VOLATILITY (IV) This is the volatility that the underlying would need to have for the pricing model to produce the same theoretical option price as the actual option price. The term *implied volatility* comes from the fact that options imply the volatility of their underlying, just by their price. A computer model starts with the actual market price of an option, and measures IV by working the option fair value model backward, solving for volatility (normally an input) as if it were the unknown.

INDEX The compilation of stocks and their prices into a single number.

INDEX OPTION An option that has an index of assets serving as the underlying contract.

IN-THE-MONEY (ITM) Term used when the strike price of an option is less than the price of the underlying for a call option, or greater than the price of the underlying for a put option. In other words, the option has an intrinsic value greater than zero.

INTRINSIC VALUE Amount of any favorable difference between the strike price of an option and the current price of the underlying (i.e., the amount by which it is in the money). The intrinsic value of an out-of-the-money option is zero.

LAST TRADING DAY The last business day prior to the options expiration during which purchases and sales of options can be made. For equity options, this is generally the third Friday of the expiration month.

LEAPS Long-Term Equity Anticipation Securities, also known as long-dated options. Calls and puts with expiration as long as two to five years. Only about 10 percent of equities have **LEAPS**. Currently, equity **LEAPS** have two series at any time, always with January expirations. Some indexes also have **LEAPS**.

LEG Term describing one side of a spread position.

LEGGING Term used to describe a risky method of implementing or closing out a spread strategy one side (*leg*) at a time. Instead of utilizing a *spread order* to ensure that both the written and the purchased options are filled simultaneously, an investor gambles that a better deal can be obtained on the price of the spread by implementing it as two separate orders.

LEVERAGE A means of increasing return or worth without increasing investment. This strategy involves the use of borrowed funds to increase one's investment return—for example, buying stocks on margin. Option contracts are leveraged, as they provide the prospect of a high return with little investment. The percent double parameter for each option in the matrix is a measure of leverage.

LIMIT ORDER An order placed with a brokerage to buy or sell a predetermined number of contracts (or shares of stock) at a specified price, or better than the specified price. Limit orders also allow an investor to limit the length of time an order can be outstanding before canceled. It can be placed as a day or **GTC** order. Limit orders typically cost slightly more than market orders but are often better to use, especially with options, because you will always purchase or sell securities at that price or better.

LIQUID A liquid market is one in which large deals can be easily traded without the dislocation of price. This is usually due to the involvement of many participants and/or a high volume of transactions.

LONG You are long if you have bought more than you have sold in any particular market, commodity, instrument, or contract. Also known as having a long position, you are purchasing an asset with the intention of selling it at a higher price in the future.

MARKET MAKER A trader or institution that plays a leading role in a market by being prepared to quote a two-way price (bid and ask) on request—or constantly in the case of some screen-based markets during normal market hours.

MARKET-ON-CLOSE (MOC) ORDER A type of order that requires that an order be executed at or near the close of a trading day on the day the order is entered. An **MOC** order, which can be considered a type of day order, cannot be used as part of a **GTC** order.

MARKET ORDER Sometimes referred to as an unrestricted order. It's an order to buy or sell a security immediately at the best available current price. A market order is the only order that guarantees execution. It should be used with caution in placing option trades, because you can end up paying a lot more than you anticipated.

MARKET PRICE The last price at which the asset traded.

MARK TO MARKET The revaluation of a position at its closing market price.

NAKED An investment in which options sold short are not matched with a long position in either the underlying or another option of the same type that expires at the same time or later than the options sold. The loss potential of naked strategies can be virtually unlimited.

NORMAL DISTRIBUTION A statistical distribution where observations are evenly distributed around the mean. Studies have shown that stock prices are very close to being lognormally distributed over time. When you choose bell curve as a price target in the program, a lognormal distribution based on price, volatility, and time until valuation date is constructed.

ONE-CANCELS-THE-OTHER (OCO) ORDER Type of order that treats two or more option orders as a package, whereby the execution of any one of the orders causes all the orders to be reduced by the same amount.

OPENING TRANSACTION An addition to, or creation of, a trading position.

OPEN INTEREST The cumulative total of all option contracts of a particular series sold, but not yet repurchased or exercised.

OPEN ORDER An order that has been placed with the broker, but not yet executed or canceled.

OPTION CHAIN The list of strike prices available in any option serial for a given underlying asset.

OUT-OF-THE-MONEY (OTM) An option whose strike price is unfavorable in comparison to the current price of the underlying. This means when the strike price of a call is greater than the price of the underlying, or the strike price of a put is less than the price of the underlying. An out-of-the-money option has no intrinsic value, only time value.

PREMIUM (AIR) The amount of excess price over the intrinsic value for an option. Out-of-the-money options are all premium.

PUT This option contract conveys the right to sell a standard quantity of a specified asset at a fixed price per unit (the strike price) for a limited length of time (until expiration).

PUT RATIO BACKSPREAD A long backspread using puts only.

REVERSAL   A short position in the underlying protected by a synthetic long. Also, the term used to describe a direction change in a given asset or derivative measured against time.

RHO   The change in the value of an option with respect to a unit change in the risk-free rate.

ROLLOVER   Moving a position from one expiration date to another further into the future. As the front month approaches expiration, traders wishing to maintain their positions will often move them to the next contract month. This is accomplished by a simultaneous sale of one and purchase of the other.

ROUND TURN   When an option contract is bought and then sold, or vice versa. It leaves the trader flat. The only residual is the debit or credit the trade created.

SHORT   An obligation to purchase an asset at some time in the future. An asset is sold short with the expectation of a decline in its price.

SHORT BACKSPREAD   It involves buying one option nearer the money and selling two (or more) options of the same type farther out of the money, with the same expiration, on the same underlying. The trade has unlimited risk and limited reward.

SHORT UNDERLYING   Selling an asset you don't own with the expectation of buying it back at a lower price.

SLIPPAGE   The combination of the bid–offer spread plus commissions. In thin markets, it makes them illiquid for the average retail trader.

SPREAD   A trading strategy involving two or more legs, the incorporation of one or more of which is designed to reduce the risk involved in the others.

SPREAD ORDER   An order for the simultaneous purchase and sale of two (or more) options of the same type on the same underlying. If placed with a limit, the two options must be filled for a specified price difference, or better. It can be critical in this type of order to specify whether it is an opening transaction or a closing transaction.

STANDARD DEVIATION   The square root of the mean of the squares of the deviations of each member of a sample population. In a normal distribution curve, it encompasses 68 percent of the possible combinations.

STOP ORDER   **Stop-loss** and **stop-limit** orders placed that are activated when the asset touches a specific price. Usually, they are used to limit risk, but can be used to open a transaction.

STRADDLE   The purchase (or sale) of both call and put options with the same strike price, same expiration, and on the same underlying. A short straddle means that both the call and put are sold short, for a credit. A long straddle means that both the call and put are bought long, for a debit.

STRANGLE   A strategy involving the purchase or sale of both call and put options with different strike prices normally of equal, but opposite, premium (Air).

A short strangle means that both the calls and puts are sold short, for a credit. A long strangle means both the calls and puts are bought long, for a debit.

STRIKE PRICE   The price at which the holder of an option has the right but not the obligation to buy or sell the underlying asset.

SYNTHETIC   A strategy that uses options to mimic the underlying asset. The long synthetic combines a long call and a short put to mimic a long position in the underlying. The short synthetic combines a short call and a long put to mimic a short position in the underlying. In both cases, both the call and put have the same strike price, the same expiration, and are on the same underlying.

THEORETICAL VALUE, THEORETICAL PRICE   The mathematically calculated value of an option. It is determined by the supply and demand for the option. A rise or fall of theoretical value in one option in a serial generally leads to a general rise or fall of all options in the serial.

THETA   The sensitivity of the value of an option with respect to the time remaining to expiration. It is the daily drop in dollar value of an option due to the effect of time alone. Theta is dollars lost per day, per contract.

TICK   The smallest unit price change allowed in trading a specific security. This varies by security, and can also be dependent on the current price of the security.

TIME DECAY   (Theta) The term used to describe how the theoretical value of an option "erodes" or reduces with the passage of time.

TRANSACTION COSTS   All charges associated with executing a trade and maintaining a position, including brokerage commissions, fees for exercise and/or assignment, and margin interest.

UNCOVERED   A short option position that has limited reward and unlimited risk.

UNDERLYING   The asset on which the option contract is based.

VEGA   Vega is the dollar amount of gain or loss you should experience if implied volatility goes up one percentage point. It is not related to time decay (theta), only to the current supply and demand for the option.

VERTICAL CREDIT SPREAD   The purchase and sale for a net credit of two options of the same type but different strike prices. They must have the same expiration and be on the same underlying.

VERTICAL DEBIT SPREAD   The purchase and sale for a net debit of two options of the same type but different strike prices. They must have the same expiration and be on the same underlying.

VOLATILITY   A measure of the amount by which an asset has fluctuated, or is expected to fluctuate, in a given period of time. Assets with greater volatility exhibit wider price swings and their options are higher in price than less-volatile assets.

VOLATILITY TRADE   A trade designed to take advantage of an expected change in volatility. It can be used during earnings season to capture the possible excess premium due to anticipated news.

VOLUME The quantity of trading in a market or security. It can be measured by dollars or units traded (i.e., number of contracts for options, or number of shares for stocks).

WRITE, WRITER Initiating a sale of an option naked. This transaction has limited reward and unlimited risk.

Mr. Robert J. Seifert has been involved in the securities industry for more than 38 years. He began his career in the municipal bond market, where he held positions in marketing and trading. In 1980, he established Fixed Income Atlanta, his own broker dealer, which specialized in fixed-income municipal and government bonds.

When interest rates spiked in the early 1980s, more emphasis was placed on the hedging of long-term bonds, employing the new financial future contracts that were being offered at the Chicago Board of Trade (CBOT). Eventually, he developed a trading model and formed Robert J. Seifert C.T.A., which managed both individual and pooled commodity trading accounts. During this period, he had two articles published in *Barron's* and the *Wall Street Journal* dealing with risk and portfolio diversification. Opportunities in the evolving derivatives and futures markets led him to the floor of the CBOT and CME in the fall of 1983.

In 1985, he started a floor trading partnership, Futrex, which eventually operated on the floors of the CME, the CBOT, and the CBOE. While at Futrex, he served in many capacities with the Chicago Mercantile Exchange (CME), including the position of Vice-Chairman Eurodollar Options, and Options Chairman of the International Monetary Market (IMM). He also served on numerous committees devoted to revising and designing option products, conducted educational seminars on behalf of the Exchange, and acted as a political lobbyist in Washington for the futures industry.

In 1996, he formed Cat in the Hat Trading (CITHT) to deal in financial futures and options on the floor of the CME. The primary trade was the Eurodollar options market, the largest short-term interest-rate market in the world. His principal function at CITHT was to provide capital and implement the strategy for the duration weighted-option positions that were traded on the floor.

Currently, Mr. Seifert is an independent options trader and is a product manager with Ablesys Corporation, where he supplies intellectual properties for software models. In addition, he conducts trading seminars and has developed individual options-trading courses for a number of clients.

Mr. Seifert graduated from West Virginia University, where he earned a bachelor's degree in Economics and Statistics.

Printed and bound by CPI Group (UK) Ltd, Croydon, CR0 4YY

16/04/2025

14658460-0001